# R.Gupta's®

## OBJECTIVE

# COMPUTER AWARENESS

A Collection of Highly Useful
Questions for Competitive Exams

**RAMESH PUBLISHING HOUSE,** New Delhi

**Published by**
O.P. Gupta *for* Ramesh Publishing House

**Admin. Office**
12-H, New Daryaganj Road, Opp. Officers' Mess,
New Delhi-110002 ① 23261567, 23275224, 23275124

E-mail: info@rameshpublishinghouse.com
Website: www.rameshpublishinghouse.com

**Showroom**
● Balaji Market, Nai Sarak, Delhi-6 ① 23253720, 23282525
● 4457, Nai Sarak, Delhi-6, ① 23918938



**Book Code: R-1031**

**ISBN: 978-81-7812-604-3**

**HSN Code: 49011010**

**16th Edition: Printed in January, 2020**

# CONTENTS

———————

# Objective
# COMPUTER
# AWARENESS

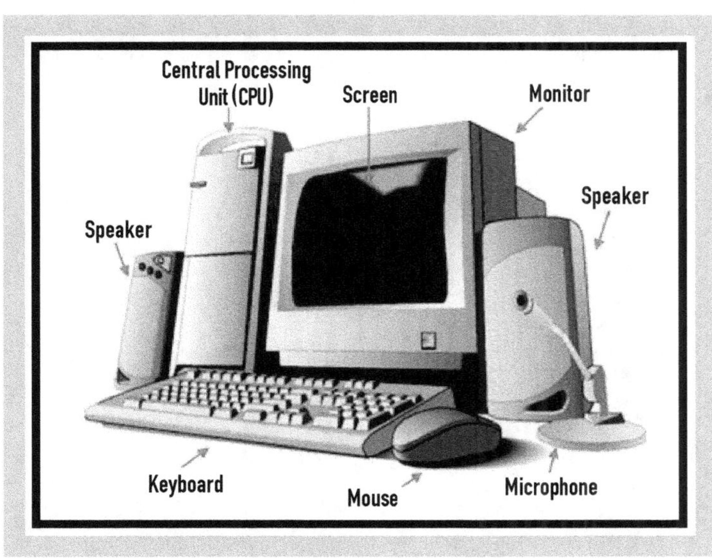

# 1. Fundamental and Applications

## COMPUTER BASICS

1. The least powerful computer is—
   A. minicomputer
   B. microcomputer
   C. mainframe computer
   D. none of the above

2. The Central Processing Unit (CPU) consists of—
   A. registers and Arithmetic Logic Unit
   B. instruction Decoding Circuit
   C. a control and timing section
   D. All of the above

3. The main purpose of the supercomputer is
   A. high speed calculations
   B. weather forecasting
   C. data Retreieval operations
   D. None of the above

4. What are the two essential parts of the Computer?
   A. Keyboard and Mouse
   B. Hardware and Software
   C. Printer and Screen
   D. Monitor and Keyboard

5. Future Generation computers will be based on
   A. online processing
   B. artificial intelligence
   C. time sharing
   D. None of the above

6. The basic operations performed by a computers are-
   A. Arithmetic operation
   B. Logical operation
   C. Storage and relative
   D. All of the above

7. The earliest calculating devices are-
   A. Abacus
   B. Clock
   C. Difference Engine
   D. None of the above

8. The Analytical Engine developed during First Generation of computers used _______ as a memory unit
   A. RAM
   B. Floppies
   C. Punch Cards
   D. Counter Wheels

9. The man who built the first Mechanical Calculator was-
   A. Joseph Marie Jacquard
   B. John Mauchly
   C. Blaise Pascal
   D. Harward Ailken

10. Punched cards were first introduced by-
    A. Powers
    B. Pascal
    C. Jacquard
    D. Herman Hollerith

11. Computers built in the First Generation of computers were-
    A. Transistor
    B. Electro-mechanical
    C. Electrical
    D. None of the above

12. Floppy Disk Drives were first introduced by which of the following computer manufacturers?
    A. IBM            B. Sony
    C. Panasonic      D. Compaq

13. Supercomputer were primarily designed by
    A. Seymour Cray   B. IBM
    C. Hewlett-Packard   D. C-DAC

14. The floppy drive have
    A. Magnetic coating   B. Silver coating
    C. Gold coating       D. Lead coating

15. Which electronic component was use in second generation?
    A. Vacuum tubes   B. transistors
    C. IC chips       D. all above

16. VLSI (Very-large scale integration) Integration Circuit technology was used in which generation?
    A. first generation
    B. second generation
    C. third generation
    D. fourth generation

17. IC chips was used in—
    A. first generation
    B. second generation
    C. third generation
    D. fourth generation

18. ENIAC was the computer of—
    A. first generation
    B. second generation
    C. third generation
    D. fourth generation

19. Manchester Mark I computer was based on—
    A. stored program concept
    B. processing concept
    C. electronic change concept
    D. all

20. What was the size of chip used in third generation?
    A. less then 8 mm
    B. less then 5 mm

C. less then 2 mm
D. less then 5 mm

21. EDVAC is
    A. Electronic Detected Variable Automatic Computer-
    B. Electronic Discrete Variable Automatic Computer
    C. Electronic Discrete Valuable Automatic Computer
    D. Electronic Developed Valuable Automatic Computer

22. How many vacuum tubes was used in ENIAC
    A. 8,498      B. 19,230
    C. 17,468     D. 13,621

23. Integrated circuits contained-
    A. vaccum tube
    B. transistor
    C. condensor
    D. resistance

## DATA REPRESENTATION

24. Which number system is usually followed in a typical 32-bit computer?
    A. binary         B. decimal
    C. hexadecimal    D. octal

25. Word length of a Personal Computer is ____
    A. 4 bits
    B. 8 bits
    C. 32 bits
    D. None of the above

26. When a key is pressed on the keyboard, which standard is used for converting the keystroke into the corresponding bits -
    A. ANSI       B. ASCII
    C. EBCDIC     D. ISO

27. The ______ digits are 0 to 9 and A to F
    A. Decimal    B. Hexadecimal
    C. Binomial   D. Treinomial

28. Each digit in Binary Coded Decimal (BCD) is known as ______.
    A. Bit
    B. Byte
    C. Nibble
    D. None of the above

**29.** ASCII Code is a 7 bit code for
  A. letters, numbers and other symbols
  B. only for letters
  C. only for numbers
  D. for numbers and letters

**30.** How many numbers are there in 2 bytes?
  A. 1011100101101110
  B. 0.278
  C. 0.002
  D. 2.000

**31.** Which of the following is the binary equivalent of the octal number 13.54?
  A. 1101.1110
  B. 1011.1100
  C. 1100.1100
  D. 1011.101100

**32.** What is the range of the numbers which can be stored in an eight bit register?
  A. −127 to +127
  B. −128 to +128
  C. −128 to +127
  D. −127 to +128

**33.** What is the term used for a half byte?
  A. bit
  B. nibble
  C. bug
  D. word

**34.** What is the Gray Code for decimal 7?
  A. 0100
  B. 0101
  C. 0010
  D. 111

**35.** Calculate the binary division of $(11000)_2 \div (100)_2$
  A. 10
  B. 100
  C. 110
  D. 111

**36.** What is the maximum count that a 6-bit binary word can represent?
  A. 61
  B. 62
  C. 63
  D. 64

**37.** The number system which is not a positional notation system is—
  A. Octal
  B. Roman
  C. Decimal
  D. Binary

**38.** The ASCII is a subset of –
  A. 8-bit-EBCDIC
  B. 8-bit ECBDIC
  C. 8-bit ECBDCI
  D. 8-bit EBCDCE

**39.** What is the sign magnitude representation of binary number +1101.011?
  A. 101001.1001
  B. 01101.011
  C. 1101.0110
  D. 1100.001

**40.** What is the excess 3 code?
  A. Cyclic complimenting code
  B. Cyclic algebraic code
  C. self complimenting code
  D. self algebraic code

**41.** Where is the used of cyclic code?
  A. Logic gate
  B. processing data
  C. simultaneous error-correction and Brust error detection
  D. Networking interface

**42.** Motherboard used in computer is
  A. powerful means of communication
  B. the main circuit board also called system board on which bus structure are mounted
  C. the interactive feature of network
  D. None of the above

**43.** The oldest form of computer language is called
  A. Machine language
  B. BASIC
  C. FORTRAN
  D. COBOL

## INPUT/OUTPUT DEVICES

**44.** Which device is used as the standard pointing device in a Graphical User Environment
  A. Keyboard
  B. Mouse
  C. Joystick
  D. Track ball

**45.** What are the units used to count the speed of a printer?
  A. CPM
  B. DPI
  C. PPM
  D. BIT

**46.** Which of the following is a term related with scanners?
  A. Laser
  B. TWAIN
  C. Catridge
  D. Toner

**47.** Cursor is a _______
  A. Pixel
  B. Thin blinking line
  C. Pointing device
  D. None of the above

**48.** Which of the following is not an output device?
A. Scanner
B. Printer
C. Flat Screen
D. Mouse

**49.** A device that allows the user to enter data into the computer is called—
A. Special purpose device
B. Input device
C. Output device
D. All of the above

**50.** A tiny chip, called the _______ detects that a key has been pressed.
A. Keys sean code
B. Keyboard buffer
C. Keyboard controller
D. All of the above

**51.** Write the name of the code that the keyboard controller keeps in its memory to indicating which key is pressed.
A. Keyboard code
B. Keys sean code
C. Keyboard controller code
D. None of the above

**52.** Like double-click, when the user presses the button three-times in quick succession it is called triple-click.
A. The statement is right
B. The statement is wrong
C. No Triple-click is the computer operation
D. None of the above

**53.** The Touch Pad is a _______ device.
A. Dynamic Pointing
B. Stationary Pointing
C. Temporary Pointing
D. Sensitive Pointing

**54.** A Joystick is used as
A. Stationary pointing device
B. Flight Stimulators
C. Temporary pointing device
D. None of the above

**55.** Many engineers and architects use a different type of pen called a
A. Computer pen
B. Light pen
C. Logical pen
D. Pointer pen

**56.** Name the kind of pen used to draw directly on the digitizing tablet.
A. Puck/stylus
B. Light Pen
C. Computer Pen
D. None of the above

**57.** Universal Product Code (UPC), a pattern of bars printed on merchandise can be read by
A. Bar Code Reader
B. Code Reader
C. Card Reader
D. Product Code Reader

**58.** Laser Scanners are capable of scanning bar codes upto a distance of—
A. 50 cm
B. 10 cm
C. 25 cm
D. 75 cm

**59.** Pen scanner is also known as—
A. Wand scanner
B. Stationary scanner
C. Hand held scanner
D. LCD scanner

**60.** The OMR used is the competitive examinations stands for
A. Optical Magnetic Reader
B. Optical Mark Reader
C. Optical Memory Reader
D. Optical Monitor Reader

**61.** The interface used to recognise input from a variety of individuals in a speech recognition systems which enable physically disable people to use computer is known as—
A. VUI
B. VII
C. VIU
D. None of the above

**62.** _______ is the second type of soft copy.
A. Data output
B. Audio output
C. Logic output
D. None of the above

**63.** Name the output device which is used to draw maps from stored data having high quality colour graphics.

A. Printer
B. Plotter
C. Colour Printer
D. None of the above

64. The type of line printer that uses an oscillating row of print hammer is known as—
A. Dot Matrix
B. Line Matrix
C. Both A and B
D. None of the above

65. Which of the following device is not a printer?
A. Non-Impact Printer
B. Laser Printer
C. Inkjet Printer
D. None of the above

## COMPUTER MEMORY

66. Which device can understand difference between data & programs?
A. Input device    B. Output device
C. Memory    D. Microprocessor

67. How many write cycles are allowed to a RAM?
A. 1    B. 10
C. 100    D. 1000

68. How many write cycles are allowed to a EEPROM?
A. 1    B. 10
C. 100    D. 1000

69. Which storage device is mounted on 'reels'?
A. Floppy Disk    B. Hard Disk
C. Magnetic Tapes    D. CDROM

70. Which of the following statements is/are true?
A. Cache Memories are bigger than RAM
B. Cache Memories are smaller than RAM
C. ROM are faster than RAM
D. Information in ROM can be written by users

71. Which of the following RAM times have to be refreshed often in order to retain its contents?
A. SIMM    B. DIMM
C. SDMM    D. DSMM

72. MDR (Memory Data Register) holds the-
A. Segment number
B. Address of a memory location
C. Register of computer controlled unit
D. None of the above

73. The contents of information are stored in—
A. Memory data register
B. Memory address register
C. Memory access register
D. Memory arithmetic register

74. Memory unit is one part of—
A. Input device
B. Control unit
C. Output device
D. Central Processing Unit

75. Which of the following device can store large amounts of data?
A. Floppy Disk    B. Hard Disk
C. CDROM    D. Zip Disk

76. Which of the following is handy to carry yet can store large amounts of data?
A. Floppy Disk    B. Hard Disk
C. CDROM    D. Zip Disk

77. Data (information) is stored in computers as—
A. Files    B. Directories
C. Floppies    D. Matter

78. Which of the following is not a valid size of a Floppy Disk?
A. 8"    B. 5 1/4"
C. 3 1/2"    D. 5 1/2"

79. Memory is made up of—
A. Set of wires
B. Set of circuits
C. Large number of cells
D. All of the above

80. Primary memory stores—
A. Data    B. Programs
C. Results    D. All of the above

81. EPROM can be used for—
    A. Erasing the contents of ROM
    B. Reconstructing the contents of ROM
    C. Erasing and reconstructing the contents of ROM
    D. Duplicating ROM

82. Which of the following devices have a limitation that we can only write information on it but cannot erase or modify it -
    A. Floppy Disk        B. Hard Disk
    C. Tape Drive         D. CDROM

83. Which technology is used in Compact disks?
    A. Mechanical         B. Electrical
    C. Electro Magnetic   D. Laser

84. Which of the following is the largest manufacturer of Hard Disk Drives?
    A. IBM                B. Segate
    C. Microsoft          D. 3M

85. The memory location address are limited to—
    A. 00000 to 9ffff(16)
    B. 00001 to 9ffff(16)
    C. 00010 to 9ffff(16)
    D. 10000 to 9ffff(16)

86. What are the most important components to create the memory cell?
    A. Transistor and Register
    B. Register and Diode
    C. Diode and electric cell
    D. Transistor and Capacitor

87. DRAM stands for
    A. Decimal Randam Access Memory
    B. Direct Random Access Memory
    C. Dynamic Random Access Memory
    D. None of the above

88. Which of the following wafer used the memory cells to etched?
    A. Platinum wafer
    B. Gold Wafer
    C. Silicon Wafer
    D. Germanium Wafer

89. Which of the following is not the name of RAM?
    A. SRAM
    B. DRAM
    C. RDRAM
    D. None of the above

90. DDR SDRAM stands for
    A. Double Data Rate Synchronous Dynamic Random Access Memory
    B. Dynamic Data Rate Synchronous Dynamic Random Access Memory
    C. Decimal Double Rate Synechronous Dynamic Random Access Memory
    D. None of the above

91. EEPROM stands for
    A. Effective Erasable Programmable Read Only Memory
    B. Electrically Erasable Programmable Read only Memory
    C. Entities Erasable Programmable Read only Memory
    D. None of the above

92. Different memories can be classified according to the concept of
    A. Access mode/capacity and cost
    B. Access Time
    C. Transfer Rate
    D. All of the above

93. A set of flip flops integrated together is called ______
    A. Counter
    B. Adder
    C. Register
    D. None of the above

94. ______ is one of the oldest form of computer storage.
    A. Magnetic Disk
    B. Magnetic Tape
    C. Hard Disk
    D. None of the above

95. The processing speed of a computer is faster when the RAM size is bigger since it eliminates.
    A. need for external memory
    B. frequent disk I/Os
    C. need for ROM
    D. None of the above

**96.** _______ is a semi conductor memory.
A. Dynamic          B. Static
C. Bubble           D. Both A & B

**97.** Which of the following is a read only memory storage device.
A. Floppy disk
B. Hard disk
C. CDROM
D. None of the above

**98.** DMA stands for _______
A. Direct Memory Access
B. Distinct Memory Access
C. Direct Module Access
D. Direct Memory Allociation

## PROCESSOR

**99.** The unit kIPS (thousand instruction per second) is used to measure the speed of ___
A. Processor         B. Disk drive
C. Printer           D. Tape drive

**100.** Which of the following is not a step of CPU
A. decode            B. execute
C. fetch             D. logic

**101.** What is the name of the 64-bit Microprocessor developed by AMD?
A. Opteron           B. RISC-9000
C. iMac              D. Am 2904

**102.** Processor is the part of a computer. There are two main types of processor : CISC and _______
A. CPU – Central Processing Unit
B. DSP – Digital Signal Processor
C. RISC – Reduced Instruction Set Computer
D. None of the above

**103.** The processor can take turns going to each device and asking if they have anything they need. This is called _______ the device.
A. Interrupting
B. Transfering
C. Polling
D. All of the above

**104.** When was the first microprocessor INTEL 4004 introduced?
A. 1972              B. 1973
C. 1971              D. 1981

**105.** Machine language is a _______ which instructs the computer what to do.
A. special code
B. operation code
C. coding scheme
D. None of the above

**106.** The first part of the instruction code is called
A. Coding scheme
B. Operation Code (opcode)
C. Special Code
D. Both A & B

**107.** What is the maximum size of the virtual address space on a 32-bit machine?
A. 6 Megabytes
B. 2 Kilobytes
C. 4 Gigabytes
D. All of the above

**108.** An important feature of a microprocessor is
A. non programmable
B. micro programmble
C. macro programmable
D. All of the above

**109.** A fetch cycle is the _______ of the instruction cycle
A. Auxiliary Part
B. Fitest Part
C. Intermediate Part
D. Last Part

## BINARY ARITHMETIC

**110.** What are the binary arithmetic operations?
A. Addition operation
B. Subraction operation
C. Multiplication and Division operation
D. All of the above

**111.** Calculate the following digits 101110 and 111101 by using binary addition operation and the answer will be
A. 1101010
B. 1101011
C. 1011011
D. None of the above

**112.** What is the decimal equivalent of the binary number $(1101011)_2$?
A. 101      B. 102
C. 105      D. 107

**113.** According to rule of binary substractions the answer of 10–1 will be
A. 1
B. 0
C. either 1 or 0
D. None of the above

**114.** The result of the binary substraction of 1011 from 100000 is
A. 101011      B. 010101
C. 101010      D. 111010

**115.** N-bit sign magnitude numbers can represent quantities from ______
A. $-(2^{(N-1)}-0)$ to $+(2^{(N-2)}-0)$
B. $+(2^{(N-1)}-1)$ to $+(2^{(N-1)}-1)$
C. $+(2^{(N-1)}-1)$ to $-(2^{(N-1)}-1)$
D. $-(2^{(N-1)}-1)$ to $+(2^{(N-1)}-1)$

**116.** Calculate the 8-bit binary complement representation of –7.
A. 00000111      B. 11111000
C. 11111001      D. 0000111

**117.** Binary multiplication of 111101 by 1110 gives
A. 1101010111      B. 1101010101
C. 1101010100      D. 1101010110

**118.** Calculate the binary addition operation of 110.1101 & 100.1010, the answer is
A. 1011.0111      B. 1101.0111
C. 1010.0111      D. 1001.0111

**119.** The result of the binary division of 110111 by 1011 is
A. Quotient = 011, Remainder = 100
B. Quotient = 101, Remainder = 000
C. Quotient = 101, Remainder = 010
D. None of the above

# COMPUTER ARCHITECTURE

**120.** ______ is concerned with the structure and behaviour of the computer system.
A. Computer Design
B. Computer Organisation
C. Computer Architecture
D. Both A and B

**121.** The Physical quantities ______ represents the binary information is digital computers
A. Light
B. Signal
C. Beam
D. None of the above

**122.** Name the three Boolean functions
A. AND, OR and XOT
B. NAND, OS and AND
C. AND, OR and exclusive –OS
D. AND, OR and complement

**123.** The truth table represents the relationship between
A. function and its binary variables
B. function and its binary operation
C. Both A and B
D. None of the above

**124.** According to the De Morgan's theorem, a NOR gate that performs the $(x + y)'$ function is equivalent to ______
A. $(xy)'$      B. $(x' + y')$
C. $x'\,y'$      D. None of the above

**125.** ______ is a binary cell capable of storing one bit of information.
A. Register
B. Flip-flop
C. Clock pulse
D. Sequential circuit

**126.** Find out which one is not a Flip-flop
A. SR Flip-flop
B. D Flip-flop
C. JK Flip-flop
D. None of the above

**127.** CMOS stands for
   A. Complementary Magnetic-oxide
      Semiconductor
   B. Complementary Manganese-oxide
      Semiconductor
   C. Complementary Memory-operation
      Semiconductor
   D. Complementary      Metal-oxide
      Semiconductor

**128.** A decoder is a combinational circuit that converts binary information from the $n$ coded inputs to a maximum of _______.
   A. $2^{n+1}$                B. $n2^{n+1}$
   C. $2_n$                    D. $2^n$

**129.** An encoder has _______ input lines and _______ output lines.
   A. $2^n$ or less, $n$
   B. $2^{n+1}$, $n+1$
   C. $2^{n+1}$, $n+1$
   D. Both A & B

**130.** A register organized to allow to move left or right operation is called _______
   A. Counter
   B. Loader
   C. Adder
   D. Shift register

**131.** Which of the following are the cheapest memory devices in terms of Cost/Bit?
   A. Semiconductor Memories
   B. Magnetic Disks
   C. Magnetic Tapes
   D. Compact Disks

**132.** Which of the following have the fastest access time?
   A. Semiconductor Memories
   B. Magnetic Disks
   C. Magnetic Tapes
   D. Compact Disks

## SOFTWARE/HARDWARE

**133.** Which technology is used in a CDROM Drive?
   A. Mechanical
   B. Electromechanical
   C. Optical
   D. Fiber Optical

**134.** MOS stands for _______
   A. Metal Oxide Semiconductor
   B. Most Often Store
   C. Method Organised Stack
   D. None of the above

**135.** The unit kIPS used to measure the speed of—
   A. Processor          B. Disk drive
   C. Printer            D. Tape drive

**136.** IC are classified on the basis of _______
   A. Manufacturing company
   B. Type of computer
   C. Number of transistors
   D. None of the above

**137.** The programs which are as permanent as hardware and stored in ROM are known as-
   A. Hardware
   B. Software
   C. Firmware
   D. ROMware

**138.** A Compiler is _______
   A. a combination of computer hardware
   B. a program which translates machine code into hight level language
   C. a program which translates high-level language to a machine code
   D. None of the above

**139.** Computer software includes _______
   A. Application software
   B. System software
   C. Both A and B
   D. All of the above

**140.** Machine language is _______
   A. 1st generation language
   B. 2nd generation language
   C. 3rd generation language
   D. 4th generation language

**141.** Assembly language _______
   A. uses alphabetic codes in place of binary numbers used in machine language
   B. is the High-level language to write programs
   C. Low level language for programming computer
   D. None of the above

**142.** A source code is ________
- A. a program written in a machine language
- B. a program to be translated into machine language
- C. a machine language translation of a program
- D. None of the above

**143.** Direct X is a
- A. Computer part
- B. Software that drives graphic hardware
- C. A user interface
- D. None of the above

**144.** Payroll software used for the salaries of the employees is a type of ________
- A. Utility software
- B. Application software
- C. System software
- D. Both A and B

**145.** Name the lowest level of computer language
- A. Symbolic language
- B. Assembly language
- C. Machine language
- D. None of the above

**146.** Which one is the correct set of instruction of Machine Language?
- A. Controlled – Load, Read, Jump, Write
- B. Controlled – Load, Store, Jump, instructions
- C. Controlled – Read and Write
- D. Controlled – Halt, start and end

**147.** Write which one is the advantage of the Assembly language over Machine language
- A. Symbolic representation of numerical code
- B. It is numerical representation of machine code
- C. Assembling the computer hardwares
- D. None of the above

**148.** Which one is not a high level language.
- A. COBOL
- B. C++
- C. ALGOL
- D. None of the above

**149.** Name the language whose main application area in Time Sharing System.
- A. RPG
- B. PL/1
- C. APL
- D. BASIC

**150.** Name the programming language whose main application area is scientific/commercial.
- A. Procedure Programming language
- B. Problem Oriented language
- C. Protocol Oriented lanugage
- D. Interactive Programming language

**151.** ________ is not classified as high level
- A. Pascle language
- B. $C^{++}$ language
- C. C language
- D. Interpreter language

**152.** The system software that transforms a program written in procedure-oriented language into an equivalent form in machine language is called the ________.
- A. Editor
- B. Translator
- C. Compiler
- D. Assembler

**153.** How many bits are there in a byte?
- A. 2
- B. 4
- C. 16
- D. 8

**154.** Which of the following is NOT one of the six major subsystems of a PC?
- A. Speakers
- B. CPU
- C. RAM
- D. User Interface

**155.** Which of the following software is System Software?
- A. Word Processor
- B. Compiler
- C. Database System
- D. Web Browser

**156.** Motherboard is used in computers as ________.
- A. a powerful means of communication
- B. the main circuit board, also called system board, on which bus structure are mounted
- C. the interactive feature of network
- D. none of the above

## OPERATING SYSTEM

**157.** Usually, in MSDOS, the primary hard disk drives has the drive letter _______
A. A   B. B
C. C   D. D

**158.** What is the name of the latest Server Operating System developed by Microsoft?
A. Windows NT
B. Windows 2000
C. Windows XP
D. Windows 2008 R-2

**159.** Programs are executed on the basis of a priority number in a-
A. Batch processing system
B. Multiprogramming
C. Time sharing
D. None of these

**160.** The primary function of an operating system is
A. Memory Management
B. Process Manangement
C. Disks and I/O device Management
D. All of the above

**161.** Which one of the following is not an operating system?
A. UNIX   B. Windows
C. XENIX   D. APPLE

**162.** Which one of the following is not a function of operating system of PC?
A. Addition and substruction
B. Control the hardware
C. Provids a platform for application software
D. Interprets the user commands

**163.** The first version of MS-DOS was released on August 1981, which run on _______ memory.
A. 6 kB   B. 7 kB
C. 8 kB   D. 10 kB

**164.** What is the Process by which the operating system is loaded into the memory?
A. Booting
B. Processing
C. Loading
D. None of the above

**165.** Where is ROM-BIOS program located?
A. RAM   B. ROM
C. Hard Disk   D. Compact Disk

**166.** The core of UNIX opeating system is called
A. Kernel
B. Karnel
C. Kannal
D. None of the above

**167.** _______ is not a multiprogramming operating system.
A. Windows   B. DOS
C. UNIX   D. LINUX

**168.** The LINUX operating systm was first developed in the year
A. 1980   B. 1991
C. 1992   D. 1995

## MS-WORD

**169.** What is the common technique to select the entire document by using mouse click.
A. Single click in the selection bar
B. Double click in the selection bar
C. Triple click in the selection bar
D. Double click anywhere on the document

**170.** How can you select a sentence by mouse click?
A. Double click on any word
B. Single click on the particular sentence
C. Double click on the particular sentence
D. Triple click on the particular sentence

**171.** If you want to select a paragraph by mouse click technique, then _______
A. Click three times in the paragraph/ double click in the selecton bar adjacent to the paragraph.
B. Click double times in the paragraph/ three-time click in the selection bar adjacent to the paragraph
C. Click one time in the paragraph/double click in the selection bar adjacent to the paragraph.
D. All of the above

**172.** What does the tool tip mean?
A. it is the button name
B. it is the tool name
C. it is the menu name
D. it is the another name of toolbar

**173.** Which one of the following is not the measuring unit of the font size?
A. Pica
B. Unit
C. Both A & B
D. None of the above

**174.** The key feature of formating text in MS-Word is
A. Table
B. Style
C. Font
D. None of the above

**175.** There are four kinds of tabs that control the alignment of the text within a document. Find out which one is not a name of the tab
A. Bar tab
B. Center tab
C. Decimal tab
D. Binary tab

**176.** What does the 'L' symbol indicates to the left of the ruler?
A. the 'L' Symbol denotes a center tab
B. the 'L' Symbol denotes start point of text
C. the 'L' Symbol denotes a flush left-tab
D. the 'L' Symbol denotes a flush right tab

**177.** What would be the symbol if you want to use the center tab?
A. Bakward 'L' symbol
B. 'L' Symbol
C. Inverted 'T' symbol
D. None of the above

**178.** If we use inverted 'T' with a dot on the right side, what kind of tab does this represent?
A. a standard tab
B. a flush right tab
C. a decimial tab
D. a flush left tab

**179.** A blueprint for the text, graphics and formating in a document is known as____
A. Text Editor
B. Template
C. Design
D. Format

**180.** What would be the extension of the template file?
A. .doc
B. .exe
C. .tem
D. .dot

**181.** ______ is a feature that is used to link a letter with an address file.
A. Mailing labels
B. Envelope
C. Mail merge
D. Catalog

## MS-EXCEL

**182.** As text editor are used at the MS-word and ______ are used in MS-Excel.
A. work space
B. work sheet
C. work area
D. none of the above

**183.** Which of the following is not a toggle key?
A. Num lock key
B. Caps lock key
C. Both (A) & (B)
D. Ctrl key

**184.** What is the total number of rows in MS-Excel?
A. 65536
B. More than 7000
C. 63536
D. 65556

**185.** Starting letter of the column is 'A', What would be the end letter?
A. Z
B. VI
C. XFD
D. IV

**186.** What location would be described by the cell E12?
A. column E on row 12
B. column 12 on row E
C. column E
D. All of the above

187. What is the function of fill handle in MS-Excel?
    A. used to fill data automatically in cell
    B. used to set up entry key directive
    C. used to make numeric entry
    D. used to create shortcut key

188. One important function of MS-excels over MS-word is
    A. Formating numerals
    B. Decimal alignment
    C. Mathematical calculation
    D. Font Selection

189. Ms-excel record cell addresses in formula in three different ways, they are ______, and mixed.
    A. Column, Row
    B. Module, Relative
    C. Absolute, Module
    D. Absolute, Relative

190. Charts can be of two types. They are ______ and ______
    A. Embedded chart, Chart sheet
    B. Embedded chart, Chart area
    C. Both A & B
    D. None of the above

191. MS-Excel offers ______ different chart types.
    A. 11                     B. 15
    C. 20                     D. 25

## MS–POWERPOINT

192. What is the file extention of Ms-Powerpoint?
    A. .exe                   B. .xls
    C. .ppt                   D. .pst

193. What will you do if changes are required in all the slides in a presentation?
    A. Change the Master
    B. Change in each slide
    C. Both A and B
    D. None of the above

194. In ______, slides cannot be edited. They can only be copied, pasted and change positions.
    A. Master slide
    B. Slide sorter
    C. Design template
    D. None of the above

195. Which of the following can be added in a slide?
    A. Image                  B. Second
    C. Chart                  D. All of the above

196. What are the things that can be added in the slide separately using animation effects?
    A. Bullets                B. Tables
    C. Objects                D. All of the above

## DATABASE MANAGEMENT SYSTEM

197. A Collection of data for one or multiple uses is known as ______
    A. Database               B. Information
    C. Datum                  D. System

198. The known facts that can be recorded and that have implicit meaning is known as ______
    A. Related Data
    B. Data
    C. Database
    D. None of the above

199. What is the meaning of DBMS?
    A. Data-based Managements Systems
    B. Data-based Management Systems
    C. Database Management System
    D. None of the above

200. Which of the following is not a relational database?
    A. Oracle
    B. MS Access
    C. MS SQL Server
    D. None of the above

201. ______ is not a characteristic of a relational database model?
    A. Records                B. Tuples
    C. Tree                   D. Fields

**202.** The DBMs is a general-purpose software that facilitates the process of defining, constructing, manipulating and ______.
  A. destreeating
  B. retreiving
  C. restoreing
  D. sharing

**203.** The information stored in the Catalog is called ______
  A. meta-data
  B. mini-world
  C. record
  D. All of the above

**204.** Some database systems provides capabilities for defining deduction rules for inferencing new information from the stored database. Such systems are called
  A. Active Database
  B. Deductive Database
  C. Both A & B
  D. None of the above

**205.** Advantages of the DBMS approach over the traditional file system are
  A. Reduce data redundancy
  B. Data independence
  C. Sharing of data
  D. All of the above

**206.** What does DBA stands for?
  A. Database Associate
  B. Database Administrator
  C. Database Actor
  D. None of the above

## COMPUTER NETWORKS

**207.** Which of the following organizations looks at standards for representation of data on the Internet ?
  A. ISOC
  B. W3C
  C. IEEE
  D. IETE

**208.** What is the address given to a computer connected to a network called?
  A. System Address
  B. SYSID
  C. Process ID
  D. IP Address

**209.** What is the other name for a LAN Card?
  A. NIC
  B. Network Connector
  C. MODEM
  D. Internet Card

**210.** Which of the following cables can transmit data at high speeds—
  A. Coaxial Cable
  B. Optic Fibre Cable
  C. Twisted pair Cable
  D. UTP Cable

**211.** When you purchase a product over a Mobile Phone, the transaction is called—
  A. Web Commerce
  B. e-Commerce
  C. m-Commerce
  D. Mobile Purchases

**212.** The minimum number of systems required to make a network of ______
  A. 2
  B. 3
  C. 10
  D. 100

**213.** The most popular network system in the PC world is ______
  A. ARPANET
  B. NOVELL NETWARE
  C. NSFNET
  D. None of the above

**214.** Traditional LAN run at speed of ______
  A. 10 to 100 Mbps
  B. 100 to 1000 Mbps
  C. 1000 to 10,000 Mbps
  D. None of the above

**215.** ______ and ______ are two types of transmission technology.
  A. Broadcast networks, Point network
  B. Broadcast networks, multicast network
  C. Broadcast network, Point-to-Point networks
  D. None of the above

**216.** ______ (the IBM token ring) is a popular ring based LAN operating at 4 and 16 Mbps.
  A. IEEE 802.3
  B. IEEE 802.4
  C. IEEE 802.5
  D. IEEE 802.6

**217.** WAN stands for
A. Wide Area Network
B. Wireless Area Network
C. World Area Network
D. None of the above

**218.** What is the slowest transmission medium?
A. twisted pair wire
B. coaxial cable
C. fiber optic cable
D. None of the above

**219.** The Distributed Queue Dual Bus (DQDB) system is used in
A. LAN          B. MAN
C. WAN          D. PAN

**220.** Which of the following have the highest transmisson rate?
A. LAN          B. MAN
C. WAN          D. PAN

**221.** The full form of TCP/IP is
A. Transport control Protocol/Internet Protocol
B. Transmission Control Protocol/ Internet Protocol
C. Both A & B
D. None of the above

## INTERNET

**222.** Which of the following was the progenitor of internet?
A. ARPANET
B. MILNET
C. NSF NET
D. None of the above

**223.** When and what is the first graphical web browser?
A. 1993, NCSA Mosaic
B. 1969, ARPANET
C. 1987, ENQIRE
D. 1991, Gopher

**224.** Which one ofthe folloiwng is an email program?
A. MS-word
B. Eudora lite
C. Internet Explorer
D. None of the above

**225.** What is Internet address known as _____?
A. Web address          B. Web site
C. URL          D. www

**226.** What does the underlined text mean is www.education.nic.in
A. Domain name
B. Organisation name
C. Country name
D. None of the above

**227.** ISDN stands for
A. Internet Services Digital Network
B. Interface Services Digital Network
C. Integrated Services Digital Network
D. None of the above

**228.** Which one of the following is not a search engine?
A. Google
B. Yahoo
C. Altavista
D. All of the above

**229.** _____ is designed for distributing searching and retriving document over the internet
A. Veronica
B. Archie
C. Gopher
D. None of the above

**230.** Word Wide Web began from the year _____.
A. 1987          B. 1988
C. 1989          D. 1990

**231.** WWW service listens on TCP port no. _____ for incomming request.
A. 80          B. 90
C. 100          D. 120

**232.** What is the name of the software that allows us to browse through web pages called?
A. Browser          B. Mail Client
C. FTP Client          D. Messenger

**233.** Which of the following devices could not be a part of a wired LAN based on star topology ?
A. Switch          B. Repeater
C. Hub          D. Router

**234.** Which protocol needs to be installed for Internet access on a network ?
A. TCP/IP
B. TELNET
C. IPX/SPX
D. NetBEUI

## MOBILE COMPUTING

**235.** What kind of Protocol is used to provide Internet access from mobile?
A. TCP/IP
B. ISD
C. WAP
D. HTTP

**236.** An average latency is a wireless network is around _____ but can be as high as _____
A. ½ second, 10 seconds
B. 1 second, 12 seconds
C. 1 minute, 5 minutes
D. 1 hour, 12 hours

**237.** What is the full form of SIM?
A. Station Identity Module
B. System Identity Module
C. Subscriber Identity Module
D. None of the above

**238.** What language is used in Mobile computing?
A. XML
B. WML
C. DHTML
D. XHTML

## MULTIMEDIA

**239.** Multimedia is made up of two words multi and media where multi means "many" and media means _____
A. the way by which we link
B. the way by which we deal
C. the way by which we communicate
D. the way by which we transfer data

**240.** What is the full-form of JPEG?
A. Joint Photographic Experts Group
B. Joint Philosophical Experts Group
C. Joint Philosophical Exports Group
D. Joint Photographic Exports Group

**241.** What is the full-form aeromym of MPEG?
A. Motion Picture Experts Group
B. Multimedia Picture Experts Group
C. Moving Picture Experts Group
D. Motion Picture Experience Group

**242.** Which one is the tool and accessories of Multimedia?
A. Animation
B. Audio
C. Image
D. All of the above

**243.** The term 'multimedia' coined by
A. Bob goldstein
B. Tay Vaughan
C. NASA
D. Mc Graw Hills

**244.** Motion Capturing System is
A. by which motion of living things are captured & integrated into the computer
B. Various pictures are integrated in the film
C. Both A & B
D. None of the above

**245.** Rapid 3D Digitizer is the latest technology of _____.
A. Photography
B. Digital Sound
C. Scanning
D. Motion Picture

**246.** What is the full-form of VRML?
A. Virtual Reality Modeling Language
B. Video Reality Modeling Language
C. Virtual Reality Multimedia Language
D. None of the above

**247.** Video conferencing is an application of _____.
A. Motion picture
B. Multimedia
C. Cinematography
D. Two-way video and audio transmissions

**248.** What is the full-form of DAT?
A. Digital Authoring Tape
B. Digital Audio Tracking
C. Digital Audio Tape
D. None of the above

## DATA WAREHOUSING

**249.** What is the full-form of OLAP?
A. Online Analytical Processing
B. Offline Analytical Processing
C. Order Analytical Processing
D. Onshore Analytical Processing

**250.** What does ERP stands for?
A. Entreprivate Resource Planning
B. Enterprise Reform Planning
C. Enterprise Record Planning
D. Enterprise Resource Planning

**251.** Which one is the fundamental distinguishing characteristic of a data warehouse?
A. Time-variance
B. Time-versatility
C. Time-variable
D. Time-value

**252.** ______ is also a fundamental distinguishing characteristic of a data warehouse.
A. Non-volatile
B. Non-variable
C. Non-variance
D. None of the above

**253.** What is data mining?
A. Automatic extraction of pattern of information from historical data
B. Automatic extraction of data from old data
C. Automatic extrapolate data from old data
D. None of the above

**254.** Which one of the following is an analysis among the decision support system?
A. Query and Reporting
B. Non-volatility
C. Time-variance
D. Subject-Orientation

**255.** ______ is and integrated computer based system used to manage internal and external resources:
A. ERP
B. EIS
C. DSS
D. None of the above

**256.** Easy to use, yet powerful
A. It is knowledge access paradigm
B. It is Data Analysis Paradigm
C. Both A & B
D. None of the above

**257.** What does GIS stands for?
A. Geological Information System
B. Genetics Information Systems
C. Geographic Information Systems
D. Gene Information Systems

**258.** Which of the following is used as a software package of ERP?
A. Ledger SMB
B. J fire
C. Open ERP
D. All of the above

# ANSWERS

| 1 | 2 | 3 | 4 | 5 | 6 | 7 | 8 | 9 | 10 |
|---|---|---|---|---|---|---|---|---|---|
| B | D | A | B | B | D | A | C | C | D |
| 11 | 12 | 13 | 14 | 15 | 16 | 17 | 18 | 19 | 20 |
| B | A | A | A | A | D | C | B | A | B |
| 21 | 22 | 23 | 24 | 25 | 26 | 27 | 28 | 29 | 30 |
| D | C | B | A | C | B | B | C | A | A |
| 31 | 32 | 33 | 34 | 35 | 36 | 37 | 38 | 39 | 40 |
| D | C | B | A | C | C | B | A | B | C |
| 41 | 42 | 43 | 44 | 45 | 46 | 47 | 48 | 49 | 50 |
| C | B | A | B | C | B | C | A | B | C |
| 51 | 52 | 53 | 54 | 55 | 56 | 57 | 58 | 59 | 60 |
| B | A | B | B | B | A | A | C | A | B |

| 61 | 62 | 63 | 64 | 65 | 66 | 67 | 68 | 69 | 70 |
|---|---|---|---|---|---|---|---|---|---|
| A | B | B | B | D | D | A | D | C | B |
| **71** | **72** | **73** | **74** | **75** | **76** | **77** | **78** | **79** | **80** |
| B | C | A | D | B | D | A | D | C | D |
| **81** | **82** | **83** | **84** | **85** | **86** | **87** | **88** | **89** | **90** |
| C | D | D | B | A | D | C | C | D | A |
| **91** | **92** | **93** | **94** | **95** | **96** | **97** | **98** | **99** | **100** |
| B | D | C | B | A | D | C | A | A | D |
| **101** | **102** | **103** | **104** | **105** | **106** | **107** | **108** | **109** | **110** |
| A | C | C | C | C | B | C | B | A | D |
| **111** | **112** | **113** | **114** | **115** | **116** | **117** | **118** | **119** | **120** |
| B | D | A | B | D | C | D | A | A | C |
| **121** | **122** | **123** | **124** | **125** | **126** | **127** | **128** | **129** | **130** |
| B | D | A | C | B | D | D | D | A | D |
| **131** | **132** | **133** | **134** | **135** | **136** | **137** | **138** | **139** | **140** |
| D | D | C | A | A | C | C | C | C | A |
| **141** | **142** | **143** | **144** | **145** | **146** | **147** | **148** | **149** | **150** |
| C | B | B | B | C | B | A | D | C | A |
| **151** | **152** | **153** | **154** | **155** | **156** | **157** | **158** | **159** | **160** |
| D | C | D | A | B | B | C | D | B | D |
| **161** | **162** | **163** | **164** | **165** | **166** | **167** | **168** | **169** | **170** |
| D | A | C | A | B | A | B | B | C | B |
| **171** | **172** | **173** | **174** | **175** | **176** | **177** | **178** | **179** | **180** |
| A | A | C | B | D | B | C | C | B | D |
| **181** | **182** | **183** | **184** | **185** | **186** | **187** | **188** | **189** | **190** |
| C | B | D | B | C | A | A | B | D | A |
| **191** | **192** | **193** | **194** | **195** | **196** | **197** | **198** | **199** | **200** |
| A | C | A | B | D | D | A | B | C | D |
| **201** | **202** | **203** | **204** | **205** | **206** | **207** | **208** | **209** | **210** |
| C | D | A | B | D | B | B | D | A | B |
| **211** | **212** | **213** | **214** | **215** | **216** | **217** | **218** | **219** | **220** |
| C | A | B | A | C | C | A | A | B | A |
| **221** | **222** | **223** | **224** | **225** | **226** | **227** | **228** | **229** | **230** |
| B | A | A | B | C | A | C | D | A | C |
| **231** | **232** | **233** | **234** | **235** | **236** | **237** | **238** | **239** | **240** |
| A | A | C | A | C | A | C | B | C | A |
| **241** | **242** | **243** | **244** | **245** | **246** | **247** | **248** | **249** | **250** |
| C | D | A | A | C | A | D | C | A | D |
| **251** | **252** | **253** | **254** | **255** | **256** | **257** | **258** | | |
| A | A | A | A | A | A | C | D | | |

# 2. ▌ C Programming ▐



**1.** Which of the following language is predecessor to C programming language?
A. A
B. B
C. BCPL
D. C++

**2.** C programming language was developed by ________.
A. Dennis Ritchie
B. Ken Thompson
C. Bill Gates
D. Peter Norton

**3.** C language was developed in the year ___
A. 1970
B. 1972
C. 1976
D. 1980

**4.** C programe is a ___ language
A. High Level
B. Low Level
C. Middle Level
D. Machine Level

**5.** C language is available for which of the following operating systems?
A. DOS
B. Windows
C. Unix
D. All of the above

## STATEMENT OF C PROGRAM

**6.** Which of the following symbol is used to denote a pre-processor statement?
A. !
B. #
C. ~
D. ;

**7.** Which symbol is used as a statement terminator in C?
A. !
B. #
C. ~
D. ;

**8.** Which escape character can be used to begin a new line in C?
A. \a
B. \b
C. m
D. \n

**9.** Which of the following is an example of compounds assignment statement?
A. a = 5
B. a += 5
C. a = b = c
D. a = b

**10.** A compound statement is a group of statements included between a pair of ________.
A. double quote
B. curly braces
C. parenthesis
D. a pair of /'s

**11.** Which of the following statements is true?
A. C Library functions provide I/O facilities
B. C inherent I/O facilities
C. C doesn't have I/O facilities
D. Both A and C

**12.** A statement differs from expression by terminating with a ________.
A. ;
B. :
C. NULL
D. .

**13.** Identify the wrong statement.
A. putchar(65)
B. putchar('x')
C. putchar("x")
D. putchar('\n')

**14.** Which escape character can be used to beep from speaker in C?
A. \a
B. \b
C. \m
D. \n

**15.** Character constants should be enclosed between ______.
A. Single quotes
B. Double quotes
C. Both a and b
D. None of these

**16.** String constants should be enclosed between _______.
A. Single quotes
B. Double quotes
C. Both a and b
D. None of these

**17.** Which of the following is invalid?
A. ' '
B. " "
C. 'a'
D. 'abc'

## DATA TYPE

**18.** Which of the following is a "Scalar Data" type?
A. Float
B. Union
C. Array
D. Pointer

**19.** Which of the following are tokens in C?
A. Keywords
B. Variables
C. Constants
D. All of the above

**20.** What is the valid range of numbers for "int" type of data?
A. 0 to 256
B. – 32768 to +32767
C. – 65536 to +65536
D. No specific range

**21.** The maximum length of a variable in C is _______.
A. 8 bits
B. 16 bits
C. 32 bits
D. 64 bits

**22.** What will be the maximum size of a float variable?
A. 1 byte
B. 2 bytes
C. 4 bytes
D. 8 bytes

**23.** What will be the maximum size of a double variable?
A. 1 byte
B. 4 bytes
C. 8 bytes
D. 16 bytes

**24.** A declaration float a,b; occupies _______ of memory.
A. 1 byte
B. 4 bytes
C. 8 bytes
D. 16 bytes

**25.** The size of a *String* variable is _______.
A. 1 byte
B. 8 bytes
C. 16 bytes
D. None of these

**26** Symbolic constants can be defined using_______.
A. # define
B. const
C. symbols
D. None of these

**27.** Null character is represented by _______.
A. \n
B. \0
C. \o
D. \e

**28.** The meaning of conversion character for data input is _______.
A. Data item is a long integer
B. Data item is an unsigned decimal integer
C. Data item is a short integer
D. None of the above

## LOOP

**29.** C programming supports how many basic looping constructs?
A. 2
B. 3
C. 4
D. 6

**30.** What should be the expression return value for a "do-while" to terminate
A. 1
B. 0
C. –1
D. NULL

**31.** Which among the following is a unconditional control structure?
A. do-while
B. if-else
C. goto
D. for

**32.** Continue statement is used _______.
A. to go to the next iteration in a loop
B. come out of a loop
C. exit and return to the main function
D. restarts iterations from beginning of loop

**33.** The continue command cannot be used with _______.
A. for
B. switch
C. do
D. while

## FUNCTION OF C

**34.** Which of the following is character oriented console I/O function?
A. getchar() and putchar()
B. gets() and puts()
C. scanf() and printf()
D. fgets() and fputs()

**35.** The output of printf("%u", -1) is _______.
   A. -1
   B. minimum int value
   C. maximum int value
   D. Error message

**36.** In C, a Union is _______.
   A. memory location
   B. memory store
   C. memory screen
   D. None of the above

**37.** When the main function is called, it is called with the arguments
   A. argc
   B. argv
   C. Both A & B
   D. None of the above

**38.** Which pair of functions below are used for single character I/O?
   A. Getchar() and putchar()
   B. Scanf() and printf()
   C. Input() and output()
   D. None of the above

**39.** The printf() function retures which value when an error occurs?
   A. Positive value
   B. Zero
   C. Negative value
   D. None of the above

**40.** With every use of a memory allocation function, what function should be used to release allocated memory which is no longer needed?
   A. unalloc()          B. dropmem()
   C. dealloc()          D. free()

## OPERATOR

**41.** The operator && is an example for _______ operator.
   A. Assignment        B. Increment
   C. Logical           D. Rational

**42.** The operator & is used for _______.
   A. Bitwise AND       B. Bitwise OR
   C. Logical AND       D. OR

**43.** The operator / can be applied to _______.

**43.** (continued)
   A. integer values
   B. float values
   C. double values
   D. All of the above

**44.** The equality operator is represented by _______.
   A. :=                B. .E
   C. =                 D. ==

**45.** Operators have hierarchy. It is used to know which operator?
   A. is most important
   B. is used first
   C. is faster
   D. operates on large numbers

**46.** The bitwise AND operator is used for _______.
   A. Masking           B. Comparison
   C. Division          D. Shifting bits

**47.** The bitwise OR operator is used to _______.
   A. set the desired bits to 1
   B. set the desired bits to 0
   C. divide numbers
   D. multiply numbers

**48.** Which of the following operator has the highest precedence?
   A. *                 B. ==
   C. =>                D. +

**49.** The associativity of ! operator is _______.
   A. Right to Left
   B. Left to Right
   C. (A) for Arithmetic and (B) for Relational
   D. (A) for Relational and (B) for Arithmetic

**50.** Which operator has the lowest priority?
   A. ++                B. %
   C. +                 D. ||

**51.** Which operator has the highest priority?
   A. ++                B. %
   C. +                 D. ||

**52.** Operators have precedence. A precedence determines which operator is _______.
   A. faster
   B. takes less memory
   C. evaluated first
   D. takes no arguments

**53.** Integer Division results in ______.
  A. rounding the fractional part
  B. truncating the fractional part
  C. floating value
  D. an Error is generated

**54.** Which of the following is a ternary operator?
  A. ?          B. *
  C. sizeof     D. ^

**55.** What will be the output of the expression 11 ^ 5?
  A. 5          B. 6
  C. 11         D. None of these

**56.** The type cast operator is ______.
  A. (type)     B. cast()
  C. //         D. " "

**57.** Explicit type conversion is known as ______.

  A. Casting        B. Conversion
  C. Disjunction    D. Separation

**58.** The operator + in a+=4 means ______.
  A. a = a + 4      B. a + 4 = a
  C. a = 4          D. a = 4 + 4

**59.** p++ executes faster than p+1 because ______.

  A. p uses registers
  B. p++ is a single instruction
  C. ++ is faster than +
  D. None of the above

**60.** Which operator in C programming is called a ternary operator?
  A. if..then       B. ++
  C. ?              D. ()

**61.** The conversion characters for data input means that the data item is ______.
  A. an unsigned decimal integer
  B. a short integer
  C. a hexadecimal integer
  D. a string followed by white space

**62.** An expression contains relational, assignment and arithmetic operators. If Parenthesis are not present, the order will be ______.
  A. assignment, arithmetic, relational
  B. relational, arithmetic, assignment
  C. assignment, relational, arithmetic
  D. arithmetic, relational, assignment

**63.** Which of the following is a key word used for a storage class?
  A. printf        B. external
  C. auto          D. scanf

**64.** In the C language 'a' represents
  A. a digit       B. an integer
  C. a character   D. a word

**65.** The number of the relational operators in the C language is ______.
  A. Four          B. Six
  C. Three         D. One

## ARRAY AND POINTER

**66.** A multidimensional array can be expressed in terms of ______.
  A. array of pointers rather than as pointers to a group of contiguous array
  B. array without the group of contiguous array
  C. data type arrays
  D. None of the above

**67.** C programming allows arrays of greater than two dimensions, who will determined this?
  A. programmer
  B. compiler
  C. parameter
  D. None of the above

**68.** A pointer to a pointer is a form of ______.
  A. multiple indirection
  B. a chain of pointers
  C. both A and B
  D. None of the above

**69.** Pointers are of ______.
  A. integer data type
  B. character data type
  C. unsigned integer data types
  D. None of the above

**70.** Maximum number of elements in the array declaration int a[5][8] is ______.
  A. 28            B. 32
  C. 35            D. 40

71. If the size of the array is less than the number of initializers then, ______.
    A. Extra values are being ignored
    B. Generates an error message
    C. Size of Array is increased
    D. Size is neglected when values are given

72. Array subscripts in C language always start at ______.
    A. –1
    B. 1
    C. 0
    D. Value provided by user

73. Identify the invalid pointer arithmetic in C programming.
    A. Addition of float value to a pointer
    B. Comparison of pointers that do not point to the element of the same array
    C. Subtracting an integer from a pointer
    D. Assigning the value 0 to a pointer variable

## HEADER FILE

74. Header files in C contains ______
    A. Compiler commands
    B. Library functions
    C. Header information of C programs
    D. Operators for files

75. Which header file is essential for using strcmp( ) function?
    A. string.h        B. strings.h
    C. text.h          D. strcmp.h

76. malloc() function used in dynamic allocation is available in which header file?
    A. stdio.h         B. stdlib.h
    C. conio.h         D. mem.h

77. File manipulation functions in C are available in which header file?
    A. streams.h       B. stdio.h
    C. stdlib.h        D. files.h

78. Which of the following header file is required for strcpy() function?
    A. string.h        B. strings.h
    C. files.h         D. strcpy()

79. A linker is
    A. a compiler
    B. an active debugger
    C. a C interpreter
    D. a analyzing tool in C

## PROGRAMMING

80. Code: int z,x=5,y=-10,a=4,b=2;
    z = x++ - —y * b / a;
    Calculate the value of 'z' from the above equation.
    A. 5               B. 6
    C. 10              D. 11

81. With every use of a memory allocation function, what function should be used to release allocated memory which is no longer needed?
    A. unalloc()       B. dropmem()
    C. dealloc()       D. free()

82. Code:
    ```
    void *ptr;
    myStruct myArray[10];
    ptr = myArray
    ```
    Which of the following is the correct way to increase the variable "ptr"?
    A. ptr = ptr + sizeof(myStruct);
    B. ++(int*)ptr;
    C. ptr = ptr + sizeof(myArray);
    D. increment(ptr);

83. Code:
    ```
    char* myFunc (char *ptr)
    {
     ptr += 3;
     return (ptr);
    }
    int main()
    {
     char *x, *y;
     x = "HELLO";
     y = myFunc (x);
     printf ("y = %s \n", y);
     return 0;
    }
    ```

What will be the print output when the above sample code is executed?

A. y = HELLO    B. y = ELLO
C. y = LLO      D. y = LO

84. "My salary was increased by 15%!" Select the statement which will EXACTLY reproduce the line of text above.

A. printf("\"My salary was increased by 15/%\!\"\n");

B. printf("My salary was increased by 15%!\n");

C. printf("My salary was increased by 15'%'!\n");

D. printf("\"My salary was increased by 15%%!\"\n");

85. What is the difference between a declaration and a definition of a variable?

A. Both can occur multiple times, but a declaration must occur first.

B. There is no difference between them.

C. A definition occurs once, but a declaration may occur many times.

D. A declaration occurs once, but a definition may occur many times.

86. int testarray[3][2][2] = {1, 2, 3, 4, 5, 6, 7, 8, 9, 10, 11, 12};

What value does testarray[2][1][0] in the sample code above contain?

A. 3       B. 5
C. 7       D. 11

87. Code:

```
int a=10,b;
b=a++ + ++a;
printf("%d,%d,%d,%d",b,a++,a,++a);
```

What will be the output when the following code is executed?

A. 12,10,11,13      B. 22,10,11,13
C. 22,11,11,11      D. 22,13,13,13

## ANSWERS

| 1 | 2 | 3 | 4 | 5 | 6 | 7 | 8 | 9 | 10 |
|---|---|---|---|---|---|---|---|---|---|
| B | A | B | A | D | B | D | D | B | B |

| 11 | 12 | 13 | 14 | 15 | 16 | 17 | 18 | 19 | 20 |
|---|---|---|---|---|---|---|---|---|---|
| D | A | C | B | B | A | D | A | A | B |

| 21 | 22 | 23 | 24 | 25 | 26 | 27 | 28 | 29 | 30 |
|---|---|---|---|---|---|---|---|---|---|
| D | C | C | C | A | A | B | C | B | B |

| 31 | 32 | 33 | 34 | 35 | 36 | 37 | 38 | 39 | 40 |
|---|---|---|---|---|---|---|---|---|---|
| C | A | B | A | C | B | C | A | C | D |

| 41 | 42 | 43 | 44 | 45 | 46 | 47 | 48 | 49 | 50 |
|---|---|---|---|---|---|---|---|---|---|
| C | C | B | D | B | B | A | A | A | C |

| 51 | 52 | 53 | 54 | 55 | 56 | 57 | 58 | 59 | 60 |
|---|---|---|---|---|---|---|---|---|---|
| A | C | B | A | B | A | A | A | B | C |

| 61 | 62 | 63 | 64 | 65 | 66 | 67 | 68 | 69 | 70 |
|---|---|---|---|---|---|---|---|---|---|
| D | D | C | C | B | A | B | A | D | D |

| 71 | 72 | 73 | 74 | 75 | 76 | 77 | 78 | 79 | 80 |
|---|---|---|---|---|---|---|---|---|---|
| B | C | A | B | A | B | B | A | A | C |

| 81 | 82 | 83 | 84 | 85 | 86 | 87 | | | |
|---|---|---|---|---|---|---|---|---|---|
| D | A | D | D | C | D | D | | | |

# 3.  ██ C++ Programming ██



1. Name the program that translates a programming language instructions one line at a time
   A. Compiler
   B. Interpreter
   C. Assembler
   D. Translator

2. C++ was originally developed by _______.
   A. Nicolas Wirth
   B. Donald Knuth
   C. Bjarne Stroustrup
   D. Ken Thompson

3. C++ name was suggested by _______.
   A. Rrick Mascitti
   B. Bjarne Stroustrup
   C. Donald Knuth
   D. Ken Thompson

4. The feature that allows the same operation to be carried out differently depending on the context is
   A. polymorphism
   B. polyamy
   C. inheritance
   D. multitasking

5. The fields in a class of a C++ programs are by default _______.
   A. protected
   B. public
   C. private
   D. None of the above

6. Control structures are the basic logic components used in the programs. Find out which is not control structure.
   A. Sequence structure
   B. Selection structure
   C. Program structure
   D. Loop structure



7. The type of error that occurs when a correct word is used in wrong context.
   A. Logical error
   B. Syntax error
   C. Semantic error
   D. none of the above

8. Choose the correct statement
   A. High-level programming language allows you to take advantage of abstraction
   B. Low-level programming language allows you to take advantage of abstraction
   C. Abstraction is the process of paying attention to detail of the program
   D. None of the above

9. When we compile a program of C++, a warning appears so you think that the program should be prevented from execution?
   A. No-it won't affect to run the program
   B. Yes-because a severe error will occur that will prevent the program from executing
   C. No to stop, the program will stop automatically
   D. None of the above

10. Main ( ) in C++ is apart of _______
    A. function header
    B. function body
    C. Return type of the function under function body
    D. none of the above

11. If the main ( ) function does not pass value to other programs or receives values from outside the program
    A. then main ( ) receives and returns a void types
    B. then main ( ) receives and returns a numerical type
    C. Both A & B
    D. None of the above

12. The header int main ( ) returns O value when
    A. the int main ( ) function does not pass/receive value from outside the program
    B. the int main ( ) function pass/receive single value from outside the program
    C. the int main ( ) function pass/receive any integer number
    D. the int main ( ) function pass/receive any real numbers

13. Which one is the simplest program in $C^{++}$?
    A. int main ( )      B. int main ( )
       {                  [
       ]                  ]
    C. int main ( )      D. int main ( )
       [                  {
       }                  }

14. Choose the correct sequence of the following components of function header
    A. Return type of the function / Function name / Variable type / names enclosed in parentheses
    B. Function name / Return type of the function / Variable name
    C. Return type of the function / variable type / Variable name
    D. Function name / Function type / Variable name

15. If data type of $5 \times 2 = 10$ is integer, then what will be the new value if data type is float?
    A. 10.0          B. 0.10
    C. 10            D. none

16. Paying attention to the important properties while ignoring unessential details is known as
    A. selectiveness      B. polymorphism
    C. abstraction         D. summarizing

17. Object-oriented programmes primarily focus on
    A. procedure to be performed
    B. the step-by-step statements needed to solve a problem
    C. objects and the tasks that must be performed with those objects
    D. the physical orientation of objects within a program

18. The member function can always access the data
    A. in the class of which it is member
    B. in any object of the class of which it is a number
    C. in the object of which is a member
    D. in the public part of its class

19. Operator overloading is
    A. giving $C^{++}$ operators more than they can handle
    B. giving new meanings to existing $C^{++}$ operators
    C. making new $C^{++}$ operators
    D. none of these

20. The scope resolution operator usually
    A. specifies a particular class
    B. provide a useful conceptual framework
    C. tell us from what base class it is derived
    D. None of the above

21. A friend function can be used to
    A. increase the versatility of an overload operator
    B. allow one class to access an unrelated class
    C. Both A & B
    D. None of the above

22. The standard $C^{++}$ comment
    A. /                 B. //
    C. /* and */       D. None of these

23. The preprocessor directive # include is required if _______.
    A. Console output is used
    B. Console input is used
    C. Both console input and output is used
    D. None of these

**24.** The operator << is called _______.
A. an insertion operator
B. put to operator
C. either A or B
D. None of the above

**25.** The operator >> is called _______.
A. an extraction operator
B. a get from operator
C. either A or B
D. get to operator

**26.** When a language has the capability to produce new data type, it is called _______.
A. Extensible            B. Overloaded
C. Encapsulated          D. Reprehensible

**27.** The $C^{++}$ symbol << _______.
A. perform the action of sending the value of expression listed as its right to the outputs strewn as the left.
B. is used to indicate the action from right to left
C. is adopted to resemble an arrow
D. All of the above

**28.** What is a reference in $C^{++}$ programming?
A. an operator
B. a reference is an alias for an object
C. used to rename an object
D. None of the above

**29.** A constructor is called whenever _______.
A. a object is declared
B. an object is used
C. a class is declared
D. a class is used

**30.** State the object oriented language.
A. $C^{++}$               B. Java
C. Eiffel                 D. All of the above

**31.** Overload function in $C^{++}$ _______.
A. a group function with the same name
B. all have the same number and type of arguments
C. functions with same name and same number and type of arguments
D. All of the above

**32.** Operator overloading is _______.
A. making $C^{++}$ operators works with objects
B. giving new meaning to existing $C^{++}$ operators

C. making new $C^{++}$ operator
D. Both A & B above

**33.** A class having no name _______.
A. is not allowed
B. can't have a constructor
C. can't have a destructor
D. can't be passed as an argument

**34.** The differences between constructors and destructor are _______.
A. constructors can take arguments but destructor can't
B. constructors can be overloaded but destructors can't be overloaded
C. both A & B
D. None of these

**35.** A destructor takes _______.
A. one argument
B. two arguments
C. three arguments
D. Zero arguments

**36.** Constructors are used to _______.
A. initialize the objects
B. construct the data members
C. both A & B
D. None of these

**37.** In $C^{++}$ a function contained within a class is called _______.
A. a member function  B. an operator
C. a class function     D. a method

## ENCAPSULATION AND ABSTRACTION

**38.** The wrapping up of data and functions in a single unit is called _______.
A. Encapsulation
B. abstraction
C. data hiding
D. None of the above

**39.** _______ provides the interface between object's data and program
A. Encapsulation
B. Abstraction
C. Data hiding
D. None of the above

**40.** The insulation of data from direct access by the program is called _______.
A. Encapsulation
B. Abstraction
C. Data hiding
D. None of the above

**41.** Which represent essential features of without including the background detail or explanations is called _______?
A. Encapsulation
B. Abstraction
C. Data hiding
D. None of the above

**42.** Classes use the concept of _______.
A. Encapsulation
B. Abstraction
C. Data hiding
D. None of the above

**43.** The concept of data abstraction is also known as _______.
A. Encapsulation
B. Abstraction
C. Data hiding
D. Abstract data type

## INHERITANCE & POLYMORPHISM

**44.** _______ is the process by which object of one class acquire the properties of object of another class
A. Encapsulation
B. Polymorphism
C. Inheritance
D. None of the above

**45.** In OOP _______ provides the idea of reusability.
A. encapsulation
B. polymorphism
C. inheritance
D. None of the above

**46.** The ability to take more then one form in OPP is called _______.
A. Encapsulation
B. Polymorphism
C. Inheritance
D. None of the above

**47.** _______ plays an important role in allowing objects having different internal structure to share the same external interface.
A. Encapsulation
B. Polymorphism
C. Inheritance
D. None of the above

**48.** Polymorphism is extensively used in implementing _______.
A. encapsulation
B. class
C. inheritance
D. None of the above

**49.** The mechanism of deriving a new class from an old one is called _______.
A. inheritance
B. multiple inheritance
C. constructor
D. None of the above

**50.** A class can inherit properties from more then one class or form more then one level. A derived class with only one base class is called _______.
A. single inheritance
B. multiple inheritance
C. constructor
D. None of the above

**51.** One class inherited by more then one class is called _______.
A. single inheritance
B. multiple inheritance
C. constructor
D. None of the above

**52.** To apply two or more types of inheritance to design a program is called _______.
A. hybrid inheritance
B. single inheritance
C. multiple inheritance
D. None of the above

## INPUT/OUTPUT OPERATOR

**53.** The multiple use of << in one statement is called ______.
A. cascading
B. threading
C. multiple operation
D. None of the above

**54.** In a program, person is defined as a new data type. The class person includes two basic data type items and two functions to operate on that data . The functions are called ______.
A. member function
B. object
C. class
D. method

**55.** In a program person is defined as a new data type. The class person includes two basic data type items and two functions to operate on that data. The variable is known as ______.
A. member function  B. object
C. class              D. method

**56.** The class definition including the member function constitute the server that provides services to main program is called ______.
A. client
B. server
C. both of above
D. None of the above

**57.** Void get data(void) used to ______.
A. collect data from run time variable
B. display data on the screen
C. manipulate data
D. store data

**58.** Void display (data) used to ______.
A. collect data from run time variable
B. display data on the screen
C. manipulate data
D. store data

**59.** In C++ the main function used to create a new object with the ______.
A. class name
B. file name
C. object name
D. None of the above

**60.** Token is a collection of ______.
A. keywords          B. data type
C. identifier        D. All of the above

**61.** (::)  this operator is called ______
A. scope resolution operator
B. pointer to member declarator
C. pointer to member operator
D. none of the above

**62.** (::*) this operator is called ______.
A. scope resolution operator
B. pointer to member declarator
C. pointer to member operator
D. none of the above

**63.** (->*) this operator is called ______.
A. scope resolution operator
B. pointer to member declarator
C. pointer to member operator
D. None of the above

**64.** The scope resolution operator used to ______.
A. uncover hidden file
B. delete hidden file
C. call member function
D. None of the above

**65.** C++ permits explicit type conversion of variable of expressions using ______.
A. arithmetic operator
B. logical operator
C. bitwise operator
D. type cast operator

## FUNCTIONS

**66.** The user use same function name to create functions that perform a variety of different task called ______.
A. function overloading
B. method overloading
C. Both A and B
D. None of the above

**67.** Use same thing for different purposes is referred to as _______.
A. function polymorphism
B. method overloading
C. overloading
D. None of the above

**68.** _______ used to handle some specific task related to class
A. Friend function
B. Virtual function
C. Member function
D. Both A and B

**69.** The member functions can be define as _______.

A. outside the class definition
B. inside the class definition
C. both A and B
D. None of the above

## CLASS

**70.** _______ is a way to bind the data and its associated function together.
A. Class
B. Object
C. Function
D. None of the above

**71.** Class declaration is similar to _______.
A. structure
B. union
C. inheritance
D. None of the above

**72.** The class body contains _______.
A. function declaration
B. variable declaration
C. function and variable declaration
D. None of the above

**73.** The member that have been declared as private can be accessed _______.
A. out side the class
B. within the class
C. out side the program
D. None of the above

**74.** By default the member of a class is _______.

A. private
B. public
C. protected
D. None of the above

**75.** The variable declare inside the class is called _______.
A. function declaration
B. variable declaration
C. member function
D. None of the above

**76.** The function declaration inside the class is called _______.
A. function declaration
B. variable declaration
C. member function
D. none of the above

**77.** The binding of data and function together into a single class type variable is known as _______.
A. encapsulation
B. data hiding
C. polymorphism
D. None of the above

**78.** get data () used to _______.
A. assign value          B. call value
C. delete value          D. modify value

**79.** The data member of a class can be qualified as _______.
A. static
B. dynamic
C. float
D. None of the above

**80.** A copy of entire object is passed to the function is called _______.
A. pass by value
B. pass by reference
C. pass by method
D. None of the above

**81.** Only address of the object is transferred to the function _______.
A. pass by value
B. pass by reference
C. pass by method
D. None of the above

## CONSTRUCTOR AND DESTRUCTOR

**82.** putdata() and setvalue() is a ______.
A. member function
B. user define function
C. predefine function
D. None of the above

**83.** Which enable an object to initialize itself when it is created is called ______.
A. constructor
B. destructor
C. automatic initialization
D. None of the above

**84.** Which destroys the objects when they are no longer require is called ______.
A. constructor
B. destructor
C. automatic initialization
D. None of the above

**85.** The constructor that accepts no parameters is called the ______.
A. default constructor
B. default destructor
C. default function
D. None of the above

**86.** Which is/are the characteristics of constructor?
A. They should be declare in the public section.
B. They are invoked automatically when the objects are created.
C. They do not have return types.
D. All of the above

**87.** We must pass the initial values as arguments to the constructor function when an object is declared this can be done ______.
A. by calling the constructor explicitly
B. by calling the constructor implicitly
C. Both A and B
D. None of the above

**88.** Allocation of memory to objects at the time of their construction is known as ______.

A. dynamic constructor
B. copy constructor
C. constructor
D. destructor

**89.** Destructor can be define as ______.
A. ~integer(){}        B. integer(){}
C. ~integer            D. integer

## POINTER VIRTUAL FUNCTION AND POLYMORPHISM

**90.** The information is known to compiler at the compile time and therefore, compiler is able to select the appropriate function for a particular cell at the compile time itself. This is called ______.
A. early binding
B. static binding
C. static linking
D. All of the above

**91.** The appropriate member function could be selected while the program is running is called ______.
A. compile time polymorphism
B. runtime polymorphism
C. virtual function
D. None of the above

**92.** C++ supports a mechanism to achieve runtime polymorphism is called ______.
A. inline function
B. virtual function
C. polymorphism
D. None of the above

**93.** The function is linked with a particular class much later after the compilation, this process is known as ______.
A. late binding
B. early binding
C. virtual function
D. inline function

**94.** Pointer is denoted by ______.
A. *ptr
B. *str
C. *tpr
D. All of the above

**95.** When the same function name in both the base and derived classes , the function in base class is declared as _______.
A. inline function
B. virtual function
C. friend function
D. None of the above

**96.** Virtual functions contains some basic rules, these are _______.
A. the virtual functions must be member of some class
B. not static member
C. accessed by using object pointer
D. All of the above

## CONSOLE I/O OPERATION

**97.** General input/output stream class is _______.

A. IOS
B. IStream
C. ostram
D. all of the above

**98.** Istream function is used to _______.
A. inherit the properties of ios
B. inherit the property of class
C. inherit the property of derived class
D. none of the above

**99.** C$^{++}$ provides formatted console I/O operations the width () used to _______.
A. specify the required field size for displaying an output device
B. specify the number of digits to be displayed after the decision point of float value.
C. specify a character that is used to fill the unused portion of a field
D. clear the flags specified.

**100.** C$^{++}$ provides formatted console I/O operations the precision () used to _______.
A. specify the required field size for displaying an output device
B. specify the number of digits to be displayed after the decision point of float value.
C. specify a character that is used to fill the unused portion of a field
D. clear the flags specified.

**101.** C$^{++}$ provides formatted console I/O operations the unsetf () used to _______.
A. specify the required field size for displaying an output device
B. specify the number of digits to be displayed after the decision point of float value.
C. specify a character that is used to fill the unused portion of a field
D. clear the flags specified.

**102.** C$^{++}$ provides formatted console I/O operations the fill () used to _______.
A. specify the required field size for displaying an output device
B. specify the number of digits to be displayed after the decision point of float value.
C. specify a character that is used to fill the unused portion of a field
D. clear the flags specified.

## FUNCTIONS FOR MANIPULATION OF FILE POINTER

**103.** The seekg() used to _______.
A. move get Pointer (input) to a specified location
B. move Put pointer (output) to a specified location
C. give the current position of the get pointer
D. give the current position of the put pointer

**104.** The seekp() used to _______.
A. move get Pointer (input) to a specified location
B. move Put pointer (output) to a specified location
C. give the current position of the get pointer
D. give the current position of the put pointer

**105.** The tellg() used to ________.
- A. move get Pointer (input) to a specified location
- B. move Put pointer (output) to a specified location
- C. give the current position of the get pointer
- D. give the current position of the put pointer

**106.** The tellp() used to ________.
- A. move get Pointer (input) to a specified location
- B. move Put pointer (output) to a specified location
- C. give the current position of the get pointer
- D. give the current position of the put pointer

## ANSWERS

| 1 | 2 | 3 | 4 | 5 | 6 | 7 | 8 | 9 | 10 |
|---|---|---|---|---|---|---|---|---|---|
| B | C | A | A | C | C | B | A | A | A |

| 11 | 12 | 13 | 14 | 15 | 16 | 17 | 18 | 19 | 20 |
|---|---|---|---|---|---|---|---|---|---|
| A | A | D | A | A | C | C | C | B | A |

| 21 | 22 | 23 | 24 | 25 | 26 | 27 | 28 | 29 | 30 |
|---|---|---|---|---|---|---|---|---|---|
| B | C | C | A | A | A | A | A | A | D |

| 31 | 32 | 33 | 34 | 35 | 36 | 37 | 38 | 39 | 40 |
|---|---|---|---|---|---|---|---|---|---|
| A | B | A | A | D | A | A | A | A | C |

| 41 | 42 | 43 | 44 | 45 | 46 | 47 | 48 | 49 | 50 |
|---|---|---|---|---|---|---|---|---|---|
| B | B | D | C | C | B | B | C | A | A |

| 51 | 52 | 53 | 54 | 55 | 56 | 57 | 58 | 59 | 60 |
|---|---|---|---|---|---|---|---|---|---|
| B | A | A | A | C | A | A | B | A | D |

| 61 | 62 | 63 | 64 | 65 | 66 | 67 | 68 | 69 | 70 |
|---|---|---|---|---|---|---|---|---|---|
| A | B | C | A | D | A | C | D | C | A |

| 71 | 72 | 73 | 74 | 75 | 76 | 77 | 78 | 79 | 80 |
|---|---|---|---|---|---|---|---|---|---|
| A | C | B | A | B | A | A | A | A | A |

| 81 | 82 | 83 | 84 | 85 | 86 | 87 | 88 | 89 | 90 |
|---|---|---|---|---|---|---|---|---|---|
| B | A | C | B | A | D | C | A | A | D |

| 91 | 92 | 93 | 94 | 95 | 96 | 97 | 98 | 99 | 100 |
|---|---|---|---|---|---|---|---|---|---|
| B | B | A | A | B | D | A | A | A | B |

| 101 | 102 | 103 | 104 | 105 | 106 |
|---|---|---|---|---|---|
| D | C | A | B | C | D |

# 4.    

## BASICS OF DATA STRUCTURE

1. What is a 'rich picture'?
   A. An expensive painting.
   B. A schematic view of a problem that is to be addressed.
   C. The view of a problem from a specific perspective.
   D. A map containing a large amount of annotation.

2. What does 'crossed swords' mean in a rich picture?
   A. The site of a battle.
   B. An expression of conflict.
   C. A personal or group opinion.
   D. A tactical decision.

3. What is a 'soft systems' approach?
   A. A technique of addressing unstructured problems.
   B. A method for addressing structured and ordered problems.
   C. A method of choosing the correct software for an application.
   D. A method for approaching conflict in decision making.

4. What is a 'hard systems' approach?
   A. A technique of addressing unstructured problems.
   B. A method for addressing structured and ordered problems.
   C. A method of choosing the correct software for an application.
   D. A method for approaching conflict in decision making.

5. Which of the following phase is recognized phases in hard systems analysis?
   A. The lexical phase.
   B. The analysis phase.
   C. The parsing phase.
   D. All of the above

6. What is cartographic modelling?
   A. The sequence of modelling of real world entities in a GIS database.
   B. A way of expressing and organizing methods by which spatial operations are selected and used to develop a GIS model.
   C. The modelling of map inputs to a GIS, using natural language.
   D. A generic method of creating a GIS map data structure.

7. Expand the acronym of 'SLC'?
   A. Software Life Cycle approach.
   B. Software Leasing Costs.
   C. Systems Life Cycle approach.
   D. System Loan Costs.

8. What is the prototyping method?
   A. A method of rapid start-up of a GIS project.
   B. A method of taking user needs into account when designing GIS projects/ systems.
   C. An approach to GIS database design based on the soft systems approach
   D. A method of designing a GIS project based on previously tried and tested models

9. When we say the order of a tree is M, we mean _______.
   A. every non-leaf node must have M subtrees
   B. every non-leaf node must have M keys
   C. every non-leaf node can have at most M subtrees
   D. every non-leaf node can have at most M keys

10. In Java, we have to use "if(s1.equals(s2))" to test whether two strings, s1 and s2, are equal to each other. The reason why we cannot use "if(s1==s2)" is _______.
   A. "==" can only be used for comparing numbers
   B. "s1==s2" only compares the memory locations of s1 and s2
   C. "s1==s2" only compares the length of s1 and s2
   D. "s1==s2" only compares the first characters in s1 and s2.

11. Four statements about lists and stacks are given below. Three of them are correct. Which one is incorrect?
   A. Lists can be implemented by using arrays or linked lists
   B. A list is a sequence of one or more data items
   C. A stack is a special kind of list in which all insertions and deletions take place at one end
   D. Stacks are easier to implement than lists

12. With the "wrap around" implementation of a queue, which of the following code should be used to work out the next location of insertion?
   A. tail++
   B. tail—
   C. tail = (tail % max_queue_size) + 1
   D. tail = (tail++) % max_queue_size

13. When we say an algorithm has a time complexity of $O(n)$, what does it mean?
   A. The algorithm has n nested loops
   B. The computation time taken by the algorithm is less than n seconds
   C. The algorithm is n times slower than a standard algorithm
   D. The computation time taken by the algorithm is proportional to n

14. Can we read a data item at any location of a list within a constant time (i.e. $O(1)$?
   A. Yes
   B. Yes only if the list is implemented by pointers (i.e. linked-list)
   C. Yes only if the list is implemented by an array
   D. No, we need $O(n)$ computation steps no matter what kind of implementation is used

15. Sequential search has a time complexity of $O(n)$, and binary search has a time complexity of $O(\log(n))$, (What will be the difference when the size n is 1000?
   A. You would not notice much difference because computers run very fast anyway
   B. When n is 1000, binary search is twice as fast as sequential search
   C. When nz is 1000, binary search is 10 times as fast as sequential search
   D. When n is 1000, binary search is 100 times as fast as sequential search

**TREE**

16. The followings are four binary trees. Can you identify which one satisfies the heap condition? (one only)

```
      4           3         1          1
     / \         / \       /          / \
    5   10      9   5     5          2  4
   / \ / \     / \ / \   / \        /  / \
  6  7 9 11   9 10 6 7   3  7      8
```

   A. A               B. B
   C. C               D. D

17. The following statements explain the differences/similarities between binary search trees and heaps. Which one of the following statements is INCORRECT?
   A. Both binary search trees and heaps are binary trees

B. With heaps the smallest value is stored at the root, while with binary trees the smallest value is on the leftmost leaf

C. Both binary search trees and heaps require ascending order between sibling nodes

D. In heaps no gaps are allowed apart from the right side of the leaves' level, but in binary search trees gaps are allowed

**18.** Consider the heap array

```
0   2   1   3   7   4   6   8
```

What does this heap look like, when drawn as a tree?

```
      0           0           0           0
    /  \        /  \        /  \        /  \
   1    2      1    4      1    2      2    1
  /\  /\      /\  /\      /\  /\      /\  /\
 3 4 6 7    2 3 6 7    6 4 7 3    3 7 4 6
 /           /           /           /
8           8           8           8
```

A. A                     B. B
C. C                     D. D

**19.** Let's consider two different ways to implement priority queues: either using a heap or using an ordered list. What are their time complexities of dequeue (i.e. deleting the smallest) and enqueue (i.e. inserting an item)?

A. heap—dequeue costs $O(1)$, and enqueue costs $O(\log(n))$ ordered list - dequeue costs $O(n)$, and enqueue costs $O(n)$

B. heap—dequeue costs $O(\log(n))$, and enqueue costs $O(\log(n))$ ordered list - dequeue costs $O$   A., and enqueue costs $O(n)$

C. heap—dequeue costs $O(\log(n))$, and enqueue costs $O(\log(n))$ ordered list - dequeue costs $O(\log(n))$, and enqueue costs $O(\log(n))$

D. heap—dequeue costs $O(\log(n))$, and enqueue costs $O(\log(n))$ ordered list - dequeue costs $O(n)$, and enqueue costs $O(n)$

**20.** Which of the following heap is constructed by inserting the following sequence of values: 6, 5, 2, 4, 1, 7, and 3.

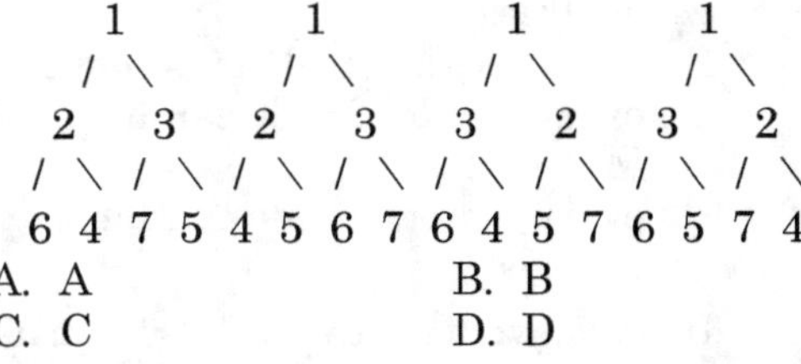

```
      1           1           1           1
    /  \        /  \        /  \        /  \
   2    3      2    3      3    2      3    2
  /\  /\      /\  /\      /\  /\      /\  /\
 6 4 7 5    4 5 6 7    6 4 5 7    6 5 7 4
```

A. A                     B. B
C. C                     D. D

**21.** Four statements about B-trees are given below. Three of them are correct. Which one is INCORRECT?

A. All B-trees are also search trees

B. The word B-tree stands for balanced tree

C. The word B-tree also stands for binary tree

D. All leaves of a B-tree must be on the same level

**22.** A B-tree of order 3 is constructed by inserting integers 1,2,3,4,... in ascending order. Which integer causes the leaves to be on level 3 for the first time? (root is on level 1)

A. 3                     B. 5
C. 7                     D. 9

**23.** For any B-tree of height H (H>1), after inserting a new key, is it possible for a key, K, which was located in a leaf-node to move up to the root? Which of the following answers is correct?

A. Yes

B. Never

C. Yes, only if H=2

D. Yes, only when the half of the keys in the root are less than K and the other half of the keys in the root are greater than K

**24.** Suppose that we have a data file containing records of famous people, and we need to build a hash table to find a record from the person's birthday. The size of the hash table is 4096. The following are hash functions which convert a birthday to an integer. Which function do you think is the best?

A. h1( day/month/year ) = day + month + year
B. h2( day/month/year ) = day + month*31 + year
C. h3( day/month/year ) = (day + month*31 + year*365) mod 4096
D. h4( day/month/year ) = (day + month*31 + year*365) mod 4093

**25.** Carry on the above question. Which is the worst hash function?
A. h1
B. h2
C. h3
D. h4

## COLLISION

**26.** Which of the following case is so-called "collision"?
A. Two different hash functions produce the same address for a given key:
B. h1( key ) = h2( key )
C. Two different hash functions produce the same address for two different keys:
D. h1( key1 ) = h2( key2 )   where key1 =\= key2

**27.** What is collision resolution with open addressing?
A. When collision happens, we create a new memory location outside of the existing table, and use a chain to link to the new memory location
B. When collision happens, we enlarge the hash table
C. When collision happens, we look for an unoccupied memory location in the existing table
D. We use an extra table to collect all collided data

**28.** According to the Birthday Paradox (which we briefly learnt last year from Analytical Modeling), if there are 23 people in a room, the chance of two people sharing a same birthday (day/month regardless of year) can reach ______.
A. 2.3 %
B. 23 %
C. 50 %
D. 90 %

**29.** When we say the order of a tree is M, we mean ______.
A. every non-leaf node must have M subtrees
B. every non-leaf node must have M keys
C. every non-leaf node can have at most M subtrees
D. every non-leaf node can have at most M keys

**30.** Let's use the "TreeNode" class defined in our coursework file. Assuming that we need to create a tree like given below, which of the following code is/are correct?

```
      y
     / \
    x   z
```

A.
```
TreeNode t = new TreeNode("y");
TreeNode t1 = new TreeNode("x");
TreeNode t2 = new TreeNode("z");
t.left = t1;
t.middle = t2;
```
B.
```
TreeNode t = new TreeNode(null);
t.value1 = "y";
t.left = new TreeNode("x");
t.middle = new TreeNode("z");
```
C.
```
TreeNode t = new TreeNode("y");
t.left = new TreeNode("x");
t.right = new TreeNode("z");
```
D. Both A and B

## SORTING

**31.** For the bubble sort algorithm, what is the time complexity of the best/worst case? (assume that the computation stops as soon as no more swaps in one pass)
A. best case: $O(n)$    worst case: $O(n*n)$
B. best case: $O(n)$    worst case: $O(n*\log(n))$
C. best case: $O(n*\log(n))$    worst case: $O(n*\log(n))$
D. best case: $O(n*\log(n))$    worst case: $O(n*n)$

**32.** For the quick sort algorithm, what is the time complexity of the best/worst case?

A. best case: $O(n)$ — worst case: $O(n*n)$

B. best case: $O(n)$ — worst case: $O(n*\log(n))$

C. best case: $O(n*\log(n))$ — worst case: $O(n*\log(n))$

D. best case: $O(n*\log(n))$ — worst case: $O(n*n)$

**33.** There are two sorted lists L1 and L2. Their lengths are n1 and n2 respectively. You are asked to design an algorithm to generate a sorted list L3 from L1 and L2. That is, for example, if L1 = [2, 6, 35] and L2 = [4, 5, 10, 23, 37] then L3 = [2, 4, 5, 6, 10, 23, 35, 37]. Which of the following method is the most efficient?
A. Taking elements from L1 one by one, and inserting them ioto L2 such that the order of L2 remains
B. Appending two lists (i.e. join one list's beginning to the other one's end), then applying quick sort to the appended list
C. Using a merge method that compares two elements at the head of both lists. The smaller one is then taken out and inserted at the end of L3 while the larger one is kept its location unchanged. Repeat this until either L1 or L2 is empty.
D. None of the above

**34.** What is the time complexity of the algorithm A in question?
A. $O(n1*n2)$  B. $O(n1*\log(n2))$
C. $O(n1+n2)$  D. $O(\max(n1,n2))$

**35.** What is the time complexity of the algorithm C in question?
A. $O(n1*n2)$  B. $O(n1*\log(n2))$
C. $O(n1+n2)$  D. $O(\max(n1,n2))$

**36.** Where does a binary search examine on each pass through?
A. start  B. end
C. midpoint  D. random point

**37.** How many steps does a selection sort take if the is length n?

A. n/s  B. n
C. n–1  D. n+1

**38.** The linear search method has an execution time of ______.
A. O(1)  B. O(n2)
C. O(n)  D. O(n3)

**39.** The big-O value of O(1) is also called ______.
A. Linear  B. Quadratic
C. Logarithmic  D. Constant

**40.** In has-a and knows-a relationship, the association between the classes is assumed to be ______.
A. one-to-one  B. many-to-one
C. one-to-many  D. two-to-one

**41.** When are implementation decisions made?
A. Analysis  B. Request
C. Testing  D. Design

**42.** Which operation on a collection visits each item?
A. cloning
B. traversal
C. removal
D. search and retrieval

**43.** Which items are dequeued first in a priority queue?
A. highest priority
B. same priority
C. lowest priority
D. first in

**44.** In a map, each item is associated with a unique ______.
A. index  B. key
C. subscript  D. object

**45.** What happens when you insert a key/value pair into a map and the key is already in the map?
A. returns null
B. An exception is thrown
C. discards the key/value pair
D. replaces the previous value with the new value and returns the previous value

**46.** Accessing array elements has a run-time complexity of:
A. O( n )
B. O( n log n )
C. O( log n )
D. O(1)

**47.** When two items share the same position after a hash function has been run, it is called a:
A. collision
B. crash
C. bump
D. impact

**48.** When the items that cause a collision are relocated to the same region within an array is called:
A. grouping
B. bundling
C. clumping
D. clustering

**49.** Which of the following is the expression for locating an items index in an array?
A. Math.abs(item.hashCode() % array.length );
B. item.hashCode() % array.length;
C. item.hashCode() / array.length
D. Math.abs( item.hashCode() / array.length );

**50.** In chaining, each item's hash code locates the _______ of the chain in which the item already resides or is to be inserted.
A. barrel
B. can
C. bucket
D. jug

**51.** To implement the level order traversal, it is convenient to schedule node visits using a(n):
A. stack
B. queue
C. tree
D. array

## ANSWERS

| 1 | 2 | 3 | 4 | 5 | 6 | 7 | 8 | 9 | 10 |
|---|---|---|---|---|---|---|---|---|---|
| B | A | A | B | D | B | A | B | C | B |
| **11** | **12** | **13** | **14** | **15** | **16** | **17** | **18** | **19** | **20** |
| B | D | D | C | D | B | C | D | B | A |
| **21** | **22** | **23** | **24** | **25** | **26** | **27** | **28** | **29** | **30** |
| C | C | A | D | A | C | C | C | C | D |
| **31** | **32** | **33** | **34** | **35** | **36** | **37** | **38** | **39** | **40** |
| A | D | C | A | C | C | C | C | D | A |
| **41** | **42** | **43** | **44** | **45** | **46** | **47** | **48** | **49** | **50** |
| A | C | B | B | B | D | A | D | A | A |
| **51** | | | | | | | | | |
| B | | | | | | | | | |

# 5.     | Networking |

## DEVICES/FIREWALL

1. A company has a large network and you have to make subnet. Which of the following devices used to separate your LAN and still protect critical resources?
   A. An internal firewall
   B. A router between subnets
   C. A switch between departments
   D. All of the above

2. Which of the following is considered to be possible components of an ethernet LAN?
   A. Coax
   B. Fiber optic
   C. STP
   D. All of the above

3. Which of the following device is specially designed to forward packets to specific ports based on the packet's address?
   A. Specialty hub
   B. Switching hub
   C. Port hub
   D. Filtering hub

4. Your company receives Internet access through a network or gateway server. Which of the following device is best suited to protect resources and subnet your LAN directly on the network server?
   A. DSL modem
   B. A multi-homed firewall
   C. VLAN
   D. A brouter that acts both as a bridge and a router

5. What are the benefits of using a firewall for your LAN?
   A. Increased access to Instant Messaging
   B. Stricter access control to critical resources
   C. Greater security to your LAN
   D. Both B and C

6. Which of the following are true about firewalls?
   A. Filters network traffic
   B. Can be either a hardware or software device
   C. Follows a set of rules
   D. All of the above

7. Which of the following are true about firewall protection when using static packet filtering on the router?
   A. Static packet filtering is less secure than stateful filtering
   B. Static packet filtering is less secure than proxy filtering
   C. Static packet filtering is more secure than dynamic packet filtering
   D. Both A and B

8. A packet filtering firewall operates at which of the following OSI layers?
   A. At the Application layer
   B. At the Transport layer
   C. At the Network layer
   D. Both B and C

9. Firewall is designed to perform all the following except _______.
   A. Limiting security exposures
   B. Logging Internet activity
   C. Enforcing the organization's security policy
   D. Protecting against viruses

10. Stateful firewalls may filter connection-oriented packets that are potential intrusions to the LAN. Which of the following types of packets can a stateful packet filter deny?
    A. UDP                B. TCP
    C. IP                 D. ICMP

11. Which of the following systems run an application layer firewall using Proxy software?
    A. Proxy NAT          B. Proxy client
    C. Client 32          D. Proxy server

12. Which of the following firewalls keeps track of the connection state?
    A. Application layer firewall
    B. Packet filtering firewall
    C. Router enhanced firewall
    D. Stateful packet filtering firewall

13. Which of the following device could not be a part of wired LAN on star topology
    A. Switch             B. Repeater
    C. Hub                D. Rouler

14. Which of the following use routers with packet filtering rules to allow or deny access based on source address, destination address, or port number?
    A. Application layer firewall
    B. Packet filtering firewall
    C. Router enhanced firewall
    D. IP enabled firewall

## ROUTERS

15. Which of following devices discriminates between multicast and unicast packets?
    A. Multicast switch
    B. Bicast switch
    C. Bicast router
    D. Multicast router

16. Your primary concern is LAN security. You want to subnet your internal network with a device that provides security and stability. Which of the following devices do you choose to meet these needs?
    A. Static router      B. Dynamic router
    C. Static switch      D. Dynamic switch

17. Which of the following will help you to improve your LAN security?
    A. Change user passwords frequently
    B. Install a firewall program
    C. Use a proxy
    D. All of the above

18. Which of the following is the most difficult to configure, but safest device to use on a LAN?
    A. Static router
    B. IP enabled router
    C. Dynamic router
    D. RIP enabled router

19. Which of the following statements are true about routers and bridges?
    A. Bridges connect two networks at the Data Link Layer
    B. Routers are improved bridges
    C. Routers connect two networks at the Network Layer
    D. Both A and C

20. Remember, routers work at the Network Layer of the International Standards Organization/Open Systems Interconnection (ISO/OSI) established sequence of OSI Layers. What is the correct and complete OSI sequence in order from user interface (Layer 7) to the delivery of binary bits (Layer 1)?
    A. Physical Layer, Network Layer, Data Link Layer, Transport Layer, Session Layer, Presentation Layer, Application Layer
    B. Application Layer, Presentation Layer, Session Layer, Transport Layer, Network Layer, Data Link Layer, Physical Layer
    C. Application Layer, Physical Layer, Session Layer, Transport Layer, Network Layer, Data Link Layer, Presentation Layer
    D. Physical Layer, Data Link Layer, Network Layer, Session Layer, Transport Layer, Presentation Layer, Application Layer

21. Most networks employ devices for routing services. Routers work at which of the following OSI layers?
    A. Transport
    B. Network
    C. Presentation
    D. Session

22. A local area network (LAN) administrator must be restricted from _______.
    A. having helpdesk responsibilities
    B. reporting to functional managers
    C. being responsible for LAN security administration
    D. having programming responsibilities.

23. A port protection device controls access to _______.

    A. Database
    B. Network
    C. System
    D. Server

## SWITCHES

24. You manage a company network and the network budget. You want to minimize costs, but desire to prevent crackers from sniffing your local network (LAN). Which of the following devices would you recommend to meet your goals?
    A. Hub
    B. Switch
    C. Router
    D. Firewall

25. Which of the following statements apply to security concerns when using a switch in the LAN?
    A. Switches use SSH to manage interfaces by default
    B. Switches use Telnet or HTTP to manage interfaces
    C. Switches should be placed behind a dedicated firewall
    D. Both B and C

26. Which of following is a type of hub that forwards packets to an appropriate port based on the packet's address?
    A. Smart hub
    B. Switching hub
    C. Routing hub
    D. Porting hub

## WIRELESS/MODEMS/ RAS/TELECOM/PBX

27. Which of the following is actually considered a critical wireless device?
    A. AP
    B. WAP
    C. WEP
    D. WLAN

28. Which of the following are true statements about modems?
    A. Modems use the telephone lines
    B. Modem stands for modulator and demodulator
    C. Modems are no longer used in secure networks
    D. Both A and B

29. Modems can be configured to automatically answer any incoming call. Many user computers have modems installed from the manufacturer. What is the greatest security risk when dealing with modems in this situation?
    A. Remote access without network administrator knowledge
    B. Local access without network administrator knowledge
    C. Client access without network administrator knowledge
    D. Server access without network administrator knowledge

30. Which of the following terms defines RAS?
    A. Random Access Security
    B. Remote Access Security
    C. Random Access Service
    D. Remote Access Service

31. Usually, a RAS connection is a dial-up connection. What network connections also apply to RAS?
    A. ISDN
    B. VPN
    C. DSL
    D. All of the above

32. Your company has gone through several phone company changes to reduce costs. Last week, two new phone company employees indicated that they needed remote access to your company network and wanted to establish a permanent guest account on your RAS server for continued maintenance support. Which of the

following actions are your best recommendations for this situation?
A. Agree with their requests so that maintenance costs are reduced
B. Recommend that user accounts be verified with strong authentication
C. Remove the guest account and create verifiable remote accounts
D. Both B and C

**33.** Which of the following applies to PBX?
A. PBX stands for Private Branch Exchange
B. PBX allows for analog, digital, and data to transfer over a high-speed phone system
C. Both A and B
D. PBX is used to carry analog messages and modem communication originating at the phone company

## VPN/IDS

**34** You want to have a private communication between two sites that also allows for encryption and authorization. Which of the following is the best choice in this instance?
A. Modem
B. Firewall
C. VPN
D. Bastion Host

**35.** VPN tunnels have end points. Which of the following methods is used to offer Strong Authentication at each end point?
A. DES
B. Block cipher
C. Stream cipher
D. Diffie-Hellman

**36.** VPNs transfer encrypted data through tunneling technology. Which of the following performs fast data encryption and may be used with VPNs?
A. Stream cipher
B. RSA
C. DES
D. IPSec

**37.** You desire to secure a VPN connection. Which protocols should you use?
A. TLS
B. IPSec
C. L2TP
D. Both B and C

**38.** What does the acronym IDS stand for?
A. Intrusion Detection System
B. Internet Detection Standard
C. Internet Detection System
D. Intrusion Detection Standard

**39.** Which of the following devices is used to monitor network traffic, including DoS attacks in real time?
A. A host-based Intrusion Detection System
B. A network-based Intrusion Detection System
C. A router-based Intrusion Detection System
D. A server-based Intrusion Detection System

**40.** Which of the following security devices acts more like a detective rather than a preventative measure?
A. IDS
B. DMZ
C. NAT
D. Proxy

## NETWORK MONITORING/ DIAGNOSTIC/ WORKSTATIONS/SERVERS

**41.** Which of the following protocols is used to monitor network devices such as hubs, switches, and routers?
A. SMTP
B. SNMP
C. RIP
D. OSPF

**42.** You have been using a network monitor or protocol analyzer to monitor ethernet packets. One of the messages sent has an IP header protocol field value of "1". What does this value classify?
A. UDP
B. ICMP
C. IGMP
D. TCP

**43.** You have been using a network monitor or protocol analyzer to monitor ethernet packets. One of the messages sent has an IP header protocol field value of "6". What does this value classify?
A. UDP
B. ICMP
C. IGMP
D. TCP

**44.** Which of the following LAN devices is frequently a source of security concern because of its ability to process applications, share files, and perform network services in a peer-to-peer network?
A. SQL Servers
B. Routers
C. Switches
D. Workstations

**45.** You want to prevent users from downloading software on company workstations. What is this called?
A. Desktop lookup
B. Desktop lockup
C. Desktop lockdown
D. Desktop lookdown

**46.** Which of the following is a group of independent servers that are grouped together to appear like one server?
A. Proxy Server
B. SQL Server
C. Server Array
D. Server Cluster

**47.** Which of the following devices have similar security concerns because they provide file sharing, network connection, and application services?
A. Switches
B. Workstations
C. Servers
D. Both B and C

## MOBILE DEVICES/MEDIA/ COAX/ UTP/STP/FIBER

**48.** Many mobile devices use wireless technology and may lack security. Which of the following devices are considered mobile devices used to connect to a network?
A. PDR
B. PDA
C. Pager
D. Both B and C

**49.** Which one of the following is a small network device that is a security concern for network administrators because the device is easily misplaced?
A. Workstation
B. Server
C. Mobile device
D. VPN

**50.** Which of the following are types of network cabling?
A. Twisted pair
B. Fiber optic
C. Coaxial
D. All of the above

**51.** For which one of the following situations would a crossover cable be effective?
A. Between a modem and a computer
B. Between a hub and a computer
C. Between two computers
D. Between a switch and a router

**52.** What does CSMA represent?
A. Carrier Sensing Minimal Access
B. Carrier Sensing Multiple Access
C. Carrier Sense Minimal Access
D. Carrier Sense Multiple Access

**53.** Which of the following is a type of coax cabling transmission method?
A. Baseband
B. Broadband
C. Both A and B
D. CSMA/CA

**54.** Which of the following is the greatest advantage of coax cabling?
A. High security
B. Physical dimensions
C. Long distances
D. Easily tapped

**55.** Which one of the following types of coax cabling has two outer conductors, or shields, and offers greater resistance and decreased attenuation?
A. STP coax
B. Dual-shielded coax
C. Multi-shielded coax
D. Bi-coax

**56.** Which of the following can transmit data at speeds of up to 16 Mbps?
A. Category 1 UTP
B. Category 2 UTP
C. Category 3 UTP
D. Category 4 UTP

**57.** Which of the following is not a property of twisted-pair cabling?
A. Twisted-pair cabling is a relatively low-speed transmission
B. The wires can be shielded
C. The wires can be unshielded
D. Twisted-pair cable carries signals as light waves

**58.** What is the media standard for most local network installations?
   A. Fiber optic
   B. CAT 3
   C. CAT 5
   D. Thinnet

**59.** Which of the following is not a property of fiber optic cabling?
   A. Transmits at faster speeds than copper cabling
   B. Easier to capture a signal from than copper cabling
   C. Very resistant to interference
   D. Carries signals as light waves

**60.** What does fiber use to transmit data?
   A. Vibrations
   B. Sound
   C. Electrical current
   D. Light

**61.** Which of the following network cabling would you choose to install around a noisy room where machines were constantly running?
   A. Fiber optic      B. STP
   C. Coax             D. UTP

**62.** You've been told about radio frequency dropping and want to protect your network from this threat. Which of the following media types would you choose in this situation?
   A. UTP              B. STP
   C. Coax             D. Fiber optic

**63.** Which of the following is most resistant to electrical and noise interference?
   A. STP              B. UDP
   C. Coax             D. Fiber optic

**64.** Which of the following is capable of conducting modulated light transmissions?
   A. Category 3 UTP
   B. Category 5 UTP
   C. Fiber optic
   D. Coax

**65.** Which of the following is the most expensive to install and terminate?

   A. Fiber optic
   B. Coaxial cable
   C. Category 4 UTP
   D. Category 5 UTP

## REMOVABLE MEDIA/TAPE/ CDR/HARD DRIVES/ DISKETTES/FLASHCARDS

**66.** What is the best way to avoid a catastrophic loss of computer data?
   A. Make backup copies of data
   B. Save all data to floppy disks
   C. Encrypt the data and backup to CD-R
   D. Check for viruses and worms

**67.** Which of the following are examples of magnetic storage media?
   A. Zip disk          B. CD-ROM
   C. Floppy disk       D. Both A and C

**68.** Which of the following has the largest storage capacity for removable media?
   A. Floppy disk
   B. CD-ROM
   C. DVD
   D. Partitioned space

**69.** Which of the following are concerns when using tape as a backup method?
   A. You are unable to reuse the data
   B. If a crash occurs, you may have to reenter data
   C. Data transfers during restores may be slow
   D. Both B and C

**70.** Which of the following media is one of the oldest media designed to store data, but should be carefully checked with antivirus software before restoration?
   A. Magnetic tape     B. Laptops
   C. Hard drives       D. CDR

**71.** Which of the following media is a relatively new media designed to store data, but should be carefully checked with antivirus software before restoration?
   A. Magnetic tape     B. Laptops
   C. Hard drives       D. CDR

72. Your company has decided to dispose of a few of the older computers that once stored critical data. What should you do first?
    A. Use Western Digital Clear (wdclear) to low-level format the hard disk
    B. Use FIPS to overwrite all data on the hard disk with zeroes
    C. Use a demagnetizer to demagnetize the hard disk
    D. Remove all the files and folders on the hard disk

73. Which of the following media is used for fault tolerant RAID arrays?
    A. Magnetic tape        B. Laptops
    C. Hard drives          D. CDR

74. Which of the following are one of the greatest sources of viruses, which are also a small type of media that are frequently carried from one computer to another?
    A. Hard drives          B. Smartcards
    C. Flashcards           D. Diskettes

75. Which of the following devices are also known as memory sticks?
    A. Flashcards           B. Hard drives
    C. CDR                  D. Diskettes

## SMARTCARDS/SECURITY TOPOLOGIES/SECURITY ZONES/DMZ

76. Which of the following devices provides secure, mobile storage of users' Private keys in a PKI?
    A. Flashcard            B. Smartcard
    C. Public key           D. Session key

77. Which one of the following is the most dependable authentication tool?
    A. Flashcards
    B. Smartcards
    C. Memory cards
    D. Authentication cards

78. Which of the following are known as the registered ports, according to the IANA?
    A. Ports 1 to 255
    B. Ports 255 to 1024
    C. Ports 1024 to 49151
    D. Ports 1025 to 65535

79. Which of the following terms could be considered security zones?
    A. Intranet             B. Internet
    C. DMZ                  D. All of the above

80. You have decided to create a DMZ to allow public access to your business assets. Which of the following should you place within the DMZ?
    A. Web server           B. Proxy server
    C. Email server         D. All of the above

## INTRANET/EXTRANET/VLANS

81. Which of the following security zones is considered to be a private company network?
    A. Forward lookup zone
    B. Internal lookup zone
    C. Intranet
    D. Internet

82. Which of the following characteristics of an intranet are true?
    A. An intranet can be a part of a Local Area Network (LAN)
    B. An intranet can work with Wide Area Networks (WAN)
    C. An intranet may be restricted to a community of users
    D. All of the above

83. Which of the following security zones is designed to allow one company to connect to another company through trust relationships and possible tunneling technology?
    A. Intranet
    B. DMZ
    C. Extranet
    D. Internet

84. When you think of Virtual Local Area Networks (VLANs), how are workstations connected?
    A. Same functional department
    B. Same group of users
    C. Same application
    D. All of the above

85. Which one of the following is software used to logically connect workgroups, thereby improving network performance for group members in different physical locations?
    A. Virtual Private Network (VPN)
    B. Virtual Local Area Network (VLAN)
    C. Remote Authentication Dial-in User Service (RADIUS)
    D. Network Address Translation (NAT)

86. You are in charge of a large network and have been using many devices. You finally want to subnet your network and allow users from the sales department in one office to communicate with sales representatives in another city. Which device should you use to improve connectivity?
    A. Router           B. VLAN
    C. Brouter          D. Bridge

## NAT

87. A company desires to use a private addressing scheme for their LAN users. What solution should they implement?
    A. NAT              B. Honey pot
    C. IDS              D. Proxy server

88. Which of the following is relatively more secure than proxy, because it assigns private IP addresses to the clients on your LAN, acting as a firewall?
    A. RADIUS
    B. Internet Control Message Protocol (ICMP)
    C. Network Address Translation (NAT)
    D. ICMP Router Discovery Protocol (IRDP)

89. What is the primary purpose for Network Address Translation (NAT)?
    A. Multiple users sharing one IP address for Instant Messenger (IM)
    B. Hiding the IP addresses of the internal network from those outside of the network
    C. Showing the IP addresses of the external network to clients on the internal network
    D. Single users gaining access to multiple email accounts

90. Which of the following are true statements about Network Address Translation (NAT)?
    A. Provides for private addressing ranges for internal network
    B. Hides the true IP addresses of internal computer systems
    C. Translates private IP addresses into registered Internet IP addresses
    D. All of the above

91. Which of the following is an example of a private IP address, which is not to be used on the Internet?
    A. 10.13.40.15         B. 131.10.42.5
    C. 129.101.22.15       D. 193.10.143.105

92. Which of the following is an example of a private IP address, which is not to be used on the Internet?
    A. 171.15.40.32        B. 172.46.32.2
    C. 171.90.22.1         D. 172.16.12.5

93. Which of the following is an example of a private IP address, which is not to be used on the Internet?
    A. 172.111.12.15
    B. 192.168.141.15
    C. 192.165.142.15
    D. 19.176.134.15

## TUNNELING/SECURITY BASELINES/OS/NOS HARDENING/FILE SYSTEM UPDATES

94. Which of the following applies to the networking concept of tunneling?
    A. Private network data is encapsulated or encrypted
    B. Private data is transmitted over a public network
    C. Private network data is lost in a black hole
    D. Both A and B

**95.** There are several tunneling protocols. Which of the following are types of VPN remote computing tunneling protocols? (Select all that apply.)

A. L2F          B. L2TP
C. PPTP       D. All of the above

**96.** Which of the following items relates to the fundamental principle of implementing security measures on computer equipment to ensure that minimum standards are being met?

A. Security baselines
B. Security policies
C. Security standards
D. Security countermeasures

**97.** You have just installed a Network Operating System (NOS) and want to establish a security baseline. Which of the following tasks should you perform to harden your new NOS?

A. Check the installation CD for a valid expiration date
B. Check the manufacture's Web site for any additional service patches for the NOS
C. Disable any unused services
D. Both B and C

**98.** Which of the following file systems allows for both file and folder level permissions?

A. FAT
B. FAT16
C. FAT32
D. NTFS

**99.** You want to harden your Linux file system by modifying folder permissions. Which command allows you to change folder permissions on a Linux system?

A. chmod       B. ls
C. ls -l         D. top

**100.** When would you consider restoring a clean version of a file from a backup?

A. When you are in a financial position to do so
B. When you have time to do so
C. When things are quiet at night
D. When a system file has become infected

**101.** You frequently browse the Internet for new products and updates. You notice that one of your computer manufacturers has distributed a new security patch. When should you install this update?

A. As soon as possible to prevent catastrophic security threats
B. After you have tested the security patch on a non-production server
C. After you have called the manufacturer to verify the source
D. After you have verified that patch for safety on a production server

## NETWORK HARDENING/ FIRMWARE/ CONFIGURATION/SERVICES AND PROTOCOLS

**102.** Even in a large, mixed environment, TCP/IP is the protocol of choice for most networks. Which of the following protocols would you want to deny passage over your Firewall?

A. TCP         B. IP
C. IPX/SPX     D. NetBEUI

**103.** Which of the following terms refers to actions taken by a programmer to fix logic errors in a program under development before actual production?

A. Compiling     B. Compressing
C. Debugging    D. Degaussing

**104.** Which of the following steps might be appropriate to harden your network system?

A. Configure ACL settings on select servers
B. Configure your servers to have unused services disabled
C. Configure your servers to all run NAT
D. Both A and B

**105.** Which of the following is the best method to disable services?
A. Verify the dependencies of all unused services before removing
B. Verify the dependencies of all active services before removing
C. Verify the dependencies of all unused services after removing
D. Verify the dependencies of all active services after removing

**106.** There are several common TCP and UDP ports, some of which you may wish to disable. List the matching service provided by ports 20, 21, 23, 25, 42, 53, 67, 70, 80, 110, 119, 135, 139, 161, and 443. How many common ports do you recognize?
A. At least 13 of the 15 ports
B. At least 10 of the 15 ports
C. At least 5 of the 15 ports
D. At least 2 of the 15 ports

**107.** Your network administrator has found one of your unused server services enabled. What should you do?
A. Disable the unused service for security reasons after verifying dependencies
B. Monitor the unused service for security reasons before verifying dependencies
C. Troubleshoot the unused service for security reasons and functionality
D. Maintain the enabled unused service for security reasons and functionality

## ACCESS CONTROL LISTS/ APPLICATION HARDENING/ UPDATES/WEB SERVERS

**108.** Which of the following hardening methods gives you the capability to deny access to one individual computer by IP address or computer name?
A. NTFS permissions
B. Authentication keys
C. PKI
D. Access control lists

**109.** Which of the following relates best to application hardening?
A. Buying the most recent application version available
B. Buying the most recent software package available
C. Configuring network applications with the most recent updates and service packs
D. Testing the most recent hotfixes, service packs, and patches after purchasing

**110.** You are responsible for your network security. Where would you go to ensure that you have the most current network updates, including hotfixes, service packs, and patches?
A. Your purchasing manager
B. Your CEO
C. The manufacturer's Web site
D. Your network administrator

**111.** You have added a new Web server to your network. Which of the following are sound practices when checking a Web server for security features?
A. Check with the vendor for the latest security patches for the Web software
B. Check the Web Server for any additional unused services
C. Check the Internet for any reports of software vulnerabilities
D. All of the above

**112.** Your small company is growing and has decided to host a Web page and dedicate a server for email. What protocol is used to support email traffic?
A. ARP
B. DNS
C. SMTP
D. IM

**113.** Which of the following functions has an email message relay agent?
A. SMTP               B. SNMP
C. S/MIME             D. LDAP

**114.** You desire to protect your email server. What should you configure to protect your email server?
A. SMTP relay settings
B. Antivirus software
C. Access control permissions
D. All of the above

## FTP, DNS, NNTP, FILE/PRINT AND DHCP SERVERS

**115.** What is the primary purpose of an FTP server?
A. Simplify storage of files
B. Allow for backup storage of files
C. Report security violations of files
D. Facilitate transfer of files

**116.** Which of the following is frequently used to send and receive text-based files and messages, including router configurations and ACL information?
A. File Transport Protocol (FTP)
B. Trivial File Transfer Protocol (TFTP)
C. Fast File Transfer Protocol (FFTP)
D. Trivial Transport Protocol (TTP)

**117.** What is the primary function of a DNS server?
A. Resolve 32-bit addresses in IPv4
B. Find other DNS servers
C. Resolve Fully Qualified Domain Names to IP addresses
D. Find MAC, 48-bit hardware addresses

**118.** Which of the following is one of the most important tasks to perform when hardening a DNS server?
A. Check the forward lookup zone for proper connections
B. Perform a DNS recursive query
C. Check the reverse lookup zone for proper connections
D. Restrict zone transfers to authorized computers

**119.** Which of the following servers allows for a high volume of group network traffic and is a potential source for malicious code or DoS?
A. FTP server
B. NNTP server
C. DNS server
D. File and Print server

**120.** Which one of the following is an easy way to protect an NNTP server from malicious attacks?
A. Implement a firewall protection plan on the NNTP server
B. Use a bastion host on the NNTP server
C. Implement virus scanning on the NNTP server
D. Turn off the NNTP server, because there is no way to protect a NNTP server from malicious attacks

**121.** Because networks were created to share resources, file and print servers announce network shares by default. Which of the following provides the best hardening technique for file and print servers?
A. Limit access to less than ten users at a time
B. Configure network shares to the default settings
C. Evaluate and set each folder share for the appropriate file and folder permissions
D. Audit all folders for successful access

**122.** What is the primary network security concern with DHCP servers?
A. Statically configured clients have the same address as DHCP clients
B. A cracker pretending to be the DHCP server, maliciously spoofs DHCP clients
C. The DNS server can be vulnerable to DHCP changes, causing clients to disconnect
D. The router is no longer available to DHCP clients

**123.** Which of the following could pose a conflict of IP addressing for clients on your network, thereby removing them from your zone?
A. A primary DHCP server
B. A secondary DHCP server
C. A rogue DHCP server
D. An Active Directory DHCP server

## DATA REPOSITORIES/ DIRECTORY SERVICES/ DATABASES

**124.** Which of the following are used as large Data Repositories?
A. SAN
B. NAS
C. DEN
D. All of the above

**125.** Which of the following is considered a Directory Service?
A. Lightweight Directory Access Protocol (LDAP)
B. Heavyweight Directory Access Protocol (HDAP)
C. Hierarchical Directory Access Protocol (HDAP)
D. Local Directory Access Protocol (LDAP)

**126.** Which of the following databases have this default security vulnerability: The "sa" account is established with a blank password?
A. LDAP
B. SQL
C. Proxy
D. Exchange

**127.** Which of the following is the best definition for the term polyinstantiation?
A. Many instances or copies of a file
B. Keeping database information hidden
C. Many instances or copies of a database
D. Lower-level databases have access to many upper-level databases

## ANSWERS

| 1 | 2 | 3 | 4 | 5 | 6 | 7 | 8 | 9 | 10 |
|---|---|---|---|---|---|---|---|---|---|
| D | D | B | B | D | D | D | D | D | B |
| **11** | **12** | **13** | **14** | **15** | **16** | **17** | **18** | **19** | **20** |
| D | D | B | B | D | A | C | A | D | B |
| **21** | **22** | **23** | **24** | **25** | **26** | **27** | **28** | **29** | **30** |
| B | D | C | B | D | B | A | D | A | D |
| **31** | **32** | **33** | **34** | **35** | **36** | **37** | **38** | **39** | **40** |
| D | D | C | C | D | C | D | A | B | A |
| **41** | **42** | **43** | **44** | **45** | **46** | **47** | **48** | **49** | **50** |
| B | B | D | D | C | D | D | D | C | D |
| **51** | **52** | **53** | **54** | **55** | **56** | **57** | **58** | **59** | **60** |
| C | D | C | C | C | D | D | C | B | D |
| **61** | **62** | **63** | **64** | **65** | **66** | **67** | **68** | **69** | **70** |
| A | D | D | C | C | A | D | C | D | A |
| **71** | **72** | **73** | **74** | **75** | **76** | **77** | **78** | **79** | **80** |
| D | C | C | D | D | B | B | C | D | D |
| **81** | **82** | **83** | **84** | **85** | **86** | **87** | **88** | **89** | **90** |
| C | D | C | D | B | B | A | C | B | D |
| **91** | **92** | **93** | **94** | **95** | **96** | **97** | **98** | **99** | **100** |
| A | D | B | D | D | A | D | D | A | D |
| **101** | **102** | **103** | **104** | **105** | **106** | **107** | **108** | **109** | **110** |
| C | B | C | D | A | A | A | D | C | C |
| **111** | **112** | **113** | **114** | **115** | **116** | **117** | **118** | **119** | **120** |
| D | C | A | D | D | B | C | D | B | C |
| **121** | **122** | **123** | **124** | **125** | **126** | **127** | | | |
| C | D | C | D | A | B | B | | | |

# 6. Database Management System (DBMS)

## BASICS OF DBMS

**1.** The processing of an application between a client and a _______ processor.
A. Front end
B. Back end
C. Both A and B
D. None of the above

**2.** Relationship between one master table to more then child table is the concept of
A. one to one relationship
B. one to many relationship
C. many to many relationship
D. None of the above

**3.** The _______ is not formal enough to be implemented directly in a programming language.
A. Analysis model
B. E R model
C. Object oriented model
D. Object oriented data mode

**4.** Size of a database are usually measured in terms of
A. Terabytes
B. Megabytes
C. Data bytes
D. Gigabytes

**5.** In databases, Locking level is also called as _______.
A. Gramulority
B. S lock
C. X lock
D. Dead lock

**6.** HSAM stands for _______
A. Hierarchic Sequential Access Method
B. Hierarchic Standard Access Method
C. Hierarchic Sequential and Method
D. Hierarchic Standard and Method

**7.** Threats to data security may be _______ threats to the database.
A. Direct
B. Indirect
C. Both Direct and Indirect
D. None of the above

**8.** Which of the following is not a logical database structure?
A. Chain
B. Network
C. Tree
D. Relational

**9.** An organized collection of logically related data is known as _______.
A. Data
B. Meta data
C. Database
D. Data versus Information

## RDBMS

**10.** The advantages of Standard Query Language (SQL) include which of the following in relation to GIS databases?
A. It is simple and easy to understand.
B. It uses a pseudo-English style of questioning.
C. It is good at handling geographical concepts.
D. It is widely used.

**11.** Which of the following are characteristics of an RDBMS?
A. Queries are possible on individual or groups of tables.
B. It cannot use SQL.
C. Data are organized in a series of two-dimensional tables each of which contains records for one entity.
D. Tables are linked by common data known as keys.

**12.** What is a 'tuple'?
A. Another name for the key linking different tables in a database.
B. A row or record in a database table.
C. Another name for a table in an RDBMS.
D. An attribute attached to a record.

**13.** Which of the following are issues to be considered by users of large corporate GIS databases?
A. The need for multiple views or different windows into the same databases.
B. The need for concurrent access and multi-user update.
C. The need to manage long transactions.
D. The need for multiple copies of the same data and subsequent merging after separate updates.

**14.** A key is completely arbitrary having no function and meaning other then identification of row is called _______.
A. primary key
B. foreign key
C. non-intelligent key
D. intelligent key

**15.** RDBMS provides _______.
A. one to one relationship
B. one to many relationship
C. many to many relationship
D. all of the above

**16.** Which of the following is not a database application?
A. dBase       B. Edit
C. FoxPro      D. Access

**17.** Which of the following is a database management tool developed by Microsoft?
A. dBase       B. Access
C. Personal Oracle    D. Sybase

**18.** Which is/are the quality of RDBMS
A. accuracy
B. timelines
C. relevance
D. all of the above

## ORACLE/SQL SERVER

**19.** The following program is submitted.

```
data test;
 input name $ age;
cards;
John +35
;
run;
```

Which values are stored in the output data set?

A.
| name | age |
| --- | --- |
| John | 35 |

B.
| name | age |
| --- | --- |
| John | (missing value) |

C.
| name | age |
| --- | --- |
| (missing value) | (missing value) |

D. The DATA step fails execution due to data errors.

**20.** The following observation is stored in a SAS data set named EMPLOYEES:

| LNAME | FNAME | JOBCODE |
| --- | --- | --- |
| Whitley | Sam | na1 |

If the DATA step below is executed, what will be the value of the variable JOBDESC in the output SAS data set when this observation is processed:

```
data navigate;
 set employees;
 if jobcode = 'NA1' then jobdesc =
'Navigator';
run;
```

A. navigator
B. Navigator
C. NAVIGATOR
D. a missing value

**21.** Which of the following is not normally used as a server-side scripting language?
A. PHP         B. Java Applets
C. PERL        D. ASP

**22.** Client-side scripting programs are executed by:
   A. the web browser before making a HTTP request.
   B. the web server after receiving a HTTP request, but before HTML is generated.
   C. the web browser after receiving a HTTP response containing HTML.
   D. the web server after generating HTML but before sending a HTTP response.

**23.** MySQL is
   A. a hierarchical model.
   B. a RDBMS.
   C. a relational model.
   D. a database scheme

**24.** An attribute or set of attributes that uniquely identify an entity is called
   A. a primary key
   B. a relation
   C. a one-to-many relationship
   D. a many-to-many relationship

**25.** Which of the following is not a valid character type in MySQL?
   A. CHAR              B. VARCHAR
   C. STRING            D. TEXT

**26.** Which of the following is not a type of SQL statement?
   A. SELECT            B. INSERT
   C. MODIFY            D. CREATE

**27.** When querying information stored on two different tables by means of a common column, we use ______.
   A. the DISTINCT operator
   B. an Aggregate Function
   C. an ORDER BY clause
   D. a Join

**28.** Which function is not used when accessing MySQL from PHP?
   A. The mysql select db function
   B. The mysql update function
   C. The mysql connect function
   D. The mysql query function

**29.** Given that the data set named ONE contains 10 observations and the data set named TWO contains 10 observations, how many observations will be contained in the data set named COMBINE that is created in the following DATA step?
data combine;
set one two;
run;
   A. 10
   B. 20
   C. 0, the DATA step will fail due to syntax errors
   D. 10 to 20, depending on how many observations match

**30.** Primary key is a ______.
   A. common key
   B. unique key
   C. input key
   D. None of the above

## SQL/PLUS

**31.** Structural components which are used to build the model are______.
   A. relational          B. attributes
   C. tuples              D. All of the above

**32.** SQL was standardized by ______.
   A. ANSI                B. IBM
   C. ORACLE             D. Microsoft

**33.** SQL introduced by ______.
   A. ANSI                B. Oracle
   C. Microsoft          D. IBM

**34.** Trigger is executed on ______.
   A. insert              B. delete
   C. update             D. All of the above

**35.** The cache of system global area is/are ___.
   A. server process
   B. user process
   C. background process
   D. All of the above

**36.** Grant and Revoke used for ______.
   A. data access control
   B. data definition language
   C. data manipulation language
   D. All of the above

**36.** User name of PL/SQL is ______.
A. trigger   B. tiger
C. oracle   D. scott

**37.** Password of PL/SQL is ______.
A. tiger   B. lion
C. dog   D. cat

## NETWORK DATABASE MODEL

**38.** The primary advantage of auditing around the computerize that this ______.
A. takes less time
B. is oriented towards results
C. has no logical constraints
D. requires little technical knowledge.

**39.** The part of a computer system controlling data manipulation is the:
A. Operating system
B. Arithmetic-logic unit
C. Primary storage
D. Job control program

**40.** DB2, SQL Server, Ingress, Informix & Sybase are ______.
A. Library system
B. Access control system
C. Programming language
D. Database managers

## FOXPRO

**41.** The maximum number of field assented in a table ______.
A. 156   B. 229
C. 256   D. 255

**42.** FoxPro provides maximum width of a field is ______.
A. 62500
B. 65500
C. 35555
D. None of the above

**43.** The maximum record can be stored in a field is ______.
A. 1 billion
B. 2 billion
C. 10 thousand
D. None of the above

**44.** The extension of Foxpro file is ______.
A. .ftp   B. .fdb
C. .dbf   D. .fbf

**45.** The extension of memo file is ______.
A. .fpt   B. .mem
C. .mpt   D. .dbf

**46.** A field where all character, number and special character and symbols can be stored ______.
A. logical   B. float
C. numeric   D. character

**47.** The logical field stores maximum character ______.
A. 254   B. 1
C. 2   D. 20

**48.** Memo type field acquire the space in database file ______.
A. 5000   B. 254
C. 10   D. 1

**49.** Date type field acquire the space in database file ______.
A. 6   B. 5
C. 2   D. 8

**50.** The maximum width of numeric type field is ______.
A. 20   B. 18
C. 10   D. 8

**51.** The column of a database is called ______.
A. record   B. field
C. database file   D. data

**52.** Each line of database is called ______.
A. field
B. data
C. record
D. information

**53.** Foxpro is a modified version of ______.
A. FoxBase+
B. DBASE I
C. DBASE II
D. None of the above

**54.** The smallest component of data base is
_______.
  A. field
  B. record
  C. file
  D. record number

**55.** What is the process of Exit form FoxPro database?
  A. File ' Exit        B. Quit
  C. Alt+ F4            D. All of the above

**56.** Through which command data can be displayed _______.
  A. display           B. list
  C. browse            D. All of the above

**57.** The record pointer presents on _______.
  A. EOF
  B. BOF
  C. any records
  D. All of the above

**58.** Pack command used to _______.
  A. delete the record
  B. permanent delete the record
  C. temporary delete the record
  D. None of the above

**59.** Which command used for delete all records
_______.
  A. delete             B. pack
  C. zap                D. All of the above

**60.** Which command used to print the name of day _______.
  A. dow                B. cdow
  C. cdaw               D. day

**61.** The extension name of label file is _______.
  A. .lbx
  B. .ibx
  C. .lbl
  D. None of the above

**62.** Which command use to create program file _______.
  A. modify command
  B. modi comm.
  C. both A and B
  D. None of the above

**63.** Extension name of program file is _______.
  A. .prg
  B. .prog
  C. .prig
  D. None of the above

## ANSWERS

| 1 | 2 | 3 | 4 | 5 | 6 | 7 | 8 | 9 | 10 |
|---|---|---|---|---|---|---|---|---|----|
| C | B | A | D | A | A | A | A | C | C |

| 11 | 12 | 13 | 14 | 15 | 16 | 17 | 18 | 19 | 20 |
|----|----|----|----|----|----|----|----|----|----|
| B | B | A | C | D | B | B | D | A | B |

| 21 | 22 | 23 | 24 | 25 | 26 | 27 | 28 | 29 | 30 |
|----|----|----|----|----|----|----|----|----|----|
| B | C | B | A | C | C | D | B | B | B |

| 31 | 32 | 33 | 34 | 35 | 36 | 37 | 38 | 39 | 40 |
|----|----|----|----|----|----|----|----|----|----|
| D | A | D | D | D | D | D,A | A | D | D |

| 41 | 42 | 43 | 44 | 45 | 46 | 47 | 48 | 49 | 50 |
|----|----|----|----|----|----|----|----|----|----|
| D | B | A | C | A | D | B | C | D | A |

| 51 | 52 | 53 | 54 | 55 | 56 | 57 | 58 | 59 | 60 |
|----|----|----|----|----|----|----|----|----|----|
| B | C | A | A | D | D | D | B | B | B |

| 61 | 62 | 63 |
|----|----|----|
| A | C | A |

# 7. Operating System



1. ........... runs on computer hardware and serve as platform for other software's to run on _______.
   A. Operating System
   B. Application Software
   C. System Software
   D. All of the above

2. ........ is the layer of a computer system between the hardware and the user program _______.
   A. Operating environment
   B. Operating system
   C. System environment
   D. None of the above

3. The primary purpose of an operating system is _______.
   A. to make the most efficient use of the computer hardware
   B. to allow people to use the computer
   C. to keep systems programmers employed
   D. to make computers easier to use

4. _______ transforms one interface into another interface
   A. Hardware
   B. Software
   C. Data
   D. None of the above

5. _______ system is built directly on the hardware.
   A. Environment
   B. Both A and B
   C. Operating
   D. None of the above

6. Multiprogramming systems _______.
   A. are easier to develop than single programming systems
   B. execute each job faster
   C. execute more jobs in the same time period
   D. are used only one large mainframe computers.

7. _______ is the first program run on a computer when a computer is booting
   A. System software
   B. Operating system
   C. System operations
   D. None of the above

8. _______ interface consists of things like program counter, registers, interrupts and terminals.
   A. Hardware
   B. Software
   C. Data
   D. None of the above

9. _______ shares characteristics with both hardware and software.
   A. Operating system
   B. Software
   C. Data
   D. None of the above

**10.** Which of the following best describes a Spooler?
A. The software that schedule privileged instructions for input/output
B. The take up real on tape drive
C. A buffer between input/output devices and the computer
D. The priority indicator from the job scheduler

**11.** MTBF means
A. Mean Time Between Failure
B. Master Time Buffer Feature
C. Most Treated Buffer Time
D. Master Test Board Feature

**12.** A register organized to allow to move left or right operations is called a ____
A. Counter
B. Loader
C. Adder
D. Shift register

## OPERATING SYSTEM STRUCTURE

**13.** Swapping
A. works best with may many small partitions
B. allows many programs to use memory simultaneously
C. allows each program in turn to use the memory
D. does not work with overlaying

**14.** Which of the following operating system does not implement multitasking truly?
A. Windows 98
B. Windows NT
C. Windows XP
D. MS DOS

**15.** When a computer is first turned on or restarted, a special type of absolute loader called ______ is executed.
A. Compile and Go loader
B. Boot loader
C. Bootstrap loader
D. Relating loader

**16.** Poor response times are usually caused by ______.

A. Busy process
B. high I/O rates
C. high paging rates
D. All of the above

**17.** Which of the following program is not a utility?
A. Debugger
B. Editor
C. Spooler
D. All of the above

**18.** A co-processor ______.
A. is relatively easy to support in software
B. causes all processors to function equally
C. works with any application
D. is quite common in modern computers

**19.** Which of the following operating systems do you choose to implement a Client-Server network.
A. Windows 3.1
B. Windows 95
C. Windows 3.1X
D. Windows 2000

**20.** Page stealing ______.
A. is a sign of an efficient system
B. is taking page frames from other working sets
C. should be the tuning goal
D. is taking larger disk spaces for pages paged out

**21.** The operating system manages ______.
A. Memory
B. Processes
C. Disks and I/O devices
D. All of the above

## MS-DOS

**22.** The DOS 1.0 operating system developed by ______.
A. Microsoft
B. IBM
C. apple talk
D. None

**23.** Who was the programmer of MS-DOS operating system?
A. R.Jhon
B. Bill Gates
C. Dennis Ritchi
D. Tim pelerson

**24.** Which was the last version of MS-DOS that was released separately?
A. 7.2
B. 6.22
C. 6.11
D. 7.1

**25.** Which file in MS-DOS contains internal commands that are loaded during booting process?

# 8. | Visual Basic |

## INTEGRATED DEVELOPMENT ENVIRONMENT (IDE)

1. Event-driven languages are ______.
   A. FORTRAN based
   B. used  to write procedural languages
   C. OOP
   D. designed to make programming GUI easier

2. IDE is ______.
   A. Independent Development Enterprise
   B. a development environment for machine language
   C. a software project management tool
   D. an Integrated Development Environment for Visual Basic

3. Which of the following is not part of the IDE?
   A. Code editor window
   B. Properties window
   C. Form layout window
   D. General window

4. The application name always appears in the ______.
   A. properties window
   B. intermediate window
   C. code window
   D. title bar

5. The color of a button is ______.
   A. one of its properties
   B. not updateable
   C. defined in the project
   D. defined in the intermediate window

6. Code is ______.
   A. updateable in the form editor
   B. instructions
   C. seldom used
   D. an object

7. Controls are ______.
   A. code
   B. part of the menus
   C. rules
   D. objects

8. In the IDE, which of following is used to design the layout of an application?
   A. Form Designer window
   B. Project Explorer window
   C. Context Menu
   D. Form Layout window

9. The location of the form on the desktop during execution is determined by the ______.
   A. form Designer window
   B. project Explorer window
   C. context Menu
   D. form Layout window

10. The Object Browser ______.
    A. displays the command buttons and textboxes, etc.
    B. shows frequently used shortcuts as objects
    C. is a Context Menu
    D. displays the object libraries and their combinations of data and code

11. The first procedure-oriented language was ______.
    A. FORTRAN      B. BASIC
    C. COBOL        D. ADA

12. C is ______.
    A. a language widely used in UNIX
    B. a language based on BASIC
    C. used primarily for business applications
    D. a GUI

13. COBOL is ______.
    A. one of the oldest programming languages
    B. still widely used
    C. not suitable for business applications
    D. None of the above

14. Object Oriented languages ______.
    A. are procedural languages
    B. are task oriented
    C. are based on actions happening to objects
    D. are natural language techniques

15. Visual Basic projects are identified by a ______.

    A. ".vbp" suffix        B. ".mak" suffix
    C. ".vbg" suffix        D. All the above

16. Visual Basic forms are identified by a ______.

    A. ".frm" suffix        B. ".mak" suffix
    C. ".for" suffix        D. special icon

17. To run an application in Visual Basic ______.

    A. click on the start button (blue arrow)
    B. use the File Menu
    C. use the Project Menu to select Run
    D. none of the above

18. To exit Visual Basic ______.
    A. click Alt-Q
    B. use the File Menu to select Quit
    C. use the Window Menu to select Exit
    D. click on the diskette icon

19. The reference library of Visual Basic books is called:
    A. MSDN library        B. help library
    C. contents            D. topic pane

## VARIABLES

20. What is the storage range of integer variable in VB?
    A. –32768 to +32767
    B. whole number in the range + or –2 billion
    C. single but held 15 digit
    D. + or – 900000

21. What is the storage range of long variable?
    A. –32768 to +32767
    B. whole number in the range + or –2 billion
    C. single but held 15 digit
    D. + or –900000

22. What is the storage size of single variable?
    A. –32768 to +32767
    B. whole number in the range + or –2 billion
    C. single point number held accuracy to 7 digits
    D. + or –900000

23. What is the storage range of double integer?
    A. –32768 to +32767
    B. whole number in the range + or –2 billion
    C. single but held 15 digit
    D. + or –900000

24. The storage range currency data type?
    A. –32768 to +32767
    B. whole number in the range + or –2 billion
    C. single but held 15 digit
    D. + or – 900000

25. The storage size of string is ______.
    A. –32768 to +32767
    B. whole number in the range + or –2 billion
    C. single but held 15 digit
    D. 65000 character

26. The variable can be define as ______.
    A. dim num1 as integer
    B. num1 as integer
    C. dim as integer num1
    D. All of the above

**27.** In visual basic an Array can be define as
______.
 A. dim result(50) as integer
 B. dim integer X(50)
 C. dim result Array(50) as integer
 D. none of the above

**28.** ______ array used to change their size
during the execution of the program.
 A. Redim
 B. Global
 C. Dim
 D. All of the above

## OPERATORS

**29.** ______ operator used with a single
expression, to reverse its value so that
true becomes false and vice versa.
 A. NOT                    B. AND
 C. OR                     D. XOR

**30.** EOQ operator use if ______.
 A. both expression True
 B. both expression False
 C. both expression True or False
 D. None of the above

**31.** Visual basic use QB and RBG color for
color property. What is the QBcode of
Black & White?
 A. 8-15                   B. 15-24
 C. 5-12                   D. 7-9

**32.** Back End is a ______.
 A. program file
 B. RDBMS file
 C. VB Code properties
 D. All of the above

## VISUAL BASIC CONTROLS

**33.** Visual basic program provides extra
facility to the system. They are loaded
automatically by ______.
 A. autoload .mak
 B. .vbx
 C. .mdb
 D. None of the above

**34.** The command dialog and Grid controls are
made available through the ______.
 A. autoload .Mak
 B. .vbx
 C. .mdb
 D. cmdialog.vbx

**35.** OLE stands for ______.
 A. Object Linking Embedding
 B. Object Link Environment
 C. Object Link Enhancement
 D. None of the above

**36.** Where you set the properties of objects?
 A. Property windows
 B. Form layout
 C. Windows explorer
 D. All of the above

**37.** ______ provides a way to move and resize
forms and controls.
 A. Pointer                B. Picture Box
 C. Label                  D. Frame

**38.** ______ control displays bitmap, icons or
windows meta file.
 A. Pointer                B. Picture Box
 C. Label                  D. Frame

**39.** ______ provides an area to enter or
display text
 A. Pointer                B. Picture Box
 C. Label                  D. Text

**40.** ______ Control carries out a command or
action when a user choose it.
 A. Pointer
 B. Picture Box
 C. Command Button
 D. Text

**41.** ______ displays a true/ false or Yes/No
option. User can check any number of
check boxes on a form at one time.
 A. Pointer              B. Check box
 C. Command button  D. Text

**42.** Combines text boxes with a list box .That
allows a user to type in a selection or select
an item from a drop-down list called.
 A. combo box
 B. list box
 C. dir list box
 D. None of the above

43. ______ executes timer events at specified time interval.
    A. Combo box
    B. Timer
    C. Dir list box
    D. None of the above

44. ______ to connect an existing database and display information from it on forms.
    A. Data
    B. OLE
    C. Custom control
    D. None of the above

45. Who contains the separate file with file extension .VBX and .OCX?
    A. Data
    B. OLE
    C. Custom control
    D. None of the above

46. Visual basic modules is/are ______.
    A. Class module
    B. Standard module
    C. Form module
    D. All of above

47. BOF stands for ______.
    A. Beginning of File
    B. Beginning of Form
    C. Bank of File
    D. None of the above

48. EOF stands for ______.
    A. End of File
    B. Extend of File
    C. Eliminate of File
    D. None of the above

49. What is ODBC?
    A. Open Database Connectivity
    B. Open Dictionary Connectivity
    C. Open Database Costing
    D. Open Disk Data Connectivity

50. RDO stands for ______.
    A. Remote Data Object
    B. Rule Data Object
    C. Remote Dictionary Object
    D. None of the above

51. ______ is used to read and update in relational database management system.
    A. Remote Data Object
    B. Remote Data Control
    C. Both A and B
    D. None of the above

52. ActiveX is based on an old technology known as ______.
    A. ODBC
    B. OLE
    C. OCX
    D. None of the above

53. ______ provides a standard set of dialog boxes for operations such as opening and saving file.
    A. Common dialog
    B. Data bound combo box
    C. Apex data bound grid control
    D. None of the above

54. ______ provides a spreadsheet like bound control that display a series of rows and columns representing records and fields from a record set object.
    A. Common dialog
    B. Data bound combo box
    C. Apex data bound grid control
    D. None of the above

55. The extension of user control object file is ______.
    A. .CTL
    B. .OCX
    C. .EXE
    D. .PPT

## REPORTS

56. ______ is used to assign a data format and format text
    A. Data bound combo box
    B. Apex data bound grid control
    C. Text box control
    D. None of the above

57. ______ allows to place labels on the report to identify fields or sections.
   A. Common dialog
   B. Data bound combo box
   C. Apex data bound grid control
   D. Label control

58. ______ enables you to place graphics on the report. This control cannot be bound to a data field.
   A. Common dialog
   B. Data bound combo box
   C. Apex data bound grid control
   D. Image control

59. Which of the following provides Data Link Properties?
   A. Microsoft OLE DB provider ODBC driver
   B. Microsoft Jet 3.51 OLEDB provider
   C. Apex data bound grid control
   D. Microsoft OLE DB simple provider

60. A statement that cannot execute properly in a VB project is a result of a ______.
   A. Syntax Error
   B. Logic Error
   C. Compile Error
   D. Run-time Error

61. An IIS application is a visual basic application that lives on a ______ and responds to request from the browser.
   A. Web server
   B. Client server
   C. Web and client server
   D. All of the above

## LIBRARY FUNCTIONS

62. ______ returns a string consisting of the specified number of spaces.
   A. Space          B. Str
   C. String         D. Length

63. What version of Visual Basic have you been working with in your labs on this course?
   A. The Enterprise Edition
   B. The Learning Edition
   C. The Licensed Edition
   D. None of the above

64. In an If statement, when the condition is true?
   A. only the Else clause is executed
   B. only the ElseIf clause is executed
   C. only the End If statement is executed
   D. only the Then clause is executed

65. The text property of a text box behaves like a
   A. string         B. numeric
   C. variant        D. function

66. ______ returns a specified number of characters from the right side of the string
   A. str
   B. right
   C. string
   D. None of the above

67. ______ returns a specified number of characters from the left side of the string.
   A. Left
   B. Right
   C. Len
   D. None of the above

68. ______ returns the position of the first occurrence of one string within another.
   A. Instr          B. Str
   C. Right          D. Left

69. ______ returns a copy of string without leading space and without trailing spaces.
   A. LTrim
   B. RTrim
   C. Both A and B
   D. None of the above

70. Which returns a string that has been converted to Uppercase?
   A. Lcase          B. Ltrim
   C. RTrim          D. Ucase

71. ______ returns a string that has been converted to Lowercase.
   A. Lcase          B. Ltrim
   C. Rtrim          D. Ucase

72. ______ returns the number containing in a string.
    A. Val
    B. Sgn
    C. Rnd
    D. None of the above

73. ______ returns an integer indicating the sign of a number.
    A. Val
    B. Sgn
    C. Rnd
    D. None of the above

74. ______ returns a random number.
    A. Val
    B. Sgn
    C. Rnd
    D. None of the above

75. ______ Returns the integer portion of a number.
    A. Int
    B. Fix
    C. Int Fix
    D. None of the above

76. ______ returns a string representing the hexadecimal value of a number.
    A. Hex
    B. MyHexx
    C. Oct
    D. All of the above

77. ______ represents a string representing the octal value of a number.
    A. Hex              B. MyHexx
    C. Oct              D. All of the above

78. ______ returns the current date and time according to system's date and time.
    A. Now
    B. Time
    C. Date
    D. None of the above

79. ______ returns a whole number between 0 and 59 inclusive, representing the minute of the hour.
    A. Now              B. Time
    C. Date             D. Minute

80. ______ returns the whole number representing colour value.
    A. QBColor          B. RBG
    C. XYG              D. RTY

81. Which is not a button argument?
    A. VbOkOnly         B. VbOkCancle
    C. VbYesNo          D. VbThankY

82. Which one is used for warning message icon?
    A. VbQuestion
    B. VbYesNoCancle
    C. VbInformation
    D. None of the above

83. Which one code used for this message "File Not Found"?
    A. 53               B. 78
    C. 43               D. 23

84. Which property used for the help context is?
    A. helpcontext
    B. helpfile
    C. LastDll error
    D. None of the above

85. ______ property used to A string corresponding to the internal error number returned by the number property if this string exists.
    A. Description      B. helpcontext
    C. helpfile         D. LastDll error

86. A variable or constant that must be passed to a function in this manner is called ______.
    A. Library
    B. Argument
    C. Typecasting
    D. None of the above

87. Microsoft design the DLL files such that other applications like VB will also be able to use these functions from the windows DLL file. These functions are called ______.
    A. Application program interface
    B. Graphical user Interface
    C. System user Interface
    D. None of the above

**88.** RTF stands for ______.
  A. Random Text File
  B. Rich Text File
  C. Restore Text File
  D. Remove Text File

**89.** In Visual Basic which one of the following is a property of a scroll bar control?
  A. Internal
  B. Cancel
  C. Fore color
  D. Max

## ANSWERS

| 1 | 2 | 3 | 4 | 5 | 6 | 7 | 8 | 9 | 10 |
|---|---|---|---|---|---|---|---|---|---|
| D | D | D | D | A | B | D | A | D | D |

| 11 | 12 | 13 | 14 | 15 | 16 | 17 | 18 | 19 | 20 |
|---|---|---|---|---|---|---|---|---|---|
| A | A | D | C | D | A | A | A | A | A |

| 21 | 22 | 23 | 24 | 25 | 26 | 27 | 28 | 29 | 30 |
|---|---|---|---|---|---|---|---|---|---|
| B | C | C | D | D | A | A | A | A | C |

| 31 | 32 | 33 | 34 | 35 | 36 | 37 | 38 | 39 | 40 |
|---|---|---|---|---|---|---|---|---|---|
| A | B | A | D | A | A | A | A | D | C |

| 41 | 42 | 43 | 44 | 45 | 46 | 47 | 48 | 49 | 50 |
|---|---|---|---|---|---|---|---|---|---|
| B | A | B | A | C | D | A | A | A | A |

| 51 | 52 | 53 | 54 | 55 | 56 | 57 | 58 | 59 | 60 |
|---|---|---|---|---|---|---|---|---|---|
| A | B | A | C | A | C | D | D | B | C |

| 61 | 62 | 63 | 64 | 65 | 66 | 67 | 68 | 69 | 70 |
|---|---|---|---|---|---|---|---|---|---|
| A | A | A | D | A | B | A | A | C | D |

| 71 | 72 | 73 | 74 | 75 | 76 | 77 | 78 | 79 | 80 |
|---|---|---|---|---|---|---|---|---|---|
| A | A | B | C | C | A | C | A | D | B |

| 81 | 82 | 83 | 84 | 85 | 86 | 87 | 88 | 89 |
|---|---|---|---|---|---|---|---|---|
| D | A | A | A | A | B | A | B | D |

# 9. | Software Engineering |



1. Support systems that allow employees to communicate with each other and with customers and suppliers are called ______.
   A. Transaction Processing Systems (TPS)
   B. Decision Support Systems (DSS)
   C. Office Support Systems
   D. Communication Support Systems

2. Which of the following is the analyst's approach to problem solving?
   A. Verify that the benefits of solving the problem outweigh the costs, then research and understand the problem.
   B. Develop a set of possible solutions, then verify that the benefits of solving the problem outweigh the costs.
   C. Verify that the benefits of solving the problem outweigh the costs, then define the requirements for solving the problem.
   D. Implement the solution, then define the details of the chosen solution.

3. An example of a project phase is ____.
   A. gathering information about the user's needs
   B. performing a project cost/benefit analysis
   C. planning the project
   D. designing the system interface

4. Users are typically more involved in the project during which two phases?
   A. Analysis and design
   B. Planning and analysis
   C. Design and implementation
   D. Analysis and implementation

5. A ______ is a representation of an important aspect of the real world.
   A. methodology          B. tool
   C. technique            D. model

6. Which of the following encourages developers to combine the best of eXtreme programming (XP) with the best of UP?
   A. Risk model
   B. Agile modeling
   C. Extreme programming (XP)
   D. Spiral model

7. By showing which tasks can be done concurrently, a ____ assists in assigning staff.
   A. Data Flow Diagram (DFD)
   B. Project Evaluation and Review Technique (PERT) Chart
   C. Gantt Chart
   D. Work Breakdown Structure (WBS)

8. Which of the following indicates the current date and percentage of work completed for each task?
   A. Cost/benefit analysis
   B. Critical path
   C. Work breakdown structure
   D. Tracking Gantt chart

## PROJECT PLANNING

9. ____ feasibility asks the question: "Is the anticipated value of the benefits greater than projected costs of development?"
   A. Technological        B. Economic
   C. Cultural             D. Organizational

10. Questions that have a simple, definitive answer are called _______ questions.
    A. opinion
    B. closed-ended
    C. open-ended
    D. multiple choice

11. _______ prototypes are not built with the intent of being fully functional, but to check the feasibility of certain approaches to the business need.
    A. Functional
    B. Discovery
    C. Workflow
    D. Logical

12. Which of the following statements is correct?
    A. Questionnaires are well suited to help you learn about processes, workflows, or techniques.
    B. Stakeholders always return questionnaires that contain many open-ended questions.
    C. Questionnaires have a limited and specific use in information gathering.
    D. CASE tools cannot be used to develop prototypes.

13. A series of formulas that describe technical aspects of a system is a _______ model.
    A. concrete
    B. descriptive
    C. graphical
    D. mathematical

14. Narrative memos, reports, or lists that describe some aspect of a system is a _______ model.
    A. descriptive
    B. concrete
    C. mathematical
    D. graphical

15. Diagrams and schematic representations of some aspect of a system are examples of a _______ model.
    A. logical
    B. graphical
    C. mathematical
    D. descriptive

16. Checks or safety procedures are put in place to protect the integrity of the system. This is referred to as _______.
    A. perfect technology assumption
    B. risk control assumption
    C. system controls
    D. technology protection

17. A synonym for cardinality (often used with the object-oriented approach) is _______.
    A. relationship
    B. multiplicity
    C. unary relationship
    D. class

18. A(n) _______ is a process or file with a data input that is never used to produce a data output.
    A. black hole
    B. information overload
    C. fragment
    D. context diagram

## PROBLEM IDENTIFICATION

19. Which of the following is the rule of model design that limits the number of model components or connections among components to no more than nine?
    A. Minimization interfaces
    B. Rule of $7 \pm 2$
    C. Rule of balancing
    D. Black hole

20. Which of the following is a table that describes the relationship between processes and the locations in which they are performed?
    A. Location diagram
    B. Black hole
    C. Activity-location matrix
    D. Activity-data matrix

21. Which of the following is a diagram or map that identifies all of the processing locations of a system?
    A. Black hole
    B. Location diagram
    C. Activity-location matrix
    D. Activity-data matrix

22. _______ are drawn after the event table and context diagram are complete.
    A. DFD fragments
    B. Class diagrams
    C. System sequence diagrams
    D. Use cases

23. _______ was developed by James Martin in the early 1980s.
    A. Information Engineering (IE)
    B. Minimization of Interfaces
    C. CRUD
    D. Event-partitioned system model

24. Which of the following is a component of a traditional systems analysis model?
    A. Use case
    B. Process definitions
    C. Objects
    D. Decision table

25. Fact-finding activities are also referred to as ______.
    A. discovery activities
    B. sequence activities
    C. interaction activities
    D. messaging

26. A use case diagram can be derived from a(n) ______.
    A. class diagram
    B. sequence diagram
    C. event table
    D. context diagram

27. Which of the following describes the inputs and outputs that occur within a use case?
    A. System Sequence Diagrams (SSDs)
    B. Data flow definitions
    C. Context diagrams
    D. DFD fragments

28. ______ on a systems sequence diagram means multiplicity, or many.
    A. {}
    B. *
    C. ()
    D. [ ]

29. A high ______ occurs when the system takes over, as much as possible, the processing of a function.
    A. level of scope
    B. Business Process Reengineering (BPR)
    C. level of strategic planning
    D. level of automation

## REQUIREMENT OF COMPONENTS FOR IMPLEMENTATION

30. Scope creep refers to ______.
    A. rating the importance of each function
    B. deferring some functions until later
    C. determining the priority of each function
    D. requests to add new functions after decisions have been finalized

31. Which of the following would most likely be included in the "Overview of need" section of a Request For Proposal (RFP)?
    A. Expected business benefits
    B. Background on company
    C. Performance requirements
    D. Maintenance and support

32. Which of the following would most likely be included in the "Introduction and background" section of a Request For Proposal (RFP)?
    A. Request for statement of work
    B. Overview of industry/business
    C. Specification of primary functions
    D. Documentation and training

33. Which of the following types of contracts will most likely put most of the risk on the vendor?
    A. Cost-plus-incentive
    B. Cost-plus-percentage
    C. Cost-plus
    D. Fixed-dollar

34. Which of the following would most likely be included in the "Description of technical requirements" section of a Request For Proposal (RFP)?
    A. Description of business need
    B. Hardware specifications
    C. Maintenance and support
    D. Background on company

## DESIGN

35. High-level design that defines the overall structure of a system is called ______ design.
    A. system
    B. nodal
    C. architectural
    D. functional

**36.** A diagram that shows the hierarchical relationship between the modules of a computer program is called a(n) _______.
A. system flow chart
B. design class diagram
C. data flow diagram (DFD)
D. structure chart

**37.** What is the name given to the primary output data flow in a set of processes used in transform analysis?
A. Output stream
B. Afferent data flow
C. Efferent data flow
D. Primary information flow

**38.** Modules with poor cohesion tend to have high _______.
A. data flow
B. coupling
C. iterations
D. program calls

**39.** In software development, the detailed design specifications are primarily done by _______.
A. business analysts
B. project managers
C. software design experts
D. users of the system

**40.** Most method signatures are developed during the design of the _______ diagrams.
A. package
B. interaction
C. domain
D. design class

## SOFTWARE QUALITY TESTING

**41.** Which of the following is not a perspective of quality?
A. Transcendent
B. Product-based
C. Translucent
D. User-based

**42.** Which of the following is not one of Deming's 14 points for management?
A. Adopt a new philosophy
B. Eliminate slogans, exhortations, and targets for the work force
C. Mobility of management
D. Create constancy of purpose

**43.** Defects are least costly to correct at what stage of the development cycle?
A. Requirements
B. Analysis & Design
C. Construction
D. Implementation

**44.** What type of change do you need before you can obtain a behavior change?
A. Lifestyle
B. Vocabulary
C. Internal
D. Management

**45.** Software testing accounts for what per cent of software development costs?
A. 10-20
B. 40-50
C. 70-80
D. 5-10

**46.** The purpose of software testing is to
A. demonstrate that the application works properly
B. detect the existence of defects
C. validate the logical design
D. None of the above

**47.** Which of the following are characteristics of testable software?
A. Observability
B. Simplicity
C. Stability
D. All of the above

## WHITE BOX TESTING

**48.** The testing technique that requires devising test cases to demonstrate that each program function is operational is called _______.
A. black-box testing
B. glass-box testing
C. grey-box testing
D. white-box testing

**49.** The testing technique that requires devising test cases to exercise the internal logic of a software module is called _______.
A. behavioral testing
B. black-box testing
C. grey-box testing
D. white-box testing

## SOFTWARE ERROR TESTING

**50.** What types of errors are missed by black-box testing and can be uncovered by white-box testing?
   A. behavioral errors
   B. logic errors
   C. typographical errors
   D. Both B and C

**51.** The cyclomatic complexity metric provides the designer with information regarding the number of
   A. cycles in the program
   B. errors in the program
   C. independent logic paths in the program
   D. statements in the program

**52.** Condition testing is a control structure testing technique where the criteria used to design test cases is that they ______.
   A. rely on basis path testing
   B. exercise the logical conditions in a program module
   C. select test paths based on the locations and uses of variables
   D. focus on testing the validity of loop constructs

**53.** Real-time applications add a new and potentially difficult element to the testing mix ______.
   A. performance      B. reliability
   C. security         D. time

**54.** Loop testing is a control structure testing technique where the criteria used to design test cases is that they ______.
   A. rely basis path testing
   B. exercise the logical conditions in a program module
   C. select test paths based on the locations and uses of variables
   D. focus on testing the validity of loop constructs

**55.** Black-box testing attempts to find errors in which of the following categories ______.
   A. incorrect or missing functions
   B. interface errors
   C. performance errors
   D. All of the above

**56.** Fault-based testing is best reserved for ______.
   A. conventional software testing
   B. operations and classes that are critical or suspect
   C. use-case validation
   D. white-box testing of operator algorithms

**57.** Testing OO class operations is made more difficult by ______.
   A. encapsulation      B. inheritance
   C. polymorphism       D. Both B and C

**58.** Scenario-based testing ______.
   A. concentrates on actor and software interaction
   B. misses errors in specifications
   C. misses errors in subsystem interactions
   D. Both A and B

**59.** Deep structure testing is not designed to ______.
   A. examine object behaviors
   B. exercise communication mechanisms
   C. exercise object dependencies
   D. exercise structure observable by the user

**60.** Which of these techniques is not useful for partition testing at the class level?
   A. attribute-based partitioning
   B. category-based partitioning
   C. equivalence class partitioning
   D. state-based partitioning

**61.** Tests derived from behavioral class models should be based on the ______.
   A. data flow diagram
   B. object-relation diagram
   C. state diagram
   D. use-case diagram

## OPERATIONAL STAGE

**62.** Which one of the following is not typically provided by Source Code Management software?
   A. Synchronisation
   B. Versioning and revision history
   C. Syntax highlighting
   D. Project forking

**63.** Which one is most important activity of operational stage _______.
A. delivery
B. designing
C. operating
D. postmortem

**64.** Which one eliminates deviations form the specification _______.
A. corrective change
B. testing
C. adaptive change
D. All of the above

**65.** Which one responsible for alteration of hardware or operating system _______.
A. corrective change
B. adaptive change
C. perfective change
D. All of the above

**66.** _______ provides another procedure to allow the system to continue working in a manner not envisioned in the original design.
A. workaround
B. patch
C. authoritative person
D. developer

**67.** The module performs several functions that all relates to a particular portion of the execution called _______.
A. procedural
B. temporal
C. logical
D. sequential

**68.** Which is the quality of hanging together, A kind of atomicity that makes further division difficult _______.
A. coupling
B. decoupled
C. cohesion
D. None of the above

**69.** Primary stage of software project acquisition is _______.
A. professional
B. developer
C. cost estimation
D. hardware requirement

**70.** A tool of input of source code in a specific implementation language is _______.
A. flow chart generator
B. syntax detected editor
C. form generator
D. profiler

**71.** To allow a programmer to specify the appearance of a screen is _______.
A. form generator
B. spelling checker
C. test harness
D. cross reference analyzer

**72.** If the number of conditions in a decision table is $n$, the maximum number of rules (columns) possible is:
A. $n$
B. $2n$
C. $2^n$
D. $\log_2 n$

**73.** Which of the following software engineering concept does Ada language support?
A. Abstraction
B. Generic
C. Information hiding
D. All of the above

**74.** In unit testing of a module, it is found that for a set of test data, at the maximum 90% of the code alone were tested with the probability of success 0.9. The reliability of the module is:
A. greater than 0.9
B. equal to 0.9
C. at most 0.81
D. at least 1/0.81

**75.** Which of the following testing methods is normally used as the acceptance test for a software system?
A. Regression testing
B. Integration testing
C. Unit testing
D. Functional testing

**76.** A computer program can often be a very satisfactory ........... of a physical system such as road traffic conditions.
A. solution
B. replacement
C. simulation
D. model

**77.** An important aspect in coding is:
A. readability
B. productivity
C. to use as small a memory space as possible
D. brevity

**78.** One way to improve readability in coding is to:
A. avoid goto statements
B. name variables and functions according to their use
C. modularize the program
D. all of the above

**79.** The data flow model of an application mainly shows:
A. the underlying data and the relationship among them
B. processing requirements and the flow of data
C. decision and control information
D. communication network structure

**80.** Assertions are conditions which are true at the point of execution:
A. always
B. sometimes
C. many times
D. no time

**81.** Design phase includes:
A. data, architectural and procedural designs only
B. architectural, procedural and interface desings only
C. data, architectural and interface desings only
D. data, architectural, interface and procedural desings

**82.** Assuming the existence of a start and end nodes for a program graph, the total number of paths is equivalent to the........ set of test data required to test the software.
A. minimum
B. maximum
C. optimum
D. supremum

**83.** According to Brooks, if $n$ is the number of programmers in a project team then the number of communication paths is:
A. $n(n-1)/2$
B. $n\log n$
C. $n$
D. $n(n+1)/2$

**84.** The extent to which the software can continue to operate correctly despite the introduction of invalid input is called as:
A. reliability
B. robustness
C. fault-tolerance
D. portability

**85.** Design phase will usually be:
A. top-down
B. bottom-up
C. random
D. centre fringing

**86.** Structured programming codes include:
A. sequencing
B. alteration
C. iteration
D. all of the above

**87.** Information hiding is to hide from user, details:
A. that are relevant to him
B. that are not relevant to him
C. that may be maliciously handled by him
D. that are confidential

**88.** A good specification should be:
A. unambiguous
B. distinctly specific
C. functional
D. all of the above

**89.** In object-oriented design of software, objects have:
A. attributes and name only
B. operations and name only
C. attributes, name and operations
D. none of the above

**90.** To increase reliability, fault tolerance is included in the system in the form of multiple modules. If the problem can be solved by 5 different modules, each with probability of success 0.7, the probability that it can be solved even if 4 modules fail is approximately:
A. 0.3
B. 0.03
C. 0.49
D. 0.05

**91.** for (i = 0, s = 0; i < n; i++) s + = a (i);

The symbolic execution with n = 3 at i = 2, s is:
A. a0 + a1 + a2 + a3
B. a0 + a1 + a2
C. a0 + a1
D. a0 + a1 + a3

**92.** On an average, the programmer months is given by $3.6 \times (KDSI)^{1.2}$. If so, a project requiring one thousand source instructions will require:
A. 3.6 PM
B. 0.36 PM
C. 0.0036 PM
D. 7.23 PM

**93.** Software testing techniques are most effective if applied immediately after:
A. requirement specification
B. design
C. coding
D. integration

**94.** Data structure suitable for the application is discussed in:
A. data design
B. architectural design
C. procedural design
D. interface design

**95.** Which of the following is a desirable property of a module?
A. Independency
B. Low cohesiveness
C. High coupling
D. Multi functional

**96.** Which of the following is a tool in design phase?
A. Abstraction
B. Refinement
C. Information hiding
D. all of the above

**97.** Let $M$ be a node that represents a if-then-else node in a Program Graph. Let the number of paths from its if part of the end node is $y$, and from the else part to the end node is $z$. If the number of paths from the start node to the node $M$ is $x$, then the total number of paths through $M$ is:
A. $xy + z$
B. $xz + y$
C. $x + y + z$
D. $x(y + z)$

**98.** If X is a case statement in a Program Graph with $n$ cases instead of an if-then-else statement in the previous question with each case leading to only one path to end node, total number of paths through X is
A. $x + n$
B. $x^6$
C. $x\log(n)$
D. $xn$

**99.** Which of the following types of maintenance takes the maximum chunk of the total maintenance effort in a typical life cycle of a software product?
A. Adaptive maintenance
B. Corrective maintenance
C. Preventive maintenance
D. Perfective maintenance

**100.** Which of the following comments about object oriented design of software, is not true?
A. Objects inherit the properties of the class
B. Classes are defined based on the attributes of objects
C. An object can belong to two classes
D. Classes are always different

**101.** Software engineering primarily aims on developing
A. reliable software
B. cost effective software
C. reliable and cost effective software
D. none of the above

**102.** The program volume of a source code that has 10 operators including 6 unique operators, and 6 operands including 2 unique operands is:
A. 48
B. 120
C. 720
D. insufficient data

**103.** Consider the following code for finding the factorial of a given positive integer.

```
IFACT = 1

DO 100 I = 2, N, 2

100 IFACT = IFACT * I * (I – 1)
```

For which values of N, the above FORTRAN code doesn't work?

A. N is even

B. N is odd

C. N is perfect number

D. N mod 3 = 0

**104.** Which of the following is not an assertion?

A. $P$ is true, $P$ and $Q$ are true and $K$ or not $(Q)$ is true implies $K$ is true

B. $P$ is true, $P$ and $Q$ are true and $K$ or not $(Q)$ is true implies $K$ is true

C. $P$ is true, $P$ and $Q$ are false and $K$ or $Q$ is true implies $K$ is true

D. $P$ is true, $P$ and $Q$ are true and $K$ or not $(K)$ is true implies $K$ is true

**105.** For the above code, using symbolic execution, after the iteration with N = 5, IFACT is:

A. 1 * 1 * 2 * 3 * 4 * 5

B. 1 * 2 * 3 * 4 * 5

C. 1 * 1 * 2 * 3 * 4

D. 1 * 2 * 3 * 4

**106.** The reliability of a program be 0.8. The reliability of an equivalent program (i.e., another program that serves the same purpose) is 0.9. The probability that both the programs give the wrong result for the same input is:

A. 0.72

B. 1.7

C. 0.1

D. 0.02

**The next 5 questions (Qs. No. 107-111) are based on the information furnished below.**

In a particular program, it is found that 1% of the code accounts for 50% of the execution time. To code the program in FORTRAN, it takes 100 man-days. Coding in assembly language is 10 times harder than coding in FORTRAN, but runs 5 times faster. Converting an existing FORTRAN program to an assembly language program in 4 times harder.

**107.** To completely write the program in FORTRAN and rewrite the 1% code in assembly language, if a project team needs 13 days, the team consists of:

A. 13 programmers

B. 10 programmers

C. 8 programmers

D. 100/13 programmers

**108.** If 99% of the program is written in FORTRAN and the remaining 1% in assembly language, the percentage increase in the programming time compared to writing the entire program in FORTRAN and rewriting the 1% in assembly language is:

A. 10      B. 5

C. 13      D. 8

**109.** If the entire program is written in FORTRAN, the percentage increase in the execution time, compared to writing the entire program in FORTRAN and rewriting the 1% in assembly language is:

A. 0.9      B. 8

C. 0.8      D. 9

**110.** If 99% of the program is written in FORTRAN and the remaining 1% in assembly language, the percentage increase in the execution time, compared to writing the entire program in FORTRAN and rewriting the 1% in assembly language is:

A. 0.9      B. 1

C. 0.1      D. 0

**111.** If a weightage of 3 is given to the programmers effort and a weightage of 2 is given to the execution time, then coding 99% in FORTRAN and the 1% in assembly language performs better than coding in FORTRAN completely and rewriting the 1% in assembly language by a factor of about:

A. 1.5

B. 1.2

C. 1.1

D. it does not perform better

# ANSWERS

| 1 | 2 | 3 | 4 | 5 | 6 | 7 | 8 | 9 | 10 |
|---|---|---|---|---|---|---|---|---|----|
| D | C | C | D | D | B | B | D | B | B |

| 11 | 12 | 13 | 14 | 15 | 16 | 17 | 18 | 19 | 20 |
|----|----|----|----|----|----|----|----|----|----|
| B | C | D | A | B | C | B | A | B | C |

| 21 | 22 | 23 | 24 | 25 | 26 | 27 | 28 | 29 | 30 |
|----|----|----|----|----|----|----|----|----|----|
| B | A | A | B | A | C | A | B | D | D |

| 31 | 32 | 33 | 34 | 35 | 36 | 37 | 38 | 39 | 40 |
|----|----|----|----|----|----|----|----|----|----|
| A | B | D | B | C | D | C | B | C | B |

| 41 | 42 | 43 | 44 | 45 | 46 | 47 | 48 | 49 | 50 |
|----|----|----|----|----|----|----|----|----|----|
| C | C | B | C | B | B | D | A | D | D |

| 51 | 52 | 53 | 54 | 55 | 56 | 57 | 58 | 59 | 60 |
|----|----|----|----|----|----|----|----|----|----|
| C | B | D | C | D | D | B | D | A | D |

| 61 | 62 | 63 | 64 | 65 | 66 | 67 | 68 | 69 | 70 |
|----|----|----|----|----|----|----|----|----|----|
| C | C | D | A | B | A | B | C | C | B |

| 71 | 72 | 73 | 74 | 75 | 76 | 77 | 78 | 79 | 80 |
|----|----|----|----|----|----|----|----|----|----|
| A | C | D | C | D | C | A | D | B | A |

| 81 | 82 | 83 | 84 | 85 | 86 | 87 | 88 | 89 | 90 |
|----|----|----|----|----|----|----|----|----|----|
| D | A | A | B | A | D | C | D | C | B |

| 91 | 92 | 93 | 94 | 95 | 96 | 97 | 98 | 99 | 100 |
|----|----|----|----|----|----|----|----|----|-----|
| B | A | B | A | A | D | D | D | D | C |

| 101 | 102 | 103 | 104 | 105 | 106 | 107 | 108 | 109 | 110 |
|-----|-----|-----|-----|-----|-----|-----|-----|-----|-----|
| C | A | B | D | C | D | C | B | C | D |

| 111 |
|-----|
| D |

# 10. ▌Systems Analysis & Design Methods▐

**TESTING AND VERIFICATION METHODOLOGY**

1. Verification is ________.
   A. checking that we are building the right system
   B. checking that we are building the system right
   C. performed by an independent test team
   D. making sure that it is what the user really wants

2. A regression test ________.
   A. will always be automated
   B. will help ensure unchanged areas of the software have not been affected
   C. will help ensure changed areas of the software have not been affected
   D. can only be run during user acceptance testing

3. If an expected result is not specified then ________.
   A. We cannot run the test
   B. It may be difficult to repeat the test
   C. It may be difficult to determine if the test has passed or failed
   D. We cannot automate the user inputs

4. Which of the following could be a reason for a failure?
   1. Testing fault
   2. Software fault
   3. Design fault
   4. Environment Fault
   5. Documentation Fault

   A. 2 is a valid reason; 1,3,4 & 5 are not
   B. 1,2,3,4 are valid reasons; 5 is not
   C. 1,2,3 are valid reasons; 4 & 5 are not
   D. 1,2,3,4, and 5 are valid reasons for failure

5. Test are prioritized so that ________.
   A. you shorten the time required for testing
   B. you do the best testing in the time available
   C. you do more effective testing
   D. you find more faults

6. Which of the following is not a static testing technique?
   A. Error guessing     B. Walkthrough
   C. Data flow analysis D. Inspections

7. Which of the following statements about component testing is not true?
   A. Component testing should be performed by development
   B. Component testing is also know as isolation or module testing
   C. Component testing should have completion criteria planned
   D. Component testing does not involve regression testing

8. During which test activity could faults be found most cost effectively?
   A. Execution
   B. Design
   C. Planning
   D. Check Exit criteria completion

9. Which, in general, is the least required skill of a good tester?
   A. Being diplomatic
   B. Able to write software
   C. Having good attention to detail
   D. Able to be relied on

10. The purpose of requirement phase is______.
    A. to freeze requirements
    B. to understand user needs
    C. to define the scope of testing
    D. All of the above

11. The process starting with the terminal modules is called ______.
    A. Top-down integration
    B. Bottom-up integration
    C. None of the above
    D. Module integration

12. The inputs for developing a test plan are taken from ______.
    A. Project plan          B. Business plan
    C. Support plan          D. None of the above

13. Function/Test matrix is a type of ______.
    A. interim test report
    B. final test report
    C. project status report
    D. management report

14. Defect Management process does not include ______.
    A. defect prevention
    B. deliverable base-lining
    C. management reporting
    D. None of the above

15. What is the difference between testing software developed by contractor outside your country, versus testing software developed by a contractor within your country?
    A. Does not meet people needs
    B. Cultural difference
    C  Loss of control over reallocation of resources
    D. Relinquishments of control

16. Software testing accounts to what percent of software development costs?

A. 10-20                B. 40-50
C. 70-80                D. 5-10

17. A reliable system will be one that
    A. is unlikely to be completed on schedule
    B. is unlikely to cause a failure
    C. is likely to be fault-free
    D. is likely to be liked by the users

18. How much testing is enough?
    A. This question is impossible to answer
    B. The answer depends on the risks for your industry, contract and special requirements
    C. The answer depends on the maturity of your developers
    D. The answer should be standardized for the software development industry

19. Which of the following is not a characteristic for testability?
    A. Operability          B. Observability
    C  Simplicity           D. Robustness

20. Cyclomatic Complexity method comes under which testing method?
    A. White box            B. Black box
    C. Green box            D. Yellow box

21. Which of these can be successfully tested using Loop Testing methodology?
    A. Simple Loops
    B. Nested Loops
    C. Concatenated Loops
    D. All of the above

22. To test a function, the programmer has to write a ______, which calls the function and passes it test data.
    A. Stub
    B. Driver
    C. Proxy
    D. None of the above

23. Equivalence partitioning is.
    A. a black box testing technique used only by developers
    B. a black box testing technique than can only be used during system testing
    C. a black box testing technique appropriate to all levels of testing
    D. a white box testing technique appropriate for component testing

24. When a new testing tool is purchased, it should be used first by ______.
    A. a small team to establish the best way to use the tool
    B. everyone who may eventually have some use for the tool
    C. the independent testing team
    D. the vendor contractor to write the initial scripts

25. Inspections can find all the following except ______.
    A. variables not defined in the code
    B. spelling and grammar faults in the documents
    C. requirements that have been omitted from the design documents
    D. how much of the code has been covered

## ANALYSIS OF SYSTEMS

26. The statement of an organization's commitment to quality is a ______.
    A. Policy            B. Vision
    C. Mission           D. Principle

27. Which of the following is not a defect metric?
    A. Location and cause
    B. Classification and Coverage
    C. Time to fix
    D. All of the above

28. The basis upon which adherence to policies is measured is ______.
    A. Standard          B. Requirement
    C. Expected result   D. Value

29. Which of the following does not form a part of a workbench?
    A. Standards
    B. Quality attributes
    C. Quality control
    D. Procedures

30. The focus on the product is highest during
    A. a walkthrough
    B. a checkpoint review
    C. an inspection
    D. None of the above

31. The Quality manager will find it difficult to effectively implement the Quality Improvement Process, unless his organization is willing to accept the Quality principles as
    A. The organization's policy
    B. A challenge
    C. The corporate vision
    D. All of the above

32. Baselines measure the ______ change.
    A. Situation prior to
    B. Expectation of benefits of
    C. Effects of
    D. Desirability of

33. Modifying existing standards to better match the need of a project or environment is ______.
    A. Definition
    B. Standard for a standard
    C. Tailoring
    D. Customization

34. Malcolm Baldridge National Quality Award has the following eligibility categories/ dimensions ______.
    A. Approach
    B. Deployment
    C. Results
    D. Manufacturing, Service and small businesses

35. The term "benchmarking" means ______.
    A. comparing with past data from your organization
    B. comparing with the results of a market survey
    C. comparing with the results of a customer survey
    D. None of the above

36. An example of deployment of a quality approach is ______.
    A. the degree to which the approach embodies effective evaluation cycles
    B. the appropriate and effective application to all product and service characteristics
    C. the effectiveness of the use of tools, techniques, and methods
    D. the contribution of outcomes and effects to quality improvement

37. The concept of continuous improvement as applied to quality means _______.
   A. employees will continue to get better
   B. processes will be improved by a lot of small improvements
   C. processes will be improved through a few large improvements
   D. the functionality of the products will be enhanced

38. The activity which includes confirming understanding, brainstorming and testing ideas is a _______.
   A. code walkthrough
   B. inspection
   C. review
   D. structured walkthrough

39. The following can be considered to measure quality
   A. customer satisfaction
   B. defects
   C. rework
   D. All of the above

40. The most common reason for the presence of a large number of bugs in a software product is _______.
   A. incompetence of the developer
   B. incompetence of the tester
   C. bad requirements
   D. wrong use of tools and techniques

41. The following is (are) not part of a data center operations
   A. Capacity planning
   B. I/O control
   C. Scheduling
   D. All of the above

42. The process of securing future processing capability with proper data for future contingencies by duplicating systems procedures and data is _______.
   A. providing a Help Desk
   B. Database Design
   C. Artificial Intelligence
   D. System Backup

43. The objective of TQM is _______.
   A. to improve processes
   B. to improve profitability
   C. All of the above
   D. None of the above

44. System Test Plan will not include _______.
   A. Approach
   B. Pass/Fail criteria
   C. Risks
   D. Suspension and Resumption criteria

45. The following is NOT a category in Malcolm Balridge National Quality Award criteria:
   A. Leadership
   B. HR Focus
   C. Quality Management
   D. Information and Analysis

46. The following are types of listening are:
   A. Descriptive listening
   B. Compensation listening
   C. Apprehensive listening
   D. All of the above

47. The method by which release from the requirements of a specific standard may be obtained for a specific situation is a _______.
   A. Tailoring
   B. Customization
   C. Force Field Analysis
   D. Waiver

48. Measures designed to minimize the probability of modification, destruction, or inability to retrieve software or data is _______.
   A. Preventive security
   B. Corrective security
   C. Protective security
   D. None of the above

49. Quality assurance is a function responsible for
   A. Controlling Quality
   B. Managing Quality
   C. Inspections
   D. Removal of Defects

**50.** The word management in quality assurance describes many different functions encompassing ______.
   A. Policy management
   B. Human resources management, safety control
   C. Component control and management of other resources and daily schedules.
   D. None of the above

**51.** Malcolm Balridge National Quality Award is an annual award to recognize U.S. companies which excel in ______.
   A. Quality Achievement
   B. Quality Management
   C. Both A and B
   D. None of the above

**52.** Statistical process control help to identify the ______ of process problems which are causing defects.
   A. Root cause
   B. Nature
   C. Person/persons involved
   D. All of the above

**53.** Statistical methods are used to differentiate random variation from ______.
   A. Standards
   B. Assignable variation
   C. Control limits
   D. Specification limits

**54.** Random causes of process problems can be ______ eliminated.
   A. Sometimes          B. Never
   C. Rarely             D. Always

**55.** Complexity measurements are quantitative values accumulated by a pre-determined method for measuring complexity of a
   A. Software engineering process
   B. Software product
   C. Data base
   D. Project team

**56.** Function points provide an objective measure of the application system ____________ that can be used to compare different kinds of application systems.

   A. size               B. complexity
   C. performance        D. operation ease

## DATA ORIENTED SYSTEM DESIGN DIRECTORIES

**57.** A data dictionary has consolidated list of data contained in
   (i) dataflows          (ii) data stores
   (iii) data outputs     (iv) processes
   Choose the correct answer from the following given codes:
   A. (i) and (iii)       B. (i) and (ii)
   C. (ii) and (iv)       D. (i) and (iv)

**58.** A data dictionary is useful as
   (i) it is a documentation aid
   (ii) it assists in designing input forms
   (iii) it contains all data in an application including temporary data used in processes
   (iv) it is a good idea in system design

   Choose the correct answer from the following given codes:
   A. (i) and (ii)        B. (i) and (iv)
   C. (i),(ii) and (iii)  D. (i) and (iv)

**59.** By metadata we mean is ______.
   A. very large data
   B. data about data
   C. data dictionary
   D. meaningful data

**60.** A data dictionary is usually developed ______.
   A. at requirements specification phase
   B. during feasibility analysis
   C. when DFD is developed
   D. when a data base is designed

**61.** A data dictionary has information about ______.
   A. every data element in a data flow
   B. only key data element in a data flow
   C. only important data elements in a data flow
   D. only numeric data elements in a data flow

**62.** A data element in a data dictionary may have ______.
A. only integer value
B. no value
C. only real value
D. only decimal value

**63.** A data element in a data flow ______.
(i)   may be an integer number
(ii)  may be a real number
(iii) may be binary
(iv)  may be imaginary
Choose the correct answer from the following given codes:
A. (i),(ii),(iv)        B. (iii),(iv),(ii)
C. (i),(ii),(iii)       D. (i) and (ii)

**64.** It is necessary to carefully design data input to a computer based system because ______.
A. it is good to be careful
B. the volume of data handled is large
C. the volume of data handled is small
D. data entry operators are not good

**65.** Errors occur more often when ______.
A. data is entered by users
B. data is entered by operators
C. when data is handwritten by users and entered by an operator
D. the key board design is bad

**66.** Good system design prevents data entry errors by
(i) Designing good forms with plenty of space to write in block capitals
(ii) By giving clear instructions to a user on how to fill a form
(iii) Reducing keystrokes of an operator
(iv) Designing good keyboard

Choose the correct answer from the following given codes:
A. (i), (ii), and (iii)     B. (i), (ii), and (iv)
C. (i) and (ii)              D. (iii) and (iv)

**67.** In on-line data entry it is possible to ______.
A. give immediate feedback if incorrect data is entered
B. eliminate all errors
C. save data entry operators time
D. eliminate forms

**68.** The main problems encountered in off-line data entry are ______.
(i) data are entered by operators
(ii) data entered by hand in forms batched and forms may be missed or misread
(iii) errors are detected after a lapse of time
(iv) data are entered by users
Choose the correct answer from the following given codes:
A. (i) and (ii)        B. (i) and (iii)
C. (ii) and (iii)      D. (iii) and (iv)

**69.** In interactive data input a menu is used to ______.
A. enter new data
B. add/delete data
C. select one out of many alternatives often by a mouse click
D. detect errors in data input

**70.** In interactive data input a template is normally used to ______.
A. enter new data
B. add/delete data
C. select one out of many alternatives often by a mouse click
D. detect errors in data input

**71.** In interactive data input terminal commands are normally used to ______.
A. enter new data
B. add/delete data
C. select one out of many alternatives often by a mouse click
D. detect errors in data input

**72.** Data inputs which required coding are ______.
A. fields which specify prices
B. key fields
C. name fields such as product name
D. fields which are of variable length

**73.** A code is useful to represent a key field because ______.
A. it is a concise representation of the field
B. it is usually done by all
C. it is generally a good idea
D. it is needed in database design

74. By the term "concise code" we understand that the code ______.
    A. conveys information on item being coded
    B. is of small length
    C. can add new item easily
    D. includes all relevant characteristics of item being coded

75. By the term "expandable code" we understand that the code ______.
    A. conveys information on item being coded
    B. is of small length
    C. can add new item easily
    D. includes all relevant characteristics of item being coded

76. By the term "meaningful code" we understand that the code ______.
    A. conveys information on item being coded
    B. is of small length
    C. can add new item easily
    D. includes all relevant characteristics of item being code

77. By the term "comprehensive code" we understand that the code ______.
    A. conveys information on item being coded
    B. is of small length
    C. can add new item easily
    D. includes all relevant characteristics of item being coded

78. A concise code is necessarily ______.
    A. precise          B. meaningful
    C. comprehensive    D. difficult

79. Serial numbers used as codes are ______.
    (i) concise
    (ii) meaningful
    (iii) expandable
    (iv) comprehensive

    Choose the correct answer from the following given codes:
    A. (i) and (ii)        B. (ii) and (iii)
    C. (ii) and (iv)       D. (i) and (iii)

80. Block codes are ______.
    (i) concise
    (ii) meaningful
    (iii) expandable
    (iv) comprehensive

    Choose the correct answer from the following given codes:
    A. (i) and (ii)        B. (ii) and (iii)
    C. (iii) and (iv)      D. (i) and (iii)

81. Group classification codes are ______.
    (i) concise
    (ii) meaningful
    (iii) expandable
    (iv) comprehensive

    Choose the correct answer from the following given codes:
    A. (i) and (ii)
    B. (i), (ii) and (iii)
    C. (ii,) (iii) and (iv)
    D. (i), (ii) and (iv)

82. Significant codes are ______.
    (i) concise
    (ii) meaningful
    (iii) expandable
    (iv) comprehensive

    Choose the correct answer from the following given codes:
    A. (i) and (ii)
    B. (i), (ii) and (iii)
    C. (ii,) (iii) and (iv)
    D. (i), (ii) and (iv)

83. In significant codes some or all parts of the code ______.
    A. are meaningful
    B. are usable
    C. are significant
    D. represent values

84. Errors in codes are detected by ______.
    A. proper design of code
    B. introducing redundant digits/characters designed to detect errors
    C. making the code concise
    D. making the code precise

# ANSWERS

| 1 | 2 | 3 | 4 | 5 | 6 | 7 | 8 | 9 | 10 |
|---|---|---|---|---|---|---|---|---|----|
| B | B | C | D | B | A | D | C | B | D |
| **11** | **12** | **13** | **14** | **15** | **16** | **17** | **18** | **19** | **20** |
| B | A | C | B | B | B | B | B | D | A |
| **21** | **22** | **23** | **24** | **25** | **26** | **27** | **28** | **29** | **30** |
| C | B | C | A | D | A | D | A | B | B |
| **31** | **32** | **33** | **34** | **35** | **36** | **37** | **38** | **39** | **40** |
| D | A | C | D | D | C | B | C | D | D |
| **41** | **42** | **43** | **44** | **45** | **46** | **47** | **48** | **49** | **50** |
| D | D | A | C | C | C | D | A | A | B |
| **51** | **52** | **53** | **54** | **55** | **56** | **57** | **58** | **59** | **60** |
| D | B | C | D | B | A | B | C | B | C |
| **61** | **62** | **63** | **64** | **65** | **66** | **67** | **68** | **69** | **70** |
| A | B | C | B | C | A | A | C | C | A |
| **71** | **72** | **73** | **74** | **75** | **76** | **77** | **78** | **79** | **80** |
| B | B | A | B | C | A | D | A | D | B |
| **81** | **82** | **83** | **84** | | | | | | |
| C | C | D | B | | | | | | |

# 11.



**1.** What is the output of the following program?
```
StringBuffer sb1 = new StringBuffer ("Amit");
StringBuffer sb2= new StringBuffer ("Amit");
String ss1 = "Amit";
System.out.println(sb1==sb2);
System.out.println(sb1.equals(sb2));
System.out.println(sb1.equals(ss1));
System.out.println("Poddar".substring (3));
```
A. false false false dar
B. false true false Poddar
C. compiler Error
D. true true false dar

Look carefully at code and answer the following questions ( Q2 to Q8).
```
1   import java.applet.Applet;
2   import java.awt.*;
3   import java.awt.event.*;
4   public class hello4 extends Applet {
5   public void init(){
6   add(new myButton("BBB"));
7   }
8   public void paint(Graphics screen) {
9   }
10  class myButton extends Button{
11  myButton(String label){
12  super(label);
13  }
14  public String paramString(){
15  return super.paramString();
16  }
17  }
18  public static void main(String[] args){
19  Frame myFrame = new Frame(
20  "Copyright Amit");
21  myFrame.setSize(300,100);
22  Applet myApplet = new hello4();
23  Button b = new Button("My Button");
24  myApplet.add(b);
25  b.setLabel(b.getLabel()+"New");
26  // myButton b1 =(new hello4()).new
        myButton("PARAMBUTTON");
27  System.out.println(b1.paramString ());
28  myFrame.add(myApplet);
29  myFrame.setVisible(true);
30  myFrame.addWindowListener(new
        WindowAdapter(){
31  public void windowClosing(Window
        Event e){
32  System.exit(0);}});
33  }
34  } //End hello4 class.
```

**2.** If you run the above program via appletviewer ( defining a HTML file), You see on screen.
A. Two buttons
B. One button with label as "BBB"
C. One button with label as "My ButtonNew"
D. One button with label as "My Button"

**3.** In the above code if line 26 is uncommented  and program runs as standalone application.
A. Compile Error
B. Run time error
C. It will print the label as PARAMBUTTON for button b1
D. None of the above

"

**4.** In the code if you compile as "javac hello4.java" following files will be generated.
   A. hello4.class, myButton.class, hello 41.class
   B. hello4.class, hello4$myButton.class, hello4$1.class
   C. hello4.class,hello4$myButton.class
   D. None of the above

**5.** If above program is run as a standalone application. How many buttons will be displayed?
   A. Two buttons
   B. One button with label as "BBB"
   C. One button with label as "My ButtonNew"
   D. One button with label as "My Button"

**6.** If from line no 14 keyword "public" is removed, what will happen.( Hint :paramString() method in java.awt.Button is a protected method. (Assume line 26 is uncommented).
   A. Code will not compile.
   B. Code will compile but will give a run time error.
   C. Code will compile and no run time error.
   D. None of the above

**7.** If from line no 14 keyword "public" is replaced with "protected", what will happen.(Hint :paramString() method in java.awt.Button is a protected method. (Assume line 26 is uncommented)
   A. Code will not compile.
   B. Code will compile but will give a run time error.
   C. Code will compile and no run time error.
   D. None of the above

**8.** If line no 26 is replaced with Button b1 = new Button("PARAMBUTTON").(Hint :paramString() method in java.awt.Button is a protected method.(Assume line 26 is uncommented).
   A. Code will not compile.
   B. Code will compile but will give a run time error.
   C. Code will compile and no run time error.
   D. None of the above

**9.** What is the output of following if the return value is "the value 0 if the argument string is equal to this string; a value less than 0 if this string is lexicographically less than the string argument; and a value greater than 0 if this string is lexicographically greater than the string argument". (Assuming written inside main)
   String s5 = "AMIT";
   String s6 = "amit";
   System.out.println(s5.compareTo(s6));
   System.out.println(s6.compareTo(s5));
   System.out.println(s6.compareTo(s6));
   A. > -32
      32
      0
   B. > 32
      32
      0
   C. > 32
      -32
      0
   D. > 0
      0
      0

**10.** What is the output? (Assuming written inside main)
   String s1 = new String("amit");
   String s2 = s1.replace('m','i');
   s1.concat("Poddar");
   System.out.println(s1);
   System.out.println((s1+s2).charAt(5));
   A. Compile error
   B. amitPoddar
      o
   C. amitPoddar
      i
   D. amit
      i

11. What is the output? (Assuming written inside main)
```
String s1 = new String("amit");
 System.out.println(s1.replace('m','r'));
System.out.println(s1);
String s3="arit";
String s4="arit";
String s2 = s1.replace('m','r');
System.out.println(s2==s3);
System.out.println(s3==s4);
```

A. arit
   amit
   false
   true
B. arit
   arit
   false
   true
C. amit
   amit
   false
   true
D. arit
   amit
   true
   true

12. Which one does not extend java.lang. Number?
   A. Integer
   B. Boolean
   C. Character
   D. Long

13. Which one does not have a value of (String) method?
   A. Integer
   B. Boolean
   C. Character
   D. Long

14. What is the output of following? (Assuming written inside main)
```
String s1 = "Amit";
String s2 = "Amit";
String s3 = new String("abcd");
String s4 = new String("abcd");
```
```
System.out.println(s1.equals(s2));
System.out.println((s1==s2));
System.out.println(s3.equals(s4));
System.out.println((s3==s4));
```
A. true
   true
   true
   false
B. true
   true
   true
   true
C. true
   false
   true
   false
D. None of the above

15. Which checkbox will be selected in the following code? (Assume with main and added to a Frame)
```
Frame myFrame = new Frame("Test");
CheckboxGroup  cbg = new Checkbox Group();
Checkbox cb1 = new Checkbox ("First", true,cbg);
Checkbox  cb2  =  new  Checkbox ("Scond",true,cbg);
Checkbox  cb3  =  new  Checkbox ("THird",false,cbg);
cbg.setSelectedCheckbox(cb3);
myFrame.add(cb1);
myFrame.add(cb2);
myFrame.add(cb3);
```
A. cb1            B. cb2,cb1
C. cb1,cb2,cb3    D. cb3

16. Which checkbox will be selected in the following code? (Assume with main and added to a Frame)
```
Frame myFrame = new Frame("Test");
CheckboxGroup  cbg = new Checkbox Group();
Checkbox cb1 = new Checkbox("First", true,cbg);
Checkbox cb2 = new Checkbox ("Scond", true,cbg);
```

```
Checkbox cb3 = new Checkbox("THird",
true,cbg);
myFrame.add(cb1);
myFrame.add(cb2);
myFrame.add(cb3);
```
A. cb1              B. cb2,cb1
C. cb1,cb2,cb3     D. cb3

**17.** What will be the output of line 5?
```
1. Choice c1 = new Choice();
2. c1.add("First");
3. c1.addItem("Second");
4. c1.add("Third");
5. System.out.println(c1.getItemCount());
```
A. 1
B. 2
C. 3
D. None of the above

**18.** What will be the order of four items added?
```
Choice c1 = new Choice();
c1.add("First");
c1.addItem("Second");
c1.add("Third");
c1.insert("Lastadded",2);
System.out.println(c1.getItemCount());
```
A. First,Second,Third,Fourth
B. First,Second,Lastadded,Third
C. Lastadded,First,Second,Third
D. None of the above

**19.** Answer based on following code
```
1. Choice c1 = new Choice();
2. c1.add("First");
3. c1.addItem("Second");
4. c1.add("Third");
5. c1.insert("Lastadded",1000);
6. System.out.println(c1.getItemCount());
```
A. Compile time error
B. Run time error at line 5
C. No error and line 6 will print 1000
D. No error and line 6 will print 4

**20.** Which one of the following does not extends java.awt.Component?
A. CheckBox      B. Canvas
C. CheckbocGroup  D. Label

**21.** What is default layout manager for panels and applets?
A. Flowlayout
B. Gridlayout
C. BorderLayout
D. None of the above

**22.** For awt components which of the following statements are not true?
A. If a component is not explicitly assigned a font, it uses the same font that it container uses.
B. If a component is not explicitly assigned a foreground color , it uses the same foreground color  that it container uses.
C. If a component is not explicitly assigned a backround color , it uses the same background color  that it container uses.
D. If a component is not explicitly assigned a layout manager , it uses the same layout manager  that it container uses.

**23.** java.awt.Component class method getLocation() returns Point (containing x and y coordinate). What does this x and y specify?
A. Specify the position of components lower-left component in the coordinate space of the component's parent.
B. Specify the position of components upper-left component in the coordinate space of the component's parent.
C. Specify the position of components upper-left component in the coordinate space of the screen.
D. None of the above

**24.** What will be the output of following:
```
{
double d1 = -0.5d;
System.out.println("Ceil for d1 " +
Math.ceil(d1));
System.out.println("Floor for d1 "
+Math.floor(d1));
}
```

A.  Ceil for d1 0
    Floor for d1 -1;
B.  Ceil for d1 0
    Floor for d1 -1.0;
C.  Ceil for d1 0.0
    Floor for d1 -1.0;
D.  Ceil for d1 -0.0
    Floor for d1 -1.0;

25.  What is the output of following

```
{
float f4 = -5.5f;
float f5 = 5.5f;
float f6 = -5.49f;
float f7 = 5.49f;
System.out.println("Round f4 is " +
Math.round(f4));
System.out.println("Round f5 is " +
Math.round(f5));
System.out.println("Round f6 is " +
Math.round(f6));
System.out.println("Round f7 is " +
Math.round(f7));
}
```

A.  Round f4 is -6
    Round f5 is 6
    Round f6 is -5
    Round f7 is 5
B.  Round f4 is -5
    Round f5 is 6
    Round f6 is -5
    Round f7 is 5
C.  Both A and B
D.  None of the above

26.  Given Integer.MIN_VALUE = 2147483648
Integer.MAX_VALUE = 2147483647
What is the output of following

```
{
float f4 = Integer.MIN_VALUE;
float f5 = Integer.MAX_VALUE;
float f7 = -2147483655f;
System.out.println("Round f4 is " +
Math.round(f4));
System.out.println("Round f5 is " +
Math.round(f5));
System.out.println("Round f7 is " +
Math.round(f7));
}
```

A.  Round f4 is -2147483648
    Round f5 is 2147483647
    Round f7 is -2147483648
B.  Round f4 is -2147483648
    Round f5 is 2147483647
    Round f7 is -2147483655
C.  Both A and B
D.  None of the above

27.
```
1  Boolean b1 = new Boolean("TRUE");
2. Boolean b2 = new Boolean("true");
3  Boolean b3 = new Boolean("JUNK");
4  System.out.println("" + b1 + b2 + b3);
```
A. Comiler error        B. RunTime error
C. true true false      D. true true true

28.  In the above question if line 4 is changed
to System.out.println(b1+b2+b3); The
output is
A. compile time error
B. run time error
C. true true false
D. true true true

29.  What is the output?
```
{
Float f1 = new Float("4.4e99f");
Float f2 = new Float("-4.4e99f");
Double d1 = new Double("4.4e99");
System.out.println(f1);
System.out.println(f2);
System.out.println(d1);
}
```
A.  Runtime error
B.  Infinity-Infinity
    4.4E99
C.  Infinity
    -Infinity
    Infinity
D.  4.4E99
    -4.4E99
    4.4E99

30.  Which of the following wrapper classes
can not take a "String" in constructor?

A. Boolean
B. Integer
C. Long
D. Character

**31.** What is the output of following
```
Double d2 = new Double("-5.5");
Double d3 = new Double("-5.5");
System.out.println(d2==d3);
System.out.println(d2.equals(d3));
```
   A.  true             B.  false
       true                false
   C.  true             D.  false
       false               true

**32.** Which one of the following always honors the components's preferred size?
   A. FlowLayout
   B. GridLayout
   C. BorderLayout
   D. None of the above

**33.** Look at the following code import java.awt.*;

```
public class visual extends java.applet.Applet{
static Button b = new Button("TEST");
public void init(){
add(b);
}
public static void main(String args[]){
Frame f = new Frame("Visual");
f.setSize(300,300);
f.add(b);
f.setVisible(true);
}
}
```

What will happen if above code is run as a standalone application
   A.  Displays an empty frame
   B.  Displays a frame with a button covering the entire frame
   C.  Displays a frame with a button large enough to accommodate its label.
   D.  None of the above

**34.** If the code in Q33 is compiled and run via applet viewer what will happen
   A.  Displays an empty applet
   B.  Displays a applet with a button covering the entire frame
   C.  Displays a applet with a button large enough to accommodate its label.
   D.  None of the above

**35.** What is the output?
```
public static void main(String args[]){
Frame f = new Frame("Visual");
f.setSize(300,300);
f.setVisible(true);
Point p =  f.getLocation();
System.out.println("x is " + p.x);
System.out.println("y is " + p.y);
}
```
   A.  x is 300         B.  x is 0
       y is 300           y is 0
   C.  x is 0          D.  None of the above
       y is 300

**36.** Which one of the following always ignores the components' preferred size?
   A. FlowLayout
   B. GridLayout
   C. BorderLayout
   D. None of the above

**37.** Consider a directory structure like this (NT or 95)
```
C:\JAVA\12345.msg  --FILE
\dir1\IO.class -- IO.class is under dir1
```
Consider the following code
```
import java.io.*;
public class IO {
public static void main(String args[]) {
    File f = new File("..\\12345.msg");
    try{
    System.out.println(f.getCanonicalPath());
    System.out.println(f.getAbsolutePath());
    }catch(IOException e){
        System.out.println(e);
    }
}
}
```

What will be the output of running "java IO" from C:\java\dir1?
   A.  C:\java\12345.msg
       C:\java\dir1\..\12345.msg
   B.  C:\java\dir1\12345.msg
       C:\java\dir1\..\12345.msg
   C.  C:\java\dir1\..\12345.msg
       C:\java\dir1\..\12345.msg
   D.  None of the above

**38.** Suppose we copy IO.class from C:\java\dir1 to c:\java?

What will be the output of running "java IO" from C:\java.
- A.  C:\java\12345.msg
     C:\java\..\12345.msg
- B.  C:\12345.msg
     C:\java\..\12345.msg
- C.  C:\java\..\12345.msg
     C:\java\\..\12345.msg
- D.  None of the above

**39.** Which one of the following methods of java.io.File throws IO Exception and why?
- A.  get Canonical Path and get Absolute Path both require file system queries.
- B.  Only get Cannonical Path as it require file system queries.
- C.  Only get Absolute Path as it require file system queries.
- D.  None of the above

**40.** What will be the output  if Consider a directory structure like this (NT or 95)
C:\JAVA\12345.msg  --FILE
\dir1\IO.class  -- IO.class is under dir1

```
    import java.io.*;
     public class IO {
     public static void main(String args[]) {
     File f = new File("12345.msg");
      String arr[] = f.list();
     System.out.println(arr.length);
         }
       }
```

- A. Compiler error as 12345.msg is a file not a directory
- B. java.lang. Null Pointer Exception at run time
- C. No error , but nothing will be printed on screen
- D. None of the above

**41.** What will be the output?
Consider a directory structure like this (NT or 95)
C:\JAVA\12345.msg  --FILE

```
import java.io.*;
public class IO {
```

```
public static void main(String args[]) {
File f1 = new File("\\12345.msg");
System.out.println(f1.getPath());
System.out.println(f1.getParent());
System.out.println(f1.isAbsolute());
System.out.println(f1.getName());
System.out.println(f1.exists());
System.out.println(f1.isFile());
    }
}
```

- A.  \12345.msg
     \
     true
     12345.msg
     true
     true
- B.  \12345.msg
     \
     true
     \12345.msg
     false
     false
- C.  12345.msg
     \
     true
     12345.msg
     false
     false
- D.  \12345.msg
     \
     true
     12345.msg
     false
     false

**42.** If in question no 41 the line
File f1 = new File("\\12345.msg"); is replaced with File f1 = new File("12345.msg");
What will be the output?
- A. 12345.msg
    \
    true
    12345.msg
    true
    true
- B. 12345.msg
    null
    true
    12345.msg
    true
    true
- C. 12345.msg
    null
    false
    12345.msg
    true
    true
- D. \12345.msg
    \
    ture
    12345.msg
    false
    false

**43.** If class A *extends* class B, class B is the ____ of class A.
- A.  parent
- B.  child
- C.  nephew
- D.  subclass

**44.** If the operator AND is used, which of the following will make the whole condition true?

A. first operand true, second operand false
B. first operand false, second operand true
C. both operands true
D. both operands false

**45.** Which of the following Boolean expressions is equivalent to:  !( p && q )
A.  !p && !q      B.  !p && q
C.  p && !q      D.  !p | | !q

**46.** How do you find the length of an array called *employees*?
A.  employees.length()
B.  employees.size()
C.  employees.size
D.  employees.length

**47.** What is the logical size of the following array: *int[] a = new int[7];*
A.  7      B.  6
C.  8      D.  0

**48.** The modifier _________ is used to designate class variables and methods.
A.  static      B.  public
C.  final      D.  const

**49.** What keyword is used to activate a parent class's constructor?
A.  parent      B.  super
C.  superClass      D.  construct

**50.** What statement allows a program to respond gracefully to an exception?
A.  try-catch      B.  try-throw
C.  try-stop      D.  try-exit

**51.** What does the *String* method *indexOf (char c)* return if the character parameter is not in the string?
A.  Array Out Of Bounds Exception
B.  -1
C.  0
D.  null

**52.** In a collaboration diagram objects of classes are represented by:
A.  arrows      B.  circles
C.  rectangles      D.  colons ( : )

**53.** Which package contains the Graphics class?
A.  java.util      B.  java.lang
C.  java.awt      D.  java.swing

**54.** When dealing directly with layouts and listeners, we must import the _________ package.
A.  javax.swing      B.  java.awt
C.  java.util      D.  java.lang

**55.** A(n) _____________ class implements an interface by providing stub methods.
A.  abstract      B.  private
C.  adapter      D.  public

**56.** All of the GUI component classes are subclasses of the abstract class in AWT called-
A.  Container      B.  J Component
C.  J Text Component      D.  Component

# ANSWERS

| 1 | 2 | 3 | 4 | 5 | 6 | 7 | 8 | 9 | 10 |
|---|---|---|---|---|---|---|---|---|---|
| A | B | C | B | C | A | C | A | A | D |
| 11 | 12 | 13 | 14 | 15 | 16 | 17 | 18 | 19 | 20 |
| A | B | C | A | D | D | C | B | D | C |
| 21 | 22 | 23 | 24 | 25 | 26 | 27 | 28 | 29 | 30 |
| A | D | B | D | B | A | C | A | B | D |
| 31 | 32 | 33 | 34 | 35 | 36 | 37 | 38 | 39 | 40 |
| D | A | B | C | B | B | A | B | B | B |
| 41 | 42 | 43 | 44 | 45 | 46 | 47 | 48 | 49 | 50 |
| D | C | A | C | D | D | D | A | A | A |
| 51 | 52 | 53 | 54 | 55 | 56 | | | | |
| B | A | C | B | C | D | | | | |

# 12. Forms, SQL, SQL*PLUS

1. A calculated item in a Form can be used to compute
   - A. sum
   - B. average
   - C. maximum
   - D. all of these

2. Which of the following button does not appear when an LOV is listed?
   - A. Find
   - B. OK
   - C. Cancel
   - D. None of these

3. Which of the following is not a type of canvas?
   - A. Content
   - B. Vertical toolbar
   - C. Tab
   - D. None of these

4. In a master-detail Form, RELATION is
   - A. an object belonging to the master data block
   - B. an object belonging to the detail data block
   - C. an object that belongs neither to the master data block nor the detail block
   - D. not an object

5. Which of the following is the plug-in that facilitates interaction between the FORMS server and the web browser?
   - A. JInitiator
   - B. JApplet
   - C. IDE
   - D. WebFor

6. A canvas is displayed when
   - A. an item in the canvas receives the input focus
   - B. the window that is associated with the canvas is opened
   - C. the data block that is associated with the canvas is opened
   - D. all of these

7. Which of the following built-ins can be used to launch a new Form from within a Form?
   - A. Call_Form
   - B. New_Form
   - C. Open_Form
   - D. None of these

8. Setting the value of the system variable MESSAGE_LEVEL to 0.
   - A. results in the suppressing of all the messages irrespective of their severity
   - B. does not suppress the display of any message
   - C. will result in syntax error
   - D. is desirable when the Form is moved from development to production

9. Which of the following list items is the worst choice to implement lists that are long?
   - A. Combo Box
   - B. Poplist
   - C. Tlist
   - D. None of these

10. In a Form, trigger cannot be defined at
    - A. form level
    - B. data block level
    - C. data item level
    - D. none of these

11. Which of the following properties of a RELATION determines how to handle record in the detail data block if the associated record in the master data block is deleted?
    - A. Deferred
    - B. Automatic Query
    - C. Delete Record Behaviour
    - D. None of these

**12.** Let BN be the block name and DIN be the data item name. To reference DIN the syntax to be used is
A. BN/DIN
B. BN.DIN
C. DIN
D. 'BN.DIN'

**13.** Choose the correct statements.
A. An unrestricted built-in can be called by any trigger code.
B. A restricted built-in can be called by any trigger code.
C. Restricted built-ins have something to do with the Form navigation.
D. Unrestricted built-ins have something to do with the Form navigation.

**14.** The value of the "Delete Record Behavior." property of a RELATION in a master-detail Form can be
A. cascading
B. isolated
C. non-isolated
D. property class

**15.** To reference a parameter ParamA that is defined in a Form, the syntax to be used is
A. :parameter, ParamA
B. parameter.ParamA
C. parameter:ParamA
D. none of these

**16.** Logically speaking, in general, it is a good idea to set the value of the "Check Box Mapping of Other Values" property to the value of the property
A. "Value When Checked"
B. "Value When Unchecked"
C. NULL
D. None of these

**17.** You want to prevent a user from navigating past the last record in a data blcok. The natural choice to enforce this, is through a
A. block level trigger
B. form level trigger
C. item level trigger
D. application level trigger

**18.** You want to prevent a user from navigating past the last record in a data block. The code used to implement this feature uses
A. parameter variable
B. global variable
C. system variable
D. none of these

**19.** Which of the following list items is a good choice to implement lists that are long?
A. Combo Box
B. Poplist
C. Tlist
D. Llist

**20.** Which of the following can be used to create variables that can be accessed by any Form executing in the current Form session?
A. System variables
B. Parameter variables
C. Global variables
D. None of these

**21.** In a master-detail Form, more number of records is usually displayed in the
A. master block
B. detail block
C. neither (A) nor (B)
D. none of these

**22.** Which of the following is typically used to inform the user of the occurrence of a specific event?
A. LOV
B. Exception
C. Alert
D. Boiler Plate

**23.** The default tab order of the items displayed in a Form is
A. determined by the physical ordering of the items in the object navigator
B. determined by the order in which they are stored in the database table
C. determined by their size
D. unpredictable

**24.** Trigger code is written in
A. SQL
B. PL/SQL
C. JAVA
D. Machine Language

**25.** During execution, the mode of a Data Block in a Form has to be

A. Normal or Query
B. Normal or Enter Query
C. Query or Enter Query
D. Normal or Query or Enter Query

26. An LOV can be populated by
A. a record group
B. a static list of values
C. an object group
D. an exception

27. A Data Block in a Form can be based on a
A. table
B. view
C. stored procedure
D. none of these

28. When a WHEN-VALIDATE-ITEM trigger fails, it
A. terminates the Form
B. displays a message in a dialog box
C. displays a message in the status line
D. none of these

29. A canvas is displayed in
A. an enclosing canvas
B. a tabbed page
C. a dialog box
D. a window

30. Which of the following triggers can be used to disable the function keys?
A. WHEN-BUTTON-PRESSED Trigger
B. KEY-NULLIFY Trigger
C. WHEN-NEW-FORM-INSTANCE Trigger
D. KEY-OTHERS Triggers

31. If the values of the properties of a RELATION in a master-detail Form violates the constraints set forth in the database tables then
A. it results in an error
B. it results in a warning
C. what is defined in the database overrides what is defined in the RELATION
D. what is defined in the RELATION overrides what is defined in the database

32. The attributes of a Form object can be found in the
A. layout editor
B. program editor
C. property navigator
D. property palette

33. A compiled form module has the extension
A. fmb          B. fmx
C. exe          D. obj

34. Which of the following is not a parameter to SET_BLOCK_PROPERTY?
A. Block Name        B. Property Name
C. Value             D. None of these

35. Which of the following is a collection of Form components?
A. Record Group      B. Record Set
C. Data Store        D. Object Group

36. Which of the following comments about HINT are correct?
A. It is an item property.
B. It is automatically displayed when the associated item receives the input focus.
C. It may not be automatically displayed when the associated item receives the input focus.
D. None of the above are correct.

37. Records retrieved by a data block can be filtered by appropriately setting the value of the
A. where clause property
B. number of records returned property
C. select clause property
D. all of these

38. You cannot navigate to a data item if it is a
A. button            B. display item
C. text item         D. check box

39. In a master-detail Form, the records in the detail data block are not retrieved immediately when the
A. deferred property is set to Yes and the Automatic Query property is set to No.

B. deferred property is set to Yes and the Automatic Query property is set to Yes.
C. deferred property is set to No and the Automatic Query property is set to No.
D. deferred property is set to No and the Automatic Query property is set to Yes.

**40.** A set of properties can be collectively assigned to an object by using
A. record group
B. object group
C. array
D. property class

**41.** The items of a data block can be grouped within a
A. record group
B. program unit
C. frame
D. data store

**42.** Choose the correct statement.
A. A data block is associated with a canvas.
B. The size of the canvas can be larger than the size of the window.
C. The size of the canvas can be smaller than the size of the window.
D. All of the above are correct.

**43.** Which of the following statements about windows, canvases, and data items is correct?
A. A window is placed on a data item, which is displayed in a canvas.
B. A canvas is placed on a data item, which is displayed in a window.
C. A data item is placed on a window, which is displayed in a canvas.
D. A data item is placed on a canvas, which is displayed in a window.

**44.** To programmatically set a RELATION property in a master-detail Form, use the
A. SET_RELATION_PROPERTY built-in
B. SET_RELATION built-in
C. DEFINE_RELATION_PROPERTY built-in
D. DEF_RELATION_PROPERTY built-in

**45.** Suppose that a WHEN-VALIDATE-ITEM trigger and a POST-TEXT-ITEM trigger are defined for a particular text item.

Which of them will be fired first?
A. POST-TEXT-ITEM
B. WHEN-VALIDATE-ITEM
C. Unpredictable
D. Both of them will be fired simultaneously

**46.** To debug a PL/SQL code that is within a Form, appropriate messages can be displayed at different points in the execution flow using the built-in
A. print
B. display
C. show
D. message

**47.** If a trigger code assigns a value to a Check Box that neither matches the "Value When Checked" nor the "Value When Unchecked", the Check Box will be
A. checked
B. unchecked
C. unpredictable
D. none of these

**48.** Suppose a procedure my_proc is created with no formal parameter. Which of the following calls is correct?
A. my_proc
B. my_proc:
C. my_proc( )
D. my_proc( ):

**49.** Which of the following cannot be anonymous?
A. Procedure
B. Function
C. Package
D. None of these

**50.** The design of PL/SQL language has a lot of similarities with the design of
A. COBOL
B. ORACLE
C. ADA
D. LISP

**51.** Which of the following formal parameter declarations (inside the definition of a PL/SQL procedure or function) are not acceptable?
A. last_name IN OUT VARCHAR2(30)
B. last_name IN VARCHAR2
C. last_name IN VARCHAR2
D. last_name OUT VARCHAR2(30)

**52.** Which of the following can be used to print the description about an error in a PL/SQL program?
A. SQLERRM
B. ERR_MESG
C. CURR_ERROR
D. DISP_ERR

**53.** If a function does not modify the database state, its purity level is
A. RNDS
B. WNPS
C. RNPS
D. WNDS

**54.** Which of the following types of triggers can be fired on DDL operations?
A. Instead-Of Trigger
B. DML Trigger
C. System Trigger
D. DDL Trigger

**55.** If a trigger is fired by an INSERT statement, the values of :old and :new are respectively
A. NULL and the value that is inserted
B. a garbage value and the value that is inserted
C. NULL and NULL
D. the value that is inserted and the value that is inserted

**56.** To have a variable in global scope, declare it inside a
A. function
B. procedure
C. package
D. none of these

**57.** In a PL/SQL code, uninitialized variables of type VARCHAR2 will have
A. garbage value
B. NULL value
C. 0 value
D. none of these

**58.** Choose the correct statements.
A. The n in CHAR(n) can be missing in the declaration.
B. The n in CHAR(n) is mandatory in the declaration.
C. If the n in CHAR(n) is missing in the declaration, it defaults to 1.
D. If a 5 character string is stored in a variable that had been declared as CHAR(10), the string will be right padded with blanks to make it a 10 character string.

**59.** Which of the following is illegal?
A. SELECT SYSDATE – SYSDATE FROM DUAL:
B. SELECT SYSDATE – (SYSDATE – 2) FROM DUAL:
C. SELECT SYSDATE – (SYSDATE + 2) FROM DUAL:
D. None of these

**60.** Which of the following are pre-defined error conditions?
A. NO_DATA_FOUND
B. TOO_MANY_ROWS
C. CASE_NOT_FOUND
D. All of these

**61.** In PL/SQL
A. a block can access variables that are declared in the enclosing block
B. a block can access variables that are declared in the enclosed block
C. a block cannot access variables that are declared in the enclosing block
D. a block cannot access variables that are declared in the enclosed block

**62.** Choose the correct statements.
A. ROWCOUNT of an implicit cursor gives the total number of rows matched by the query.
B. ROWCOUNT of an explicit cursor gives the total number of rows fetched so far.
C. ROWCOUNT of an implicit cursor gives the total number of rows fetched so far.
D. ROWCOUNT of an explicit cursor gives the total number of rows matched by the query.

**63.** Which of the following are cursor operations?
A. OPEN
B. CLOSE
C. FETCH
D. All of these

**64.** Which of the following keywords is used in the declaration of a PL/SQL funciton but not a procedure?
A. RETURN
B. BEGIN
C. END
D. EXCEPTION

**65.** Which of these are true of Collection types?
 A. They store data of the same data type.
 B. They are sparse.
 C. They are unconstrained.
 D. They can store data of different data type.

**66.** Consider the declaration

abc   tableName%ROWTYPE;

The field names of abc
 A. are undefined
 B. are $1, $2, ...
 C. will be the column names of tableName
 D. none of these

**67.** Which of the following is not a valid parameter mode?
 A. IN
 B. OUT
 C. IN OUT
 D. None of these

**68.** Which of the following is not a collection type in PL/SQL?
 A. Varrays
 B. Index-By tables
 C. Nested Tables
 D. None of these

**69.** The SELECT statement
SELECT 'Hi' FROM DUAL WHERE NULL = NULL;
outputs
 A. Hi              B. FALSE
 C. TRUE            D. nothing

**70.** The address of a customer usually spans 4 lines—Address Line 1, Address Line 2, Address Line 3 and Address Line 4. Some customers don't have Address Line 2. The invoice when printed will show an empty second line for such customers. How do you prevent this from happening?
 A. This cannot be prevented
 B. By using anchors
 C. By using format triggers
 D. By using anchors and format triggers

**71.** When a SELECT statement displays data
 A. dates and strings will be justified to the left by default
 B. numbers will be justified to the right by default
 C. dates and strings will be justified to the right by default
 D. numbers will be justified to the left by default

**72.** If the After Parameter trigger fails
 A. nothing happens
 B. the Report gets terminated abruptly
 C. you will be put in the parameter form again
 D. none of the above

**73.** Consider the query SELECT * FROM EMP WHERE deptno = :abc;

Let there be a Validation Trigger for the variable abc that is coded as follows.

IF (:abc IN (10,20,40))     THEN

                return (TRUE);

ELSE

                return (FALSE):

END  IF

During runtime, if the user enters a value other than 10, 20 or 40.
 A. the value will be discarded
 B. the user will be asked to enter another value
 C. an exception will be raised
 D. the value will be defaulted to 10

**74.** An object in a Repeating Frame must
 A. belong to its associated group or must be from a parent group and defined at report level.
 B. be from a parent group or must be defined at Report level
 C. belong to its associated group or must be from a parent group or must be defined at Report level
 D. None of these

**75.** Which command is used to get input from the user?
 A. GET             B. ACCEPT
 C. READ            D. CIN

76. What does the / command do?
    A. Does nothing
    B. Prints the character /
    C. Re-executes the non SQL*Plus command that was most recently executed
    D. Re-executes the most recently executed command

77. You are executing a SELECT statement. In the display, each row that is displayed spans more than a line and you see a line after a set of 5 records. You can fix this problem by using the
    A. SET LINESIZE command
    B. SET PAGESIZE command
    C. SET LINESIZE and SET PAGESIZE commands
    D. SET SCREENWIDTH command

78. Which of the following activities are you allowed to do after executing the DISCONNECT command?
    A. Reconnect
    B. Exit the SQL*Plus session
    C. Execute certain SQL*Plus commands
    D. None of these

79. A PL/SQL block can return data to SQL *Plus through
    A. bind variables
    B. substitution variables
    C. local variables
    D. none of these

80. Which of the following remarks about SQL*Plus are correct?
    A. It is a PL/SQL development tool
    B. It works in character mode
    C. It is an integral part of the standard Oracle installation
    D. All of these

81. The DUAL table has
    A. One row with many columns
    B. One column with many rows
    C. One row and one column
    D. Many rows and many columns

82. A script file that is executed by SQL*Plus cannot contain
    A. SQL*Plus commands
    B. SQL statements
    C. PL/SQL block
    D. None of these

83. To change the format of the date returned by SYSDATE, use the command
    A. ALTER SESSION RESET DATE
    B. ALTER SESSION CHANGE DATE
    C. ALTER SESSION SET SYSDATE
    D. ALTER SESSION SET NLS_ DATE_ FORMAT

84. Script files can be executed by the
    A. START command
    B. STA command
    C. @ command
    D. EXECUTE command

85. To interactively assign a value to a variable, precede the variable name with
    A. :              B. --
    C. getVal         D. &

86. Which of the following is not a type of data dictionary view?
    A. USER           B. ALL
    C. DBA            D. SYS

87. Which of the following is buffered by SQL*Plus?
    A. SQL statements
    B. SQL*Plus commands
    C. PL/SQL block
    D. None of these

88. What command should you try if DBMS_OUTPUT.PUT_LINE is not doing what it is supposed to do?
    A. SET ECHO ON
    B. SET TERMOUT ON
    C. SET DISPLAY ON
    D. SET SERVEROUTPUT ON

89. Which of the following data dictionary view is used by the DESCRIBE command to extract information about the columns?
    A. ALL_TABLES
    B. ALL_COLUMNS
    C. ALL_COLS
    D. ALL_TAB_COLUMNS

**90.** SQL*Plus will know you are typing a PL/SQL block when it encounters the keyword
A. PL/SQL
B. BEGIN
C. EXCEPTION
D. DECLARE

**91.** The DESCRIBE command if used on a table, will not display information about
A. Primary key
B. Default Values
C. Indexes
D. All of these

**92.** Which of the following SQL*Plus commands can be used to see the compilation errors in a PL/SQL code?
A. TRACE
B. SHOW ERRORS
C. PROFILE
D. DEBUG

**93.** Which of the following information will be displayed when you use the DESCRIBE command on functions?
A. Data type of the return value
B. Data type of the parameters
C. Mode of the parameters
D. All of these

**94.** SGA stands for
A. Show Global Area
B. Start Global Area
C. System Global Area
D. Shut Global Area

**95.** The owner of the DUAL table is
A. SYS
B. SUPERUSER
C. SCOTT
D. MANAGER

**96.** The ALL Data Dictionary view lets you access any object
A. owned by you
B. for which you have access rights
C. in the database
D. none of these

**97.** Which of the following methods cannot be used to specify a comment in SQL*Plus scripts?
A. --
B. REMARK
C. /*....*/
D. None of these

**98.** The SQL statement
SELECT SYSDATE FROM DUAL;

prints

06-FEB-05

Consider the three SQL statements
SELECT TO_DATE((LTRIM (RTRIM ('NOV 23, 2005'))), 'Mon DD, YY') FROM DUAL; — Statement 1

SELECT TO_DATE( (RTRIM (LTRIM ('NOV 23, 2005 '))), 'Mon DD, YY') FROM DUAL; —Statement 2

SELECT TO_DATE( 'NOV 23, 2005', 'Mon DD, YY') FORM DUAL; — Statement 3.

Which of these statements gives the same output?
A. Only Statement 1 and Statement 2
B. Only Statement 1 and Statement 3
C. Only Statement 2 and Statement 3
D. All the three statements give the same output

**99.** The SQL statement
SELECT SUBSTR('123456789', INSTR ('abcabcabc', 'b' ,4)) FROM DUAL;

prints
A. 2345
B. 6789
C. 56789
D. 89

**100.** The SQL statement
SELECT TRUNC (45.926, −1) FROM DUAL:
A. is illegal
B. 5
C. prints 45.9
D. prints 40

**101.** The SQL statement
SELECT SUBSTR ('abcdefghij', INSTR (*123321234*, '2', 3, 2), 2) FROM DUAL;
prints
A. gh
B. 23
C. bc
D. ab

**102.** From the following combinatons of wildcard characters, choose those that are equivalent.

A. %
B. _%
C. %_
D. _ _

**103.** The SQL statement

SELECT ROUND (45.926, −1) FROM DUAL;

A. is illegal
B. prints garbage
C. prints 045.926
D. prints 50

**104.** Which of the following must be enclosed in double quotes?

A. Dates
B. Column Alias
C. Strings
D. All of these

**105.** If the SQL statement

SELECT NEXT_DAY('01-SEP-95', 'FRIDAY') FROM DUAL;

prints
08-SEP-95

what will the SQL statement

SELECT NEXT_DAY ('01-SEP-95', 'SATURDAY') FROM DUAL;

print?

A. 09-SEP-95
B. 02-SEP-95
C. 05-SEP-95
D. 06-SEP-95

**106.** The SELECT statement

SELECT 'Hi' FROM DUAL WHERE 1 ! = NULL;

outputs

A. TRUE
B. Hi
C. FALSE
D. nothing

**107.** In SQL, 10/NULL will evaluate to

A. FALSE
B. −1
C. NULL
D. 10

**108.** Almost all the DATE functions return a value of data type DATE, except

A. MONTHS_BETWEEN
B. ROUND
C. NEXT_DAY
D. TRUNC

**109.** The SELECT statement

SELECT LOWER(*AbCd'), UPPER ('AbCd'), INITCAP('AbCd eFgh') FROM DUAL;

will print

A. abcd ABCD Abcd Efgh
B. abcd ABCD ABCD EFGH
C. abcd ABCD abcd efgh
D. abcd ABCD aBCD eFGH

**110.** NOT BETWEEN 10 AND 20

A. displays NULL values
B. does not display NULL values
C. may display NULL values
D. none of these

**111.** The SQL statement

SELECT SUBSTR (123456789', INSTR', ('abcabcabc,' 'b'), 4) FROM DUAL;

prints

A. 6789
B. 2345
C. 1234
D. 456789

**112.** The SELECT statement

SELECT 'Hi' FROM DUAL WHERE 1 = NULL;

outputs

A. Hi
B. FALSE
C. TRUE
D. nothing

**113.** Which of the following group functions ignore NULL values?

A. MAX
B. COUNT
C. SUM
D. COUNT(*)

**114.** Table Employee has 10 records. It has a non-NULL SALARY column which is also UNIQUE. The SQL statement

SELECT COUNT (*) FROM EMPLOYEE WHERE SALARY > ANY (SELECT SALARY FROM EMPLOYEE);

prints

A. 10
B. 9
C. 5
D. 0

**115.** Table Employe has 10 records. It has a non-NULL SALARY column which is also UNIQUE. The SQL statement
SELECT COUNT(*) FROM EMPLOYEE WHERE SALARY > ALL (SELECT SALARY FROM EMPLOYEE);

prints
- A. 10
- B. 9
- C. 5
- D. 0

**116.** The SQL statement
SELECT (NVL(NVL(NULL, 3), 4)) FROM DUAL;
- A. prints 3
- B. prints 4
- C. prints NULL
- D. is illegal

**117.** Let the statement

SELECT column1 FROM myTable;

return 10 rows. The statement

SELECT ALL column1 FROM myTable;

will return
- A. less than 10 rows
- B. more than 10 rows
- C. exactly 10 rows
- D. none of these

**118.** Table EMPLOYEE has 5 rows. Consider the following sequence of SQL statements.

SQL > CREATE TABLE myTable SELECT AS (SELECT * FROM EMPLOYEE);

SQL > INSERT INTO myTable SELECT * FROM myTable;

SQL > INSERT INTO myTable SELECT * FROM myTable;

SQL > INSERT INTO myTable SELECT * FROM myTable;

SQL > INSERT INTO myTable SELECT * FROM myTable;

If the SQL statement

SELECT COUNT(*) FROM MYEMP;

is executed after executing all the statements listed above, what will be printed is

- A. 80
- B. 25
- C. 20
- D. 5

**119.** The SQL statement

SELECT LPAD('abcd',10,'*') FROM DUAL;

prints,
- A. abcd******
- B. ******abcd
- C. ***abcd***
- D. **********

**120.** The SQL statement

SELECT INSTR ('abcdefg', 'c') FROM DUAL;

prints,
- A. 2
- B. 3
- C. 5
- D. 6

**121.** The SQL statement

SELECT LENGTH('') FROM DUAL; --'' is two single quotes

prints,
- A. 0
- B. a garbage value
- C. NULL
- D. 1

**122.** Choose the correct statements.
- A. ORDER BY NAME ASC, displays NULLs last
- B. ORDER BY NAME DESC, displays NULLs first
- C. ORDER BY NAME ASC, displays NULLs first
- D. ORDER BY NAME DESC, displays NULLs last

**123.** If a query involves NOT, AND, OR with no parenthesis
- A. NOT will be evaluated first; AND will be evaluated second; OR will be evaluated last.
- B. NOT will be evaluated first; OR will be evaluated second; AND will be evaluated last.
- C. AND will be evaluated first; OR will be evaluated second; NOT will be evaluated last.
- D. the order of occurrence determines the order of evaluation.

**Directions (Qs.No. 124 to 129):** *These questions are based on the following table.*

*Consider the table:*

**(train_info)**

| TrainNum | From | To | Through1 | Through2 | Through3 |
|---|---|---|---|---|---|
| 1 | Chennai | New Delhi | Vijayawada | Jhansi | Agra |
| 2 | Vijayawada | New Delhi | Jhansi | Agra | |
| 3. | Hyderabad | Kanpur | Vijayawada | Jhansi | |
| 4. | Hyderabad | Kanpur | New Delhi | Agra | |
| 5. | Vijayawada | Agra | Hyderabad | Jhansi | Kanpur |
| 6. | Chennai | Vijayawada | | | |

**124.** The SQL statement

SQL > SELECT A.From, B.From FROM train_info A, train_info B

GROUP BY(A. From, B. From)

HAVING A.From = 'Vijayawada';

will print

A. 3 records     B. 4 records
C. 5 records     D. 6 records

**125.** The SQL statement

SQL> SELECT COUNT(*) FROM train_info A, train_info B, train_info C;

will print

A. 6     B. 18
C. 12     D. 216

**126.** The SQL statement

SQL> SELECT COUNT(*) FROM train_info A, train_info B

WHERE A.start_city = B.start_city AND A.destination_city = B.destination_city AND A.trainNum <> B.trainNum;

will print

A. 0     B. 1
C. 2     D. none of these

**127.** The SQL statement

SQL> SELECT COUNT (*) FROM train_info A, train_info B

WHERE A.start_city = B.start_city AND A.destination_city = B.destination_city;

will print

A. 6     B. 7
C. 8     D. none of these

**128.** How many record(s) will be printed by the following SQL query?

SQL> SELECT A.From, B.To FROM train_info A, train_info B

WHERE A.To = B.From;

A. No record     B. 1 record
C. 2 records     D. None of these

**129.** The SQL statement
SQL> SELECT COUNT(*) FROM train_info

WHERE through1 LIKE '%ad%':

will print,

A. 1     B. 2
C. 3     D. 4

**130.** The SELECT statement

SELECT 'Hi' FROM DUAL WHERE NULL IN (NULL);

outputs,

A. TRUE     B. FALSE
C. 'Hi'     D. Nothing

**131.** Let the statement

SELECT * FROM nameList;

return 10 rows. The statement

SELECT * FROM nameList WHERE ROWNUM > 5;

will return

A. 4 rows  
B. 5 rows  
C. 6 rows  
D. none of these

132. Which of the following SQL commands can be used to modify existing data in a database table?
A. MODIFY  
B. UPDATE  
C. CHANGE  
D. NEW

133. The FROM clause—EMPLOYEE LEFT OUTER JOIN DEPARTMENT
A. includes all employees not assigned to any department
B. includes all departments having no employee
C. includes only those employees who are assigned a department
D. none of these

134. Table Employee has 10 records. It has a non-NULL SALARY column which is also UNIQUE.

The SQL statement

SELECT COUNT(SALARY) FROM EMPLOYEE WHERE SALARY NOT IN (NULL);

prints

A. 10  
B. 9  
C. 5  
D. 0

135. Which of the following combinations of wildcard characters has the same meaning as the wildcard character %?
A. %%  
B. _%  
C. %_  
D. _ _

136. The SQL statement

SELECT ROUND(45.926, −2) FROM DUAL;

A. is illegal  
B. prints garbage  
C. prints 45.92  
D. prints 0

137. The SQL statement
SELECT LPAD('abcd', 10,' 'wert') FROM DUAL;

prints

A. wertweabcd  
B. abcdwertwer  
C. wertwertab  
D. abwertwert

138. Which of the following SELECT statements print the string 56?
A. SELECT SUBSTR('123456', 5) FROM DUAL
B. SELECT SUBSTR('123456', −2) FROM DUAL
C. SELECT SUBSTR('123456', 5, 2) FROM DUAL
D. All of these

139. Choose the correct statement that is based on a SQL query that has its ORDER BY clause defined as ORDER BY name, game DESC
A. Vijay, Golf will be listed before Anand, Chess
B. Anand, Chess will be listed before Vijay, Golf
C. Bhupathi, Tennis will be listed before Anand, Chess
D. Bhupathi, Tennis will be listed before Vijay, Golf

140. Choose the correct statements.
A. FALSE AND NULL is FALSE
B. TRUE AND NULL is NULL
C. NOT NULL is NULL
D. All of these

141. The WHERE clause - WHERE city LIKE '%a_%b'

cannot display

A. ab  
B. abb  
C. a_b  
D. a_%b

142. Choose the correct statements.
A. Column alias cannot be used in the ORDER BY clause
B. Column alias can be used in the ORDER BY clause
C. Column alias can be used in the WHERE clause
D. Column alias cannot be used in the WHERE clause

143. Which of the following joins is also called as an 'inner join'?
A. Non-Equijoin  
B. Self-Join  
C. Equijoin  
D. None of these

**144.** The SQL statement

SELECT DECODE(2, 2, DECODE(3, 3, 2)) FROM DUAL;

A. is illegal
B. prints garbage
C. 3
D. 2

**145.** Which of the following SQL commands can be used to add data to a database table?

A. ADD
B. UPDATE
C. APPEND
D. INSERT

**146.** The SELECT statement

SELECT 'Hi' FROM DUAL WHERE 1 ! = NULL

outputs

A. Hi
B. FALSE
C. TRUE
D. Nothing

## ANSWERS

| 1 | 2 | 3 | 4 | 5 | 6 | 7 | 8 | 9 | 10 |
|---|---|---|---|---|---|---|---|---|---|
| D | D | D | A | A | A,B | A,B,C | B | C | D |
| **11** | **12** | **13** | **14** | **15** | **16** | **17** | **18** | **19** | **20** |
| C | B | A,C | A,B,C | A | B | A | C | A | C |
| **21** | **22** | **23** | **24** | **25** | **26** | **27** | **28** | **29** | **30** |
| B | C | A | B | D | A,B | A,B,C | D | D | D |
| **31** | **32** | **33** | **34** | **35** | **36** | **37** | **38** | **39** | **40** |
| A | D | B | D | D | A,C | A | B | AB | D |
| **41** | **42** | **43** | **44** | **45** | **46** | **47** | **48** | **49** | **50** |
| C | B,C | D | A | B | D | D | B | C | C |
| **51** | **52** | **53** | **54** | **55** | **56** | **57** | **58** | **59** | **60** |
| A,D | A | D | C | A | C | B | A,C,D | D | D |
| **61** | **62** | **63** | **64** | **65** | **66** | **67** | **68** | **69** | **70** |
| A,D | A,B | D | A | A,B,C | C | D | D | D | D |
| **71** | **72** | **73** | **74** | **75** | **76** | **77** | **78** | **79** | **80** |
| A,B | C | C | D | B | C | C | A,B,C | A | D |
| **81** | **82** | **83** | **84** | **85** | **86** | **87** | **88** | **89** | **90** |
| C | D | D | A,B,C | D | D | A,C | D | D | B,D |
| **91** | **92** | **93** | **94** | **95** | **96** | **97** | **98** | **99** | **100** |
| D | B | D | C | A | A,B | D | D | C | D |
| **101** | **102** | **103** | **104** | **105** | **106** | **107** | **108** | **109** | **110** |
| A | B,C | D | B | B | D | C | A | A | B |
| **111** | **112** | **113** | **114** | **115** | **116** | **117** | **118** | **119** | **120** |
| B | D | A,B,C | B | D | A | C | A | B | B |
| **121** | **122** | **123** | **124** | **125** | **126** | **127** | **128** | **129** | **130** |
| C | A,B | A | A | D | C | C | C | C | D |
| **131** | **132** | **133** | **134** | **135** | **136** | **137** | **138** | **139** | **140** |
| D | B | A | D | A | D | A | D | D | D |
| **141** | **142** | **143** | **144** | **145** | **146** | | | | |
| A,B | B,D | C | D | D | D | | | | |

# 13.     Computer Graphics

1. Consider the HTML table definition given below:

```
<table border = 1>
    <tr> <td rowspan=2 > ab </td>
          <td colspan=2 > cd </td>
    </tr>
    <tr> <td> ef </td>
    <td rowspan = 2> gh </td>
    </tr>
    <tr>
    <tr> <td colspan=2> ik </td>
    </tr>
</table>
```

The number of rows in each column and the number of columns in each row are:
A. <2, 2, 3> and <2, 3, 2>
B. <2, 2, 3> and <2, 2, 3>
C. <2, 3, 2> and <2, 3, 2>
D. <2, 3, 2> and <2, 2, 3>

2. A viewgraph is
A. an oversized slide designed for presentation on an overhead projector.
B. designed and created by exposing film to the output of the graphics system.
C. a hardcopy chart.
D. none of the above

3. The best suited hidden surface algorithm to deal with non-polygonal, non-planar surface patches is
A. painter's algorithm
B. Z-Buffer algorithm
C. ray tracing
D. scan-line algorithm

4. Assuming that one allows 256 depth value levels to be used, how much memory would a $512 \times 512$ pixel display require to store the Z-Buffer?
A. 512 K          B. 256 K
C. 1024 K        D. 128 K

5. The point at which a set of projected parallel lines appear to converge is called as a
A. convergence point
B. vanishing point
C. point of illusion
D. point of delusion

6. The basic elements of a picture in volume graphics is
A. pixel
B. volsel
C. voxel
D. none of the above

7. The workstation transformation that maps the normalised device screen onto a physical device, whose $x$-extent is 0 to 10 and $y$-extent is 0 to 20 where the origin is the lower left corner is

A. $\begin{pmatrix} 10 & 00 & 00 \\ 00 & 20 & 00 \\ 00 & 00 & 01 \end{pmatrix}$    B. $\begin{pmatrix} 00 & 10 & 00 \\ 20 & 00 & 00 \\ 00 & 00 & 01 \end{pmatrix}$

C. $\begin{pmatrix} 00 & 00 & 01 \\ 00 & 20 & 00 \\ 10 & 00 & 00 \end{pmatrix}$    D. $\begin{pmatrix} 10 & 00 & 00 \\ 00 & 20 & 20 \\ 00 & 00 & 01 \end{pmatrix}$

8. In the previous question, if the origin is the upper left corner, the workstation transformation matrix is

   A. $\begin{pmatrix} 10 & 00 & 00 \\ 00 & 20 & 00 \\ 00 & 00 & 01 \end{pmatrix}$     B. $\begin{pmatrix} 00 & 10 & 00 \\ 20 & 00 & 00 \\ 00 & 00 & 01 \end{pmatrix}$

   C. $\begin{pmatrix} 00 & 00 & 01 \\ 00 & 20 & 00 \\ 10 & 00 & 00 \end{pmatrix}$     D. $\begin{pmatrix} 10 & 00 & 00 \\ 00 & 20 & 20 \\ 00 & 00 & 01 \end{pmatrix}$

9. Engineering drawing commonly applies
   A. oblique projection
   B. orthographic projection
   C. perspective projection
   D. none of the above

10. The best hidden surface removal algorithm is
    A. painters
    B. depth buffer
    C. area subdivision
    D. depends on the application

11. Consider the three points, $A(3, 6, 4)$; $B(2, 5, 5)$; $C(0, 3, 7)$ and the view point $V(1, 4, 6)$. Choose the correct option(s).
    A. $c$ hides $a$ and $b$, if viewed from $V$
    B. $c$ hides $a$ but not $b$, if viewed from $V$
    C. $a$ hides $b$ but not $c$, if viewed from $V$
    D. $b$ hides $a$ but not $c$, if viewed from $V$

**The next three questions are based on this window.**

A rectangle is bound by the lines $x = 0$; $y = 0$; $x = 5$ and $y = 3$.

12. The line $2x - y + 4 = 0$, if clipped against this window will connect the points
    A. (0, 1) and (3, 3)
    B. (0, 1) and (2, 3)
    C. (1, 2) and (3, 4)
    D. none of the above

13. The line segment joining (1, 1) and (4, 2) if clipped against this window will connect the points
    A. (0, 1) and (3, 3)
    B. (0, 1) and (2, 3)
    C. (1, 1) and (4, 2)
    D. none of the above

14. The line segment joining (−1, 0) and (4, 5), if clipped against this window will connect the points
    A. (0, 1) and (3, 3)
    B. (0, 1) and (2, 3)
    C. (0, 1) and (4, 5)
    D. none of the above

15. In displaying a clipped picture, the efficient method is
    A. clipping against the window and then applying the window transformation
    B. applying window transformation and then clipping against the viewport
    C. both (A) and (B) have the same efficiency
    D. efficiency depends on whether the window is an aligned rectangle or not.

16. Which of the following points lies on the same side as the origin, with reference to the line $3x + 7y = 2$?
    A. (3, 0)          B. (1, 0)
    C. (0.5, 0.5)      D. (0.5, 0)

17. Choose the functions that are periodic.
    A. $f(x) = x - [x]$; where $[x]$ stands for the greatest integer $\leq x$
    B. $f(x) = |\cos(x)|$
    C. $f(x) = (x)\cos(x)$
    D. $f(x) = \sin(1/x)$, if $x \neq 0$; 0 otherwise

18. The subcategories of orthographic projection are
    A. cavalier, cabinet, isometric
    B. cavalier, cabinet
    C. isometric, dimetric, trimetric
    D. isometric, cavalier, trimetric

19. A frame buffer array is addressed in row-major order for a monitor with co-ordinate locations varying from (0, 0) to (100, 100). Assuming that one bit of storage is required per pixel and address of (0, 0) is 0000, the address of the co-ordinate position (5, 10) is given by
    A. 1015          B. 515
    C. 1005          D. 505

**20.** The people of the planet Mars designed a scale for measuring the temperature in which water freezes at 100 units and boils at 250 units. The people of Jupiter designed a scale in which water freezes at 75 units and boils at 300 units. A temperature of 200 units in Mars will measure _______ in Jupiter.

   A. 300             B. 225

   C. 250             D. 175

**21.** The two scales coincide at

   A. 130             B. 165

   C. 150             D. 170

**22.** A circle, if scaled in only one dimension becomes a/an

   A. parabola        B. hyperbola

   C. ellipse          D. remains a circle

**23.** A surface appearing black

   A. reflects all the incident colours

   B. reflects all the incident colours except black

   C. reflects only black and absorbs the rest

   D. reflects none

**24.** A Bezier cubic curve with control points $P_0, P_1, P_2, P_3$ is defined by the equation

$$f(u) = \sum_{i=0}^{3} P_i B_i^3(u)$$

$B_2^3$ is

   A. $(1 - u)^3$        B. $u^3$

   C. $3u(1 - u)^2$      D. $3u^2 (1 - u)$

**25.** Which one of the following is not a linear transformation?

   A. $F : R^3 \to R^2$ defined by $f(x, y, z) = (x, z)$

   B. $F : R^3 \to R^3$ defined by $f(x, y, z) = (x, y - 1, z)$

   C. $F : R^2 \to R^2$ defined by $f(x, y) = (2x, y - x)$

   D. $F : R^2 \to R^2$ defined by $f(x, y) = (y, x)$

**26.** Pixel phasing is a technique for

   A. shading

   B. anti-aliasing

   C. hidden line removal

   D. none of the above

**27.** In the raster-scan method for transformation, a 90° rotation can be performed by

   A. reversing the order of bits within each row in the frame buffer

   B. by performing XOR on the frame buffer location

   C. by copying each row of the block into a column in the new frame buffer location

   D. none of the above

**28.** The best hidden surface removal method(s) used for complex scenes with more than a few thousand surfaces is/are

   A. depth sorting method

   B. scan line alogorithm

   C. depth buffer algorithm

   D. octree method

**29.** The phenomenon of having a continuous glow of a beam on the screen even after it is removed is called as

   A. fluorescence      B. persistence

   C. phosphorescence    D. incandescence

**30.** Let the maximum number of pixels in a line be $M$. The number of subdivisions at most necessary using the mid-point subdivision method of clipping is

   A. $N = \log_2 M$

   B. $N = 2^M$

   C. $n = 2 M$

   D. none of the above

**31.** Choose the correct statement(s).

   A. Random-scan monitors draw a picture one line at a time.

   B. The components line of a random-scan picture must be refreshed in a particular order.

   C. Raster-scan monitors draw a picture one line at a time.

   D. Random-scan method is well suited for displaying shading and colour areas.

**32.** (2, 4) is a point on a circle that has centre at the origin. Which of the following point(s) is/are also on the circle?

   A. (2, –4)        B. (–2, 4)
   C. (4, –2)        D. All of these

**33.** If the eccentricity of a conic is less than one then it is a
   A. circle        B. parabola
   C. ellipse        D. hyperbola

**34.** Which of the following statement(s) is/are true?
   A. Request, sample and event are the three basic modes of input.
   B. Keyboard is a device ideally suited for use in sample mode.
   C. A mouse is typically a device for inputting an absolute position on the screen.
   D. Special graphics hardware support is essential for providing a menu-driven user interface to an application.

**35.** A bilinear transformation can be simulated by the transformations
   A. translation, rotation and stretching
   B. translation and rotation
   C. rotation, stretching and inversion
   D. rotation, stretching, inversion and translation

**36.** If $(a, b, c) \times (1, 3, 1) = (2, 1, 6)$, where $\times$ denotes the vector product, then $(a, b, c)$ is given by
   A. (0, 1, 1)
   B. $(k, 0, 1, -k)$ for any real $k$
   C. (–1, 2, –7)
   D. there exists no solution

**37.** In Sutherland-Hodgman algorithm for polygon clipping, assume $P$ (present point) lies inside the window and $S$ (previous point) lies outside the window. Then, while processing through that window boundary, we should
   A. store the intersection point of line $PS$ ($S'$) only
   B. store the points $P$ and $S'$
   C. store the point $P$ only
   D. store the points $S$ and $S'$

**38.** The clarity of a displayed image depends on the
   A. resolution
   B. floating point precision of the system
   C. associated software
   D. aspect ratio

**39.** Which display device is best suited for CAD systems?
   A. A CRT with vector refresh monitor
   B. A CRT with raster scan monitor
   C. Plasma panel display
   D. LED display

**40.** Which statement about beam penetration method for producing colour display is/are true?
   A. It is used with raster-scan monitors.
   B. It is used with random-scan monitors.
   C. By using beam penetration method a wide range of colours can be obtained.
   D. It uses three electron guns, one each for green, blue and red colours.

**41.** $x = at^2$, $y = 2at$, is the parametric equation of a/an
   A. circle
   B. rectangular hyperbola
   C. parabola
   D. ellipse

**42.** Fractals deal with curves that are
   A. irregularly irregular
   B. regularly irregular
   C. irregularly regular
   D. regularly regular

**43.** A cube of side 1 unit is placed such that the origin coincides with one of its vertices and the three axes run along three of its edges. The vertex diagonally opposite to (1, 0, 1) is
   A. (0, 0, 0)        B. (1, 1, 0)
   C. (0, 1, 1)        D. (0, 1, 0)

**44.** A raster colour display processor supports a resolution of $1024 \times 800$ with upto 16 million colours simultaneously displayable. What will be the approximate size (in bytes) of the frame buffer used in the display processor?
   A. $1.2 \times 10^6$        B. $2.4 \times 10^6$
   C. $16 \times 10^6$        D. $10^5$

**45.** Reflection of a point about $x$-axis, followed by a counter-clockwise rotation of 90°, is equivalent to reflection about the line
A. $x = -y$      B. $y = -x$
C. $x = y$      D. $x + y = 1$

**46.** The refresh rate below which a picture flickers is
A. 25      B. 30
C. 35      D. 60

**47.** In multiple transformation, which of the following are commutative?
A. Successive transformations of the same kind
B. Rotation about a fixed point and translation
C. Uniform scaling and rotation
D. A and B

**48.** All the following hidden surface algorithms employ image space approach except
A. back face removal
B. depth buffer method
C. scan line method
D. depth sort method

**49.** The entire graph of the function $f(x) = x^2 + kx - x + 9$ is strictly above the $x$-axis if and only if
A. $-3 < k < 5$      B. $-3 < k < 2$
C. $-3 < k < 7$      D. $-5 < k < 7$

**50.** The point (4, 1) undergoes the following 3 transformations successively.
I. Reflection about the line $y = x$.
II. Translation through a distance of 2 units along the positive $x$-axis.
III. Rotation through an angle of $\pi/4$ about the origin in the counter-clockwise direction.
The final position of the point will be
A. $(-1\sqrt{2}, 7/\sqrt{2})$      B. $(1, 4)$
C. $(3/\sqrt{2}, -5/\sqrt{2})$      D. $(3/\sqrt{2}, 5/\sqrt{2})$

**51.** Which of the following curves are symmetric about the line $x = y$?
A. $1 + x + y = 0$
B. $y = |x|$
C. $y = x^3$
D. $|x| + |y| = 9$

**52.** Aspect ratio is generally defined as the ratio of the
A. vertical to horizontal points
B. horizontal to vertical points
C. vertical to (horizontal + vertical) points
D. either A or B, depending on the convention followed

**53.** Parabola can be got from a right circular cone, by cutting it through a plane that is
A. parallel to the side of the cone
B. perpendicular to the axis of the cone
C. a tangent to the cone
D. parallel to the axis of the cone

**54.** Which of the following devices has a relative origin?
A. Joystick
B. Track ball
C. Mouse
D. None of the above

**55.** Choose the correct answers.
To construct the rectangle $ABCD$, it is enough if
A. the length and breadth are given
B. the vertices $A$ and $B$ are given
C. the vertex $A$ and the length of the diagonal are given
D. the vertices $A$ and $C$ are given

**56.** Which of the following transformations are non-commutative?
A. Linear followed by scaling
B. Linear followed by rotation
C. Scaling followed by rotation
D. None of the above

**57.** Random-scan monitors are also referred to as
A. vector display
B. stroke writing display
C. calligraphic display
D. none of the above

**58.** Which of the following is an odd function?
A. $f(x) = x^2 - |x|$
B. $f(x) = \sin(x) + \cos(x)$
C. $f(x) = (x)(a^x + 1)/(a^x - 1)$
D. none of the above

**59.** When the computer is not able to maintain operation and display, bright spots occur in the screen. This is called as
A. dropping out
B. snowing
C. flickering
D. blanking

**60.** Oblique projection with an angle of 45° to the horizontal plane is called as
A. cabinet projection
B. isometric projection
C. cavalier projection
D. none of the above

**61.** A line connecting the points (1, 1) and (5, 3) is to be drawn, using the DDA algorithm. Find the value of $x$ and $y$ increments.
A. $x$–increment = 1; $y$–increment = 1
B. $x$–increment = 0.5; $y$–increment = 1
C. $x$–increment = 1; $y$–increment = 0.5
D. none of the above

**62.** Find the incorrect statement(s).
A. A perspective projection produces realistic views.
B. A parallel projection preserves realistic dimensions.
C. A perspective projection preserves realistic dimensions.
D. A parallel projection gives realistic representation of 3-D objects.

**63.** The perspective anomaly in which the object behind the centre of projection is projected upside down and backward onto the viewplane is called as
A. perspective foreshortening
B. vanishing view
C. view confusion
D. topological distortion

**64.** Let $F : R^2 \to R^2$ be the mapping defined by $F(x, y) = \left(\dfrac{x}{3}, \dfrac{y}{4}\right)$. The image under $F$ of the ellipse $\dfrac{x^2}{9} + \dfrac{y^2}{16} = 1$, is

A. the circle $x^2 + y^2 = 1$
B. the line $\dfrac{x}{3} + \dfrac{x}{4} = 1$
C. the ellipse $\dfrac{x^2}{27} + \dfrac{y^2}{64} = 1$
D. none of the above

**65.** The anti-aliasing technique which allows shift of 1/4, 1/2 and 3/4 of a pixel diameter enabling a closer path of a line is
A. pixel phasing
B. filtering
C. intensity compensation
D. sampling technique

**66.** In the clipping algorithm of Cohen and Sutherland using region codes, a line is already clipped if the,
A. codes of the end points are the same.
B. logical AND of the end points code is not 0 0 0 0.
C. logical OR of the end points code is 0 0 0 0.
D. logical AND of the end points code is 0 0 0 0.

**67.** When several types of output devices are available in a graphic installation, it is convenient to use
A. bundled attributes
B. unbundled attributes
C. inquiry attributes
D. none of the above

**68.** Raster systems display a picture from a definition in a
A. display file program
B. frame buffer
C. display controller
D. none of the above

**69.** Back face removal is an example of
A. object space method
B. image space method
C. combination of both
D. none of the above

**70.** Choose the incorrect statement from the following about the basic ray tracing technique used in image synthesis.

A. In this technique, rays are cast from the eye point through every pixel on the screen.
B. In this technique, viewing transformations are not applied to the scene prior to rendering.
C. This technique removes hidden surfaces.
D. In this technique, rays are cast from the light source to the objects in the scene.

**71.** A cube with side 3 units is placed so that one of its vertices is at the origin and it has one edge along the positive X, Y and Z axes of a 3-D right handed coordinate system. What is the homogeneous co-ordinate transformation matrix, necessary to move the cube so that it has a vertex at the origin and has one edge each along the negative X, negative Y and negative Z axis.

A. $\begin{bmatrix} 1 & 0 & 0 & 0 \\ 0 & 1 & 0 & 0 \\ 0 & 0 & 1 & 0 \\ -3 & -3 & -3 & 1 \end{bmatrix}$   B. $\begin{bmatrix} 0 & 0 & 0 & 1 \\ 1 & 0 & 1 & 1 \\ 1 & 1 & 0 & 1 \\ -3 & -3 & -3 & 0 \end{bmatrix}$

C. $\begin{bmatrix} 1 & 0 & 0 & 0 \\ 0 & 1 & 0 & 0 \\ 0 & 0 & 1 & 0 \\ 3 & 3 & 3 & 1 \end{bmatrix}$   D. $\begin{bmatrix} 0 & 0 & 0 & 1 \\ 1 & 0 & 1 & 1 \\ 1 & 1 & 0 & 1 \\ 3 & 3 & 3 & 0 \end{bmatrix}$

**72.** Hue of a colour is related to its
A. luminance
B. saturation
C. incandescence
D. wavelength

**73.** On 15 × 15 raster of white squares given in figure is stored such that the first square coincides with the top left corner of the raster. The compression ratio attained by run length coding is approximately 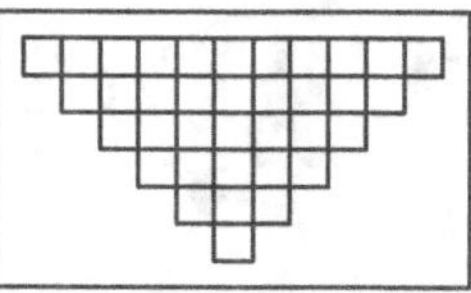
A. 1 : 2
B. 1 : 5
C. 2 : 7
D. 1 : 9

**74.** Let $R$ be the radius of a circle. The angle subtended by an arc of length $R$ at the centre of the circle is
A. 1 degree
B. 1 radian
C. 45 degrees
D. none of these

**75.** Choose the correct statement.
Given three non-collinear points,
A. it is always possible to draw a circle passing through the three points.
B. it may or may not be possible to draw a circle passing through the three points.
C. it is impossible to draw a circle passing through the three points
D. none of the above

## ANSWERS

| 1 | 2 | 3 | 4 | 5 | 6 | 7 | 8 | 9 | 10 |
|---|---|---|---|---|---|---|---|---|---|
| C | A | C | B | B | C | A | D | B | D |

| 11 | 12 | 13 | 14 | 15 | 16 | 17 | 18 | 19 | 20 |
|---|---|---|---|---|---|---|---|---|---|
| D | D | C | B | D | D | A, B | C | A | B |

| 21 | 22 | 23 | 24 | 25 | 26 | 27 | 28 | 29 | 30 |
|---|---|---|---|---|---|---|---|---|---|
| C | C | D | D | B | B | C | C, D | C | A |

| 31 | 32 | 33 | 34 | 35 | 36 | 37 | 38 | 39 | 40 |
|---|---|---|---|---|---|---|---|---|---|
| A | D | C | A | D | D | B | A, B, C | B | B |

| 41 | 42 | 43 | 44 | 45 | 46 | 47 | 48 | 49 | 50 |
|---|---|---|---|---|---|---|---|---|---|
| C | B | D | B | C | A | A, C | A | D | A |

| 51 | 52 | 53 | 54 | 55 | 56 | 57 | 58 | 59 | 60 |
|---|---|---|---|---|---|---|---|---|---|
| A, D | D | A | C | D | C | A, B, C | D | B | C |

| 61 | 62 | 63 | 64 | 65 | 66 | 67 | 68 | 69 | 70 |
|---|---|---|---|---|---|---|---|---|---|
| C | C, D | C | A | A | A, B | A | B | A | D |

| 71 | 72 | 73 | 74 | 75 |
|---|---|---|---|---|
| A | D | D | B | A |

# 14. | Automata Theory



**A.** The following abreviations are used in this chapter:

| | | |
|---|---|---|
| FSM | – | Finite State Machine |
| DFSM | – | Deterministic Finite State Machine |
| NDFSM | – | Non-Deterministic Finite State Machine |
| PDM | – | Push Down Machine |
| DPDM | – | Deterministic Push Down Machine |
| NDPDM | – | Non-Deterministic Push Down Machine |
| TM | – | Turing Machine |
| UTM | – | Universal Turing Machine |
| CFG | – | Context Free Grammar |
| CF | – | Context Free |
| CFL | – | Context Free Language |
| CSG | – | Context Sensitive Grammar |

**B.** In Transition diagrams, states are represented by circles.
The start state is represented by a circle pointed to by an arrow.
A final state is represented by a circle encircled by another.

**C.** In a CFG, unless stated otherwise, grammar symbol on the left hand side of the first production, is the start symbol.

**1.** An FSM can be used to add two given integers. This remark is
A. true
B. false
C. may be true
D. none of the above

**2.** The following grammar is
$S \rightarrow a\alpha b \mid b\alpha c \mid aB$
$S \rightarrow aS \mid b$
$S \rightarrow \alpha bb \mid ab$
$b\alpha \rightarrow bdb \mid b$
A. context free        B. regular
C. context sensitive   D. LR (k)

**3.** The statement — "A TM can't solve halting problem" is
A. true
B. false
C. still an open question
D. none of the above

**4.** A language L for which there exists a TM, T, that accepts every word in L and either rejects or loops for every word that is not in L, is said to be
A. recursive
B. recursively enumerable
C. NP-HARD
D. none of the above

**5.** CSG can be recognized by a
A. FSM
B. DPDM
C. NDPDM
D. linearly bounded memory machine

**6.** $L = \{a^n\, b^n\, a^n \mid n = 1, 2, 3,...\}$ is an example of a language that is
A. context free
B. not context free
C. not context free but whose complement is not CF
D. B and C both

**7.** Let $L(G)$ denote the language generated by the grammar G. To prove set $P = L(G)$,
   A. it is enough to prove that an arbitrary member of $P$ can be generated by grammar $G$
   B. it is enough to prove that an arbitrary string generated by G, belongs to set $P$
   C. both the above comments (A) and (B) is to be proved
   D. either of the above comments (A) and (B) is to be proved

**8.** The machine pictured in Fig.

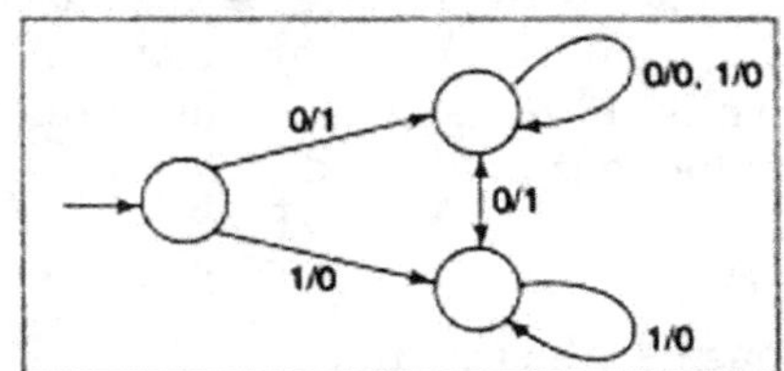


   A. complements a given bit pattern
   B. finds 2's complement of a given bit pattern
   C. increments a given bit pattern by 1
   D. changes the sign bit

**9.** The FSM pictured in Fig. recognizes.

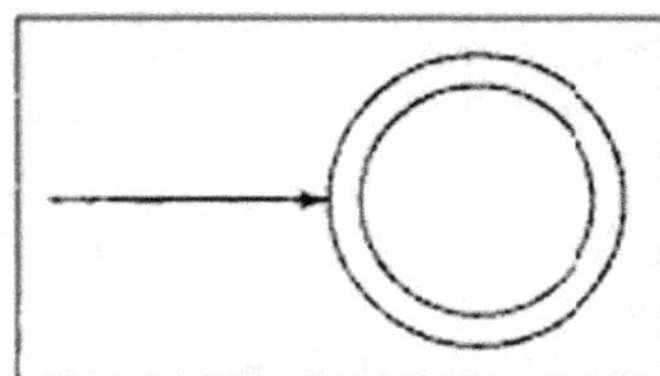

   A. all strings
   B. no string
   C. $\varepsilon$-alone
   D. none of the above

**10.** The major difference between a Moore and a Mealy machine is that
   A. the output of the former depends on the present state and the current input
   B. the output of the former depends only on the present state
   C. the output of the former depends only on the current input
   D. none of the above

**11.** Choose the correct statements.
   A. $A = \{a^n b^n \mid n = 0, 1, 2, 3,...\}$ is a regular language
   B. The set B, consisting of all strings made up of only $a$'s and $b$'s having equal number of $a$'s and $b$'s defines a regular language.
   C. $L(A^*B^*) \cap B$ gives the set A.
   D. None of the above

**12.** A finite state machine with the following state table has a single input $x$ and a single output $z$.

| *Present state* | *Next state, z* | |
|---|---|---|
| | $x = 1$ | $x = 0$ |
| A | D, 0 | B, 0 |
| B | B, 1 | C, 1 |
| C | B, 0 | D, 1 |
| D | B, 1 | C, 0 |

If the initial state is unknown, then the shortest input sequence to reach the final state C is
   A. 01       B. 10
   C. 101      D. 110

**13.** The number of states of the FSM, required to simulate the behaviour of a computer, with a memory capable of storing 'm' words, each of length 'n' bits is
   A. $m \times 2^n$
   B. $2^{mn}$
   C. $2^{m+n}$
   D. none of the above

**14.** Choose the correct statements.
   A. Set of recursively enumerable languages is closed under union.
   B. If a language and its complement are both regular, then the language must be recursive.
   C. Recursive languages are closed under complementation.
   D. All of these

**15.** Choose the correct statements.
   A. An FSM with 2 stacks is as powerful as a TM.

B. DFSM and NDFSM have the same power.
C. A DFSM with 2 stacks and an NDFSM with 2 stacks have the same power.
D. All of these

**16.** The intersection of a CFL and a regular language
A. need not be regular
B. is always regular
C. is always CF
D. B and C both

**17.** Choose the correct statements.
A. All languages can be generated by CFG.
B. Any regular language has an equivalent CFG.
C. Some non-regular languages can't be generated by any CFG.
D. B and C both

**18.** The FSM pictured in Fig. recognizes

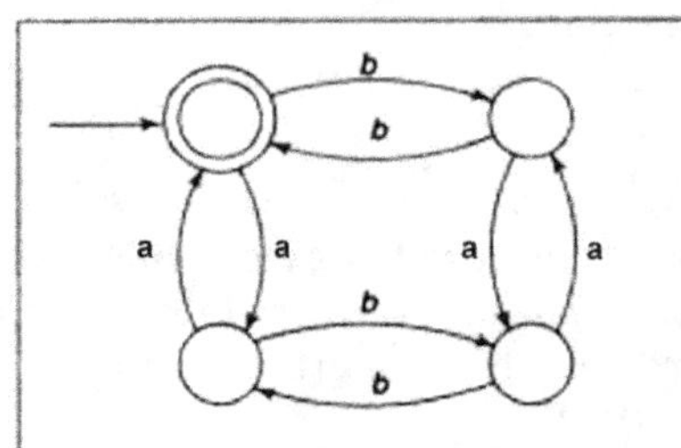


A. any string of odd number of a's
B. any string of odd number of a's and even number of b's
C. any string of even number of a's and even number of b's
D. any string of even number of a's and odd number of b's

**19.** Choose the correct statements.
A. A Mealy machine generates no language as such.
B. A Moore machine generates no language as such.
C. For a given input string, length of the output string generated by a Moore machine is one more than the length of the output string generated by that of a Mealy machine.
D. All of the above

**20.** The recognizing capability of NDFSM and DFSM
A. may be different
B. must be different
C. must be the same
D. none of the above

**21.** A CFG is said to be in Chomsky Normal Form (CNF), if all the productions are of the form A → BC or A → a. Let G be a CFG in CNF. To derive a string of terminals of length $x$, the number of productions to be used is
A. $2x - 1$     B. $2x$
C. $2x + 1$     D. $2^x$

**22.** Consider the grammar
S → PQ | SQ | PS
P → X
Q → Y
The get a string of $n$ terminals, the number of productions to be used is
A. $n^2$     B. $n + 1$
C. $2n$     D. $2n - 1$

**23.** The number of symbols necessary to simulate a TM with $m$ symbols and $n$ states is
A. $m + n$     B. $8mn + 4m$
C. $mn$     D. $4mn + m$

**24.** Which of the following is not primitive recursive but partially recursive?
A. Carnot function
B. Rieman function
C. Bounded function
D. Ackermann function

**25.** Choose the correct statements.
A. The power of DFSM and NDFSM are the same.
B. The power of DFSM and NDFSM are different.
C. The power of DPDM and NDPDM are different.
D. A and C both

**26.** The set $A = \{a^n b^n a^n \mid n = 1, 2, 3, ...\}$ is an example of a grammar that is
 A.  regular
 B.  context free
 C.  not context free
 D.  none of the above

**27.** Any string of terminals that can be generated by the following CFG

 S $\rightarrow$ XY

 X $\rightarrow$ aX | bX | a

 Y $\rightarrow$ Ya | Yb | a

 A.  has at least one b
 B.  should end in an 'a'
 C.  has no consecutive a's or b's
 D.  has at least two a's

**28.** Consider the two FSM's in Fig.

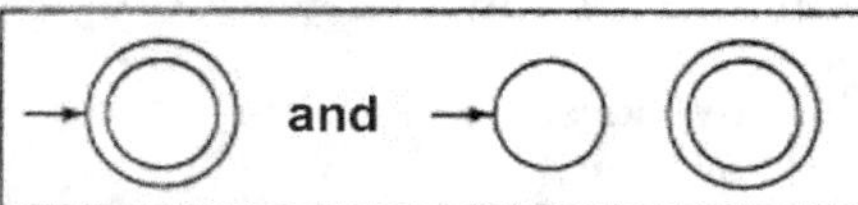


Pick the correct statement.
 A.  Both are equivalent
 B.  The second FSM accepts only $\varepsilon$
 C.  The first FSM accepts nothing
 D.  None of the above

**29.** An FSM can be considered a TM
 A.  of finite tape length, rewinding capability and unidirectional tape movement
 B.  of finite tape length, without rewinding capability and unidirectional tape movement
 C.  of finite tape length, without rewinding capability and bidirectional tape movement
 D.  of finite tape length, rewinding capability and bidirectional tape movement

**30.** Let $A = \{0, 1\}$. The number of possible strings of length 'n' that can be formed by the elements of the set A is
 A.  $n!$
 B.  $n^2$
 C.  $n^n$
 D.  $2^n$

**31.** Which of the following are not regular?
 A.  String of 0's whose length is a perfect square.
 B.  Set of all palindromes made up of 0's and 1's.
 C.  Strings of 0's, whose length is a prime number.
 D.  All of these

**32.** Choose the correct statements.

 A class of languages that is closed under
 A.  union and complementation has to be closed under intersection
 B.  intersection and complementation has to be closed under union
 C.  union and intersection has to be closed under complementation
 D.  A & B only

**33.** Any TM with $m$ symbols and $n$ states can be simulated by another TM with just 2 symbols and less than
 A.  $8mn$ states
 B.  $4mn + 8$ states
 C.  $8mn + 4$ states
 D.  $mn$ states

**34.** Choose the correct statements.
 A.  A total recursive function is also a partial recursive function.
 B.  A primitive recursive function is also a partial recursive function.
 C.  A partial recursive function is also a primitive recursive function.
 D.  A & B only

**35.** Which of the following is accepted by an NDPDM, but not by a DPDM?
 A.  All strings in which a given symbol is present at least twice.
 B.  Even palindromes (*i.e.* palindromes made up of even number of terminals).
 C.  Strings ending with a particular terminal.
 D.  None of the above

**36.** Let

 L1 = $\{a^n b^n a^m \mid m, n = 1, 2, 3, ...\}$

 L2 = $\{a^n b^n a^m \mid m, n = 1, 2, 3, ...\}$

 L1 = $\{a^n b^n a^n \mid n = 1, 2, 3, ...\}$

Choose the correct statements.

A. L3 = L1 ∩ L2
B. L1 and L2 are CFL but L3 is not a CFL
C. A & B both
D. L1 is a subset of L3

**37.** The following CFG

S → aB | bA
A → b | aS | bAA
B → b | bS | aBB

generates strings of terminals that have
A. equal number of a's and b's
B. odd number of a's and odd number b's
C. even number of a's and even number of b's
D. odd number a's and even number of a's

**38.** Set of regular languages over a given alphabet set, is not closed under
A. union
B. complementation
C. intersection
D. none of the above

**39.** TM is more powerful than FSM because
A. the tape movement is confined to one direction
B. it has no finite state control
C. it has the capability to remember arbitrary long sequences of input symbols.
D. none of the above

**40.** Choose the correct statements.
A. Moore and Mealy machines are FSM's with output capability.
B. Any given Moore machine has an equivalent Mealy machine.
C. Any given Mealy machine has an equivalent Moore machine.
D. All of these

**41.** Which of the following pairs of regular expressions are equivalent?
A. 1(01)* and (10)*1
B. $x (xx)^*$ and $(xx)^*x$
C. $x^*$ and $x^*x'$
D. All of these

**42.** Let P, Q and R be three languages. If P and R are regular and if PQ = R, then

A. Q has to be regular
B. Q cannot be regular
C. Q need not be regular
D. Q has to be a CFL

**43.** If there exists a TM which when applied to any problem in the class, terminates if the correct answer is yes, and, may or may not terminate otherwise is said to be
A. stable        B. unsolvable
C. partially solvable   D. unstable

**44.** Which of the following is not primitive recursive but computable?
A. Carnot function
B. Riemann function
C. Bounded function
D. Ackermann function

**45.** A PDM behaves like a TM when the number of auxiliary memory it has is
A. 0
B. 1 or more
C. 2 or more
D. none of the above

**46.** CFG is not closed under
A. union             B. Kleene star
C. complementation   D. product

**47.** The following CFG
$S \to aS \mid bS \mid a \mid b$
is equivalent to the regular expression
A. $(a + b)^* (a + b)$   B. $(a + b)^*$
C. $(a + b)(a + b)^*$    D. All of these

**48.** Which of the following pairs of regular expression are not equivalent?
A. $(ab)^*a$ and $a(ba)^*$
B. $(a + b)^*$ and $(a^* + b)^*$
C. $(a^* + b)^*$ and $(a + b)^*$
D. none of the above

**49.** Palindromes can't be recognized by any FSM because
A. an FSM can't remember arbitrarily large amount of information
B. an FSM can't deterministically fix the mid-point
C. even if the mid-point is known, an FSM can't find whether the second half of the string matches the first half
D. All of these

50. The word 'formal' in formal languages means
    A. the symbols used have well-defined meaning
    B. they are unnecessary, in reality
    C. only the form of the string of symbols is significant
    D. none of the above

51. Pumping lemma is generally used for proving
    A. a given grammar is regular
    B. a given grammar is not regular
    C. whether two given regular expressions are equivalent
    D. none of the above

52. Which of the following definitions generates the same language as L, where
    $L = (x^n y^n, n \geq 1)$ ?
    I. $E \to xEy \mid xy$
    II. $xy \mid x^+ xyy^+$
    III. $x^+ y^+$
    A. I only            B. I and II
    C. II and III        D. II only

53. The number of internal states of a UTM should be at least
    A. 1                 B. 2
    C. 3                 D. 4

54. Choose the correct statements.
    A. $L = (a^n b^n a^n \mid n = 1, 2, 3,...)$ is recursively enumerable.
    B. Recursive language are closed under union.
    C. Every recursive language is recursively enumerable.
    D. All of these

55. Choose the correct statements.
    A. An FSM with 1 stack is more powerful than an FSM with no stack.
    B. An FSM with 2 stacks is more powerful than a FSM with 1 stack.
    C. An FSM with 3 stacks is more powerful than an FSM with 2 stacks.
    D. A & B both

56. Which of the following conversion is not possible algorithmically?
    A. Regular grammar to context free grammar
    B. Non-deterministic FSA to deterministic FSA
    C. Non-deterministic PDA to deterministic PDA
    D. Non-deterministic Turing machine to deterministic Turing machine

57. The set $\{a^n b^n \mid n = 1, 2, 3,...\}$ can be generated by the CFG
    A. $S \to ab \mid aSb$
    B. $S \to aaSbb \mid ab \mid aabb$
    C. A & B both
    D. $S \to aaSbb \mid ab$

58. For which of the following applications regular expressions can't be used?
    A. Designing compilers
    B. Designing computers
    C. A & B both
    D. Developing text editors

59. The FSM pictured in Fig. is a

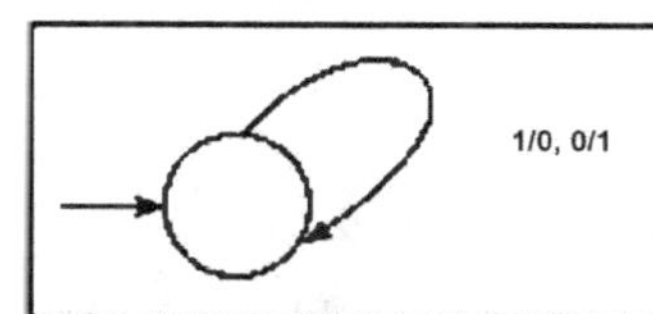


    A. Mealy machine
    B. Moore machine
    C. Kleene machine
    D. None of the above

60. The above machine
    A. complements a given bit pattern
    B. generates all strings of 0's and 1's
    C. adds 1 to a given bit pattern
    D. none of the above

61. Pick the correct statements.
    The logic of Pumping lemma is a good example of
    A. the Pigeon-hole principle
    B. the divide and conquer technique
    C. recursion
    D. iteration

62. The vernacular language English, if considered a formal language, is a

A. regular language
B. context free language
C. context sensitive language
D. none of the above

**63.** Pick the correct answers.
Universal TM influenced the concept of
A. stored-program computers
B. interpretive implementation of programming languages
C. computability
D. All of these

**64.** Bounded minimalization is a technique for
A. proving whether a primitive recursive function is Turning computable
B. proving whether a primitive recursive function is a total function
C. generating primitive recursive functions
D. generating partial recursive functions

**65.** A PDM behaves like an FSM when the number of auxiliary memory it has is
A. 0
B. 1
C. 2
D. none of the above

**66.** Which of the following CFG's can't be simulated by an FSM?
A. $S \rightarrow Sa \mid a$
B. $S \rightarrow abX$
$X \rightarrow cY$
$Y \rightarrow d \mid aX$
C. $S \rightarrow aSb \mid ab$
D. None of these

**67.** Any given Transition graph has an equivalent
A. regular expression
B. DFSM
C. NDFSM
D. All of these

**68.** The language of all words (made up of a's and b's) with at least two a's can be described by the regular expression
A. $(a + b)*a(a + b)*a(a + b)*$
B. $(a + b)*ab*a(a + b)*$
C. $b*ab*a (a + b)*$
D. All of these

**69.** The basic limitation of an FSM is that
A. it can't remember arbitrary large amount of information
B. it sometimes recognizes grammars that are not regular
C. it sometimes fails to recognize grammars that are regular
D. all of the above

**70.** FSM can recognize
A. any grammar
B. only CFG
C. any unambiguous grammar
D. only regular grammar

# ANSWERS

| 1 | 2 | 3 | 4 | 5 | 6 | 7 | 8 | 9 | 10 |
|---|---|---|---|---|---|---|---|---|---|
| B | C | A | B | D | D | C | C | C | B |
| **11** | **12** | **13** | **14** | **15** | **16** | **17** | **18** | **19** | **20** |
| C | B | B | D | D | D | D | C | D | C |
| **21** | **22** | **23** | **24** | **25** | **26** | **27** | **28** | **29** | **30** |
| A | D | D | D | D | C | D | D | B | D |
| **31** | **32** | **33** | **34** | **35** | **36** | **37** | **38** | **39** | **40** |
| D | D | A | D | B | C | A | D | C | D |
| **41** | **42** | **43** | **44** | **45** | **46** | **47** | **48** | **49** | **50** |
| D | C | C | D | C | C | D | D | D | C |
| **51** | **52** | **53** | **54** | **55** | **56** | **57** | **58** | **59** | **60** |
| B | A | B | D | D | C | C | C | A | A |
| **61** | **62** | **63** | **64** | **65** | **66** | **67** | **68** | **69** | **70** |
| A | B | D | C | A | C | D | D | A | D |

# 15. | Computer Organisation |

1. A computer uses a floating-point representation comprising a signed magnitude fractional mantissa and an excess-16 base-8 exponent. What decimal number is represented by a floating-point number whose exponent is 10011, mantissa 101000, and the sign bit set?
   A. –6250  B. –20480
   C. –320  D. –0.00122

2. The binary equivalent of the Gray code 11100 is
   A. 10111  B. 00111
   C. 01011  D. 10101

3. The minimum number of 2-input NAND gates required to implement the function $F = (x' + y') (z + w)$ is
   A. 3  B. 4
   C. 5  D. 6

4. The most relevant addressing mode to write position independent code is
   A. direct mode  B. indirect mode
   C. relative mode  D. indexed mode

5. Which of the following are CISC machines?
   A. IBM 360
   B. 80386
   C. 68030
   D. All of the above

6. Which of the following rules regarding the addition of 2 given numbers is correct, if negative numbers are represented in 2's complement form?
   A. Add sign bit and discard carry, if any.
   B. Add sign bit and add carry, if any.
   C. Don't add sign bit and discard carry, if any.
   D. Don't add sign bit and add carry, if any.

7. When INTR is encountered, the processor branches to the memory location, which is
   A. 0024H
   B. determined by the 'call address' instruction issued by the I/O device
   C. determined by the 'RST n' instruction issued by the I/O device
   D. all of the above

8. The advantage of a single bus over a multi-bus is the
   A. low cost
   B. flexibility in attaching peripheral devices
   C. high operating speed
   D. all of the above

9. The number of possible Boolean functions that can be defined for $n$ Boolean variables over $n$-valued Boolean algebra is
   A. $2^{2^n}$  B. $2^{n^2}$
   C. $n^{2^n}$  D. $n^{n^n}$

10. The ASCII code 56, represents the character
    A. V
    B. 8
    C. a
    D. carriage return

11. Parallel printer uses
    A. RS-232C interface
    B. centronics interface

C. hand-shake mode
D. synchronous data transfer mode

**12.** A microprogrammed control unit
A. is faster than a hard-wired control unit
B. facilitates easy implementation of new instructions
C. is useful when very small programs are to be run
D. usually refers to the control unit of a microprocessor

**13.** An assembler that runs on one machine but produces machine code for another machine is called
A. simulator
B. emulator
C. cross-assembler
D. boot-strap loader

**14.** When even-parity ASCII text is transmitted asynchronously at a rate of 10 characters per sec over a 110-bps line, what percentage of the received bits actually contain data (as opposed to over head)?
A. 7/11
B. 8/11
C. 700/11
D. 80/11

**15.** The output of the multiplexer circuit in Fig. can be represented by

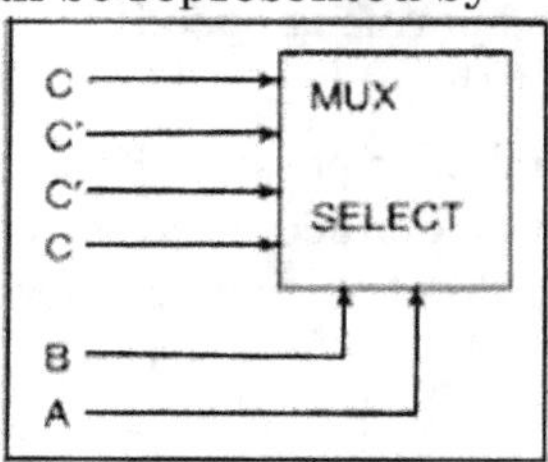


A. AB + BC' + C'A + BC
B. A + B + C
C. A + B
D. A'B'C + A'BC' + ABC

**16.** In a 11 bit computer instruction format, the size of address field is 4 bits. The computer uses expanding OP code technique and has 5 two-address instructions and 32 one-address instructions. The number of zero address instructions it can support is
A. 256
B. 2048
C. 16
D. 272

**17.** PCHL is an instruction in 8085 which transfers the contents of the register pair HL to PC. This is not a commonly used instruction as it changes the flow of control in a rather unstructured fashion. This instruction cannot be used in implementing.
A. if... then ... else construct
B. while ... do construct
C. case ... structure
D. call ... statement

**18.** To change an upper case character to a lower case character in ASCII, the correct mask and operation should be
A. 0 1 0 0 0 0 0 and NOR
B. 0 1 0 0 0 0 0 and OR
C. 0 1 0 0 0 0 0 and NAND
D. 1 0 1 1 1 1 1 and AND

**19.** The number of flip-flops needed to construct a binary modulo N counter is
A. N
B. $2^N$
C. $N^2$
D. $\log_2 N$

**20.** Multiplexing of data/address lines in an 8085 microprocessor reduces the instruction execution time. This statement is
A. true
B. false
C. most likely to be true
D. none of the above

**21.** Which of the following is unipolar, difficult to fabricate, has very high speed and offers good resistance to radiation?
A. ECL
B. GaAs
C. TTL
D. CMOS

**22.** What is A*A, if * is a Boolean operation defined by A*B = AB + A'B'?
A. A
B. B
C. 0
D. 1

**23.** If C = A*B, then C*A is
A. A
B. B
C. 0
D. 1

**24.** The Boolean variables A, B and C, that solve the Boolean equations AB + A'C = 1 and AC + B = 0 simultaneously is
A. 1, 0, 0
B. 0, 1, 1
C. 1, 0, 1
D. 0, 0, 1

**25.** If a particular idea can be implemented in hardware or software, the factor(s) that favour hardware implementation is/are
A. cost-effectiveness
B. speed of operation
C. reliability
D. frequent changes expected

**26.** Tera is 2 to the power of
A. 32
B. 30
C. 40
D. 25

**27.** Von Neumann architecture is
A. SISD
B. SIMD
C. MIMD
D. MISD

**28.** To achieve parallelism, one needs a minimum of
A. 2 processors
B. 3 processors
C. 4 processors
D. none of the above

**29.** SIMD can be used for
A. railway reservation
B. weather forecasting
C. matrix multiplication
D. all of the above

**30.** A typical application of MIMD is
A. railway reservation
B. weather forecasting
C. matrix multiplicaiton
D. all of the above

**31.** Let * be a defined as a*b = a' + b. Let m = a*b. The value of m*a is
A. a' + b
B. a
C. 0
D. 1

**32.** The correct matching for the following pairs is

(a) DMA I/O    1. High speed RAM
(b) Cache    2. Disk
(c) Interrupt I/O    3. Printer
(d) Condition Code    4. ALU
     Register
A. (a)-4, (b)-3, (c)-1, (d)-2
B. (a)-2, (b)-1, (c)-3, (d)-4
C. (a)-4, (b)-3, (c)-2, (d)-1
D. (a)-2, (b)-3, (c)-4, (d)-1

**33.** Contents of A register after the execution of the following 8085 microprocessor program is

```
MVI    A, 55h
MVI    C, 25h
ADD    C
DAA
```

A. 7Ah
B. 80h
C. 50h
D. 22h

**34.** RST 7.5 interrupt in 8085 microprocessor executes service routine from interrupt vector location
A. 0000 h
B. 0075 h
C. 003C h
D. 0034 h

**35.** Which of the following are registers?
A. Accumulator
B. Stack pointer
C. Program counter
D. All of these

**36.** (X + Y) + Z = X + (Y + Z)
A. shows that the Boolean operator OR is distributive
B. shows that the Boolean operator OR is associative
C. implies the associativity of the Boolean operator AND
D. none of the above

**37.** The Boolean expression X + X'Y equals
A. X + Y
B. X + XY
C. Y + YX
D. X'Y + Y'X

**38.** The advantage of MOS devices over bipolar devices is

A. it allows higher bit densities and also cost effective
B. it is easy to fabricate
C. its higher-impedance
D. All of these

**39.** Which of the following does not need extra hardware for DRAM refreshing?
A. 8085
B. Motorola-6800
C. Z-80
D. None of the above

**40.** Choose the correct statements.
A. Positive numbers can't be repesented in 1's complement form.
B. Whether a given piece of information is a data or not depends on the particular application.
C. Positive numbers can't be represented in 2's complement form.
D. All of these

**41.** If $(12A)_{16} = (123)_A$, then the value of A is
A. 3
B. 3 or 4
C. 2
D. none of the above

**42.** The speed imbalance between memory access and CPU operation can be reduced by
A. cache memory
B. memory interleaving
C. reducing the size of memory
D. All of these

**43.** If $(1\ 2\ 3)_5 = (A3)_{11}$, then the number of possible values of A is
A. 4
B. 1
C. 3
D. 2

**44.** Which of the following comments about the Program Counter (PC) are true?
A. It is a register
B. It is a cell in ROM
C. During execution of the current instruction, its content changes
D. None of the above

**45.** If X, Y and Z are 3 Boolean variables, then $X(Y - Z)$ equals $(X + Y)(X + Z)$, if X, Y, Z take the values
A. 1, 0, 0
B. 0, 1, 0
C. 1, 1, 0
D. 0, 1, 1

**46.** Which of the following remarks about BCD are true?
A. It is a 8–4–2–1 weighted code
B. Conversion to and from the decimal system can be done easily
C. $(12345678)_{10}$ needs 4 bytes in BCD representation
D. All of these

**47.** The first operating system used in microprocessors is
A. Zenix
B. DOS
C. CP/M
D. Multics

**48.** Which of the following remarks about PLA is/are true?
A. It produces product of sum as the output.
B. It produces sum of products as the output.
C. It is dedicated for a particular operation.
D. It is general.

**49.** The idea of cache memory is based on the
A. property of locality of reference
B. fact that only a small portion of a program is referenced relatively frequently
C. heuristic 90—10 rule
D. All of these

**50.** Which of the following is the programmable internal timer?
A. 8251
B. 8250
C. 8253
D. 8275

**51.** Bipolar devices are desirable in the fabrication of which of the following components?
A. Main memory
B. Cache memory
C. Micro program memory
D. All of the above

52. Any given truth table can be represented by a
    A. Karnaugh map
    B. sum of product of Boolean expressions
    C. product of sum of Boolean expressions
    D. All of the above

53. A number system uses 20 as the radix. The excess code that is necessary for its equivalent binary coded representation is
    A. 4          B. 5
    C. 6          D. 7

54. Choose the correct statements.
    A. Bus is a group of information carrying wires.
    B. Bus is needed to achieve reasonable speed of operation.
    C. Bus can carry data or address and it can be shared by more than one device.
    D. All of these

55. A + B can be implemented by
    A. NAND gates alone
    B. NOR gates alone
    C. AND gates alone
    D. none of the above

56. The minimum number of gates required to implement the Boolean expression AB + AB' + A'C is
    A. 1 AND gate and 1 OR gate
    B. 2 NAND gates
    C. 3 AND gates and 2 OR gates
    D. none of the above

57. The Boolean expression AB + AB' + A'C + AC is unaffected by the value of the Boolean variable
    A. A
    B. B
    C. C
    D. none of the above

58. The binary equivalent of the decimal number 0.4375 is
    A. 0.0111
    B. 0.1011
    C. 0.1100
    D. 0.1010

59. Property of locality of reference may fail if a program has
    A. many conditional jumps
    B. many unconditional jumps
    C. many operands
    D. All of the above

60. To get Boolean expression in the product of sum form, from a given Karnaugh map
    A. don't care conditions should not be present
    B. don't care conditions, if present, should be taken as zeroes
    C. one should cover all the 0's present and complement the resulting expression
    D. one should cover all the 1's present and complement the resulting expression

61. Which of the following comments about half adder are true?
    A. It adds 2 bits.
    B. It is called so because a full adder involves two half-adders.
    C. It needs two input and generates two output.
    D. All of the above

62. Which of the following weights makes the complement operation easier in BCD form?
    A. 8-4-2-1          B. Excess-3
    C. 2-4-2-1          D. 3-2-1-0

63. A byte addressable computer has a memory capacity of $2^m$ kbytes and can perform $2^n$ operations. An instruction involving 3 operands and one operator needs a maximum of
    A. $3m$ bits
    B. $3m + n$ bits
    C. $m + n$ bits
    D. none of the above

64. In the previous problem, if the computer is word addressable with the word size being 8 bytes then the answer will be
    A. $3m$ bits
    B. $3m + n$ bits
    C. $m + n$ bits
    D. none of the above

**65.** The Boolean expression (A + C) (AB' + AC) (A'C' + B') can be simplified to
A. AB
B. AB + A'C
C. A'B + BC
D. AB + BC

**66.** Any given Boolean expression can be implemented by using
A. only NAND gates
B. only NOR gates
C. only OR gates
D. only AND gates

**67.** The sequence of events that happen during a typical fetch operation is
A. PC → Mar → Memory → MDR → IR
B. PC → Memory → MDR → IR
C. PC → Memory → IR
D. PC → MAR → Memory → IR

**68.** The number of columns in a state table for a sequential circuit with '$m$' flip-flops and '$n$' input is
A. $m + n$
B. $m + 2n$
C. $2m + n$
D. $2m + 2n$

**69.** $(10110011100011110000)_2$ in base 32 is
A. 22 14 7 16
B. 11 9 23 31
C. 11 9 7 16
D. 11 14 23 16

**70.** A computer uses ternary system instead of the traditional binary system. An '$n$' bit string in the binary system will occupy
A. $3 + n$ ternary digits
B. $2n/3$ ternary digits
C. $n(\log_2 3)$ ternary digits
D. $m(\log_3 2)$ ternary digits

**71.** The combinational circuit in fig. can be replaced by a single

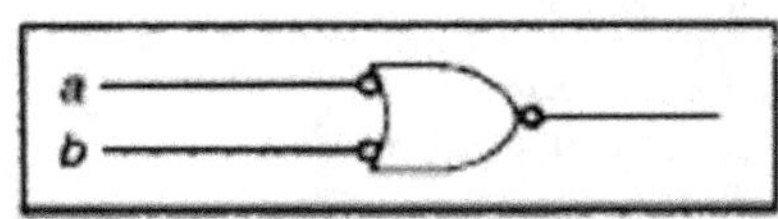

A. OR gate
B. XOR gate
C. NOR gate
D. AND gate

**72.** The Boolean expression A'BE + BCDE + BC'D'E + A'B'DE' + B'C'DE' can be simplified to BE + B'DE', if the don't care conditions are

A. ABCDE + AB'CDE'
B. ABCD + AB'CDE' + ABCD'E
C. ABC'DE + AB'CDE' + ABCD'E
D. none of the above

**73.** The addressing mode used in an instruction of the form ADD X Y, is
A. absolute
B. immediate
C. indirect
D. index

**74.** The decimal equivalent of the binary number 101.101 is
A. 5.6249
B. 5.625
C. 5.5
D. 5.25

**75.** Negative numbers cannot be represented in
A. signed magnitude form
B. 1's complement form
C. 2's complement form
D. none of the above

**76.** Which of the following does not have 8 data lines?
A. 8085
B. 8086
C. 8088
D. Z-80

**77.** The following arrangement of JK flip-flops does the function of a

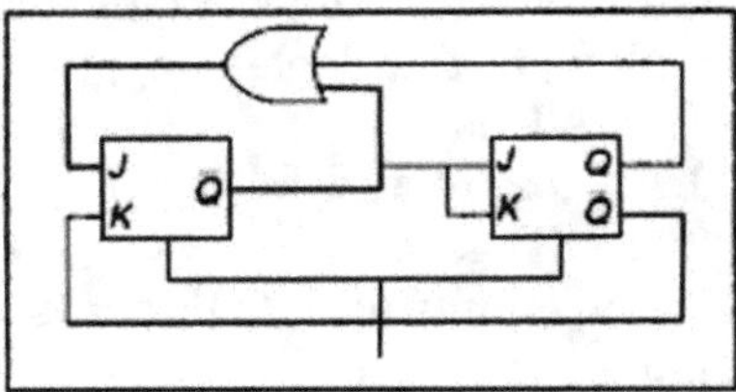

A. Shift register
B. Mod-3 counter
C. Mod-2 counter
D. none of the above

**78.** Which of the following logic families is well suited for high-speed operation?
A. TTL
B. ECL
C. MOS
D. CMOS

**79.** The XOR operator ⊕ is
A. commutative
B. associative
C. distributive over AND operator
D. none of the above

**80.** Addressing capability of 8086/88 is
A. 64 K
B. 512 K
C. 2 MB
D. 1 MB

**81.** Bubble memories are preferable to floppy disks because
A. of their higher transfer rate
B. the cost needed to store a bit is less
C. they consume less power
D. of their reliability

**82.** The following circuit produces the output sequence

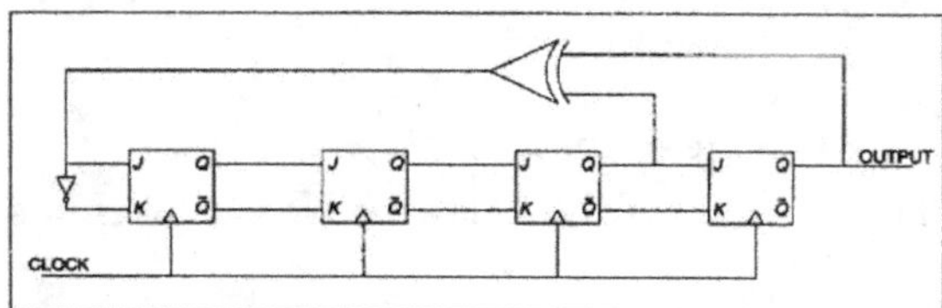


A. 1111 1111 0000 0000
B. 1111 0000 1111 000
C. 1111 0001 0011 010
D. 1010 1010 1010 1010

**83.** Which of the following operation(s) is/are not closed as regards to computers?
A. Addition
B. Subtraction
C. Multiplication & Division
D. All of the above

**84.** Which of the following units can be used to measure the speed of a computer?
A. SYPS
B. MIPS
C. BAUD
D. FLOPS

**85.** If $(11A1B)_8 = (12C9)_{16}$ (c stands for decimal 12), then the values of A and B are
A. 5, 1
B. 7, 5
C. 5, 7
D. none of the above

**86.** The total number of possible Boolean functions involving '$n$' Boolean variables is
A. infinitely many
B. $n^n$
C. $n^2$
D. none of the above

**87.** If $A \oplus B = C$ ($\oplus$ stands for the XOR operator), then
A. $A \oplus B = B$
B. $B \oplus C = A$
C. $A \oplus B \oplus C = 0$
D. All of the above

**88.** Which of the following architecture is/are not suitable for realizing SIMD?
A. Vector processor
B. Array processor
C. Von Neumann
D. All of the above

**89.** The values of $a$, $x$, $y$ if $47 \times 80$ is the 10's complement of $yaya$ 0 are
A. 4, 3, 2
B. 5, 4, 4
C. 3, 4, 5
D. 2, 4, 5

**90.** The values of $x$ and $y$, if $(x\ 567)_8 + (2y \times 5)_8 = (71yx)_8$ is
A. 4, 3
B. 3, 3
C. 4, 4
D. 4, 5

**91.** If memory access takes 20 ns with cache and 110 ns without it, then the bit-ratio, (cache uses a 10 ns memory) is,
A. 93%
B. 90%
C. 87%
D. 88%

**92.** The number of instructions needed to add '$n$' numbers and store the result in memory using only one address instructions is
A. $n$
B. $n - 1$
C. $n + 1$
D. independent of $n$

**93.** Let A be a set having '$n$' elements. The number of binary operations that can be defined on A is
A. $n^{n^2}$
B. $2^{n^n}$
C. $n^{2^n}$
D. $2^{2^n}$

**94.** How many 2-input multiplexers are required to construct a $2^{10}$ –input multiplexer?
A. 1023
B. 31
C. 10
D. 127

**95.** The Boolean expression corresponding to the circuit in fig. is

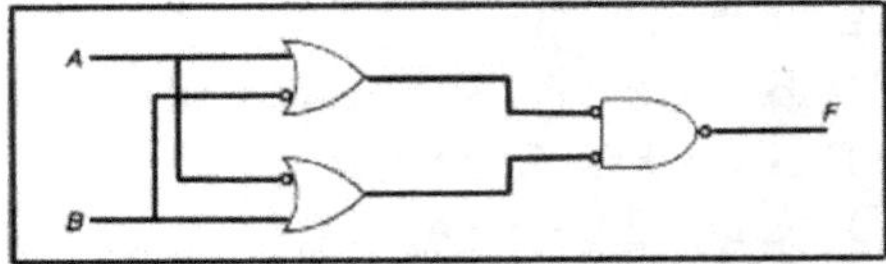

   A. a tautology
   B. an inconsistency
   C. independent of A
   D. none of the above

**96.** The clock of a microprocessor can be divided by 5 using a
   A. 3 bit counter
   B. 5 bit counter
   C. mod 5 counter
   D. mod 3 counter

**97.** The minimal cover for the maximal compatibility classes (ae, acd, ad, bd) is
   A. ae, acd, ad
   B. acd, ad, bd
   C. ae, acd, bd
   D. ae, ad, bd

**98.** The reasons for the presence of ALE pin in 8085, but not in 6800 is that
   A. 8085 uses I/O mapped I/O, whereas 6800 uses memory mapped I/O
   B. 8085 has 5 interrupt lines, whereas 6800 has only 2
   C. 8085 has multiplexed bus, whereas 6800 doesn't have
   D. none of the above

**99.** A decimal number has 25 digits. The number of bits needed for its equivalent binary representation is, approximately,
   A. 50
   B. 60
   C. 70
   D. 75

**100.** Motorola's 68040 is comparable to
   A. 8085
   B. 80286
   C. 80386
   D. 80486

**101.** The seek time of a disk is 30 ms. It rotates at the rate of 30 rotations per second. Each track has a capacity of 300 words. The access time is approximately
   A. 47 ms
   B. 50 ms
   C. 60 ms
   D. 62 ms

**102.** Consider the circuit in Fig.

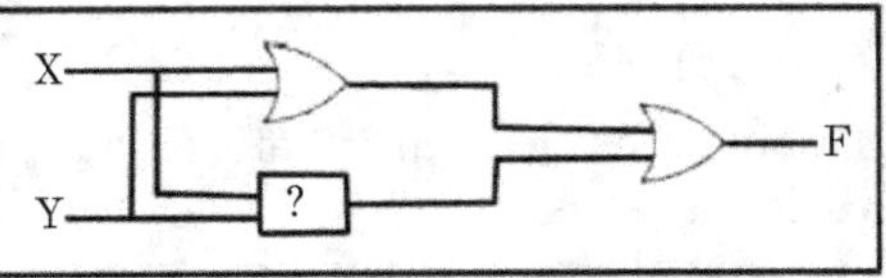

In order to make it a tautology the '?' marked box should be replaced by
   A. an OR gate
   B. an AND gate
   C. a NAND gate
   D. a NOR gate

**103.** Any instruction should have at least
   A. 2 operands
   B. 1 operand
   C. 3 operands
   D. none of the above

**104.** In which of the following instructions bus idle situation occurs?
   A. EI
   B. DAD rp
   C. INX H
   D. DAA

**105.** If the cache needs an access time of 20 ns and the main memory 120 ns, then the average access time of a CPU is (assume hit-ratio is 80%)
   A. 30 ns
   B. 40 ns
   C. 35 ns
   D. 45 ns

**106.** The number of clock cycles necessary to complete 1 fetch cycle in 8085 (excluding wait state) is
   A. 3 or 4
   B. 4 or 5
   C. 4 or 6
   D. 3 or 5

**107.** The possible number of Boolean functions of 3 variables X, Y and Z such that

$f(X, Y, Z) = f(X', Y', Z')$ is
   A. 8
   B. 16
   C. 64
   D. 32

**108.** The addressing mode used in the instruction PUSH B is
   A. direct
   B. register
   C. register indirect
   D. immediate

**109.** The difference between 80486 and 80386 is/are
   A. presence of floating point co-processor
   B. speed of operation
   C. presence of 8 K cache on chip and of memory controller
   D. All of the above

**110.** Which of the following interrupt is both level and edge sensitive?
A. RST 5.5     B. INTR
C. RST 7.5     D. TRAP

**111.** Which of the following are typical characteristics of a RISC machine?
A. Instruction taking multiple cycles
B. Highly pipelined
C. Instructions interpreted by micro-programs
D. Multiple register sets

**112.** The working of a staircase switch is a typical example of the logical operation
A. OR
B. NOR
C. Exclusive-OR
D. Exclusive-NOR

**113.** In serial communication, an extra clock is needed
A. to synchronize the devices
B. for programmed baud rate control
C. to make efficient use of RS-232
D. none of the above

**114.** The Karnaugh map for the Boolean function F of 4 Boolean variables is given in Fig. A, B, C are don't care conditions. What values of A, B, C, will result in the minimal expression?

|   |   | A |   |
|---|---|---|---|
|   | 1 | 1 |   |
| 1 | B | C |   |
|   |   | 1 |   |

A. A = B = C = 1
B. B = C = 1; A = 0
C. A = C = 1; B = 0
D. A = B = 1; C = 0

**115.** On receiving an interrupt from an I/O device, the CPU
A. halts for a predetermined time
B. hands over control of address bus and data bus to the interrupting device
C. branches off to the interrupt service routine immediately
D. branches off to the interrupt service routine after completion of the current instruction.

**116.** The exponent of a floating-point number is represented in excess-N code so that
A. the dynamic range is large
B. the precision is high
C. the smallest number is represented by all zeroes
D. overflow is avoided

**117.** If SUB A, B means B – A, then SUB 4(R0|, *5(R1) means ( (X) means content of register or memory location X)
A. ( ( ( R1 ) + 5 ) ) – ( 4 * ( R 0) )
B. ( ( ( R1 ) + 5 ) ) – ( ( R0 ) + 4)
C. ( ( R1) + 5) – ( 4 * (R0) )
D. ( (R1) + 4) – (R0 + 4)

**118.** If negative numbers are stored in 2's complement form, the range of numbers that can be stored in 8 bits is
A. –128 to + 128     B. –128 to + 127
C. –127 to + 128     D. –127 to + 127

**119.** If you want to design a boundary counter, you should prefer a flip-flop of
A. D-type     B. SR-type
C. latch     D. JK type

**120.** A subtractor is not usually present in a computer because
A. it is expensive
B. it is not possible to design it
C. the adder will take care of subtraction
D. none of the above

**121.** A computer with a 32-bit wide data bus uses $4\,K \times 8$ static RAM memory chips. The smallest memory this computer can have is
A. 32 Kb     B. 16 Kb
C. 8 Kb     D. 24 Kb

**122.** Which of the following binary numbers are not divisible by 4?
A. 1 0 1 0 1 0 1 0 1 0 1 0 1 0
B. 1 1 1 1 0 0 0 0 1 1
C. 1 1 1 0 0 0 1 1 1 0 0 0 1
D. All of the above

**123.** Which of the following 4-bit numbers equals its 1's complement?
A. 1010
B. 1000
C. No such number exists
D. None of the above

**124.** Let $a_n$, $a_{n-1}$, $...a_1a_0$ be the binary representation of an integer $b$. The integer $b$ is divisible by 3 if
A. the number of one's is divisible by 3
B. the number of one's is divisible by 3, but not by 9
C. the number of zeroes is divisible by 3
D. the difference of alternate sum, i.e., $(a_0 + a_2 + ...) - (a_1 + a_3 + ...)$ is divisible by 3

**125.** FFFF will be the last memory location in a memory of size
A. 1 k
B. 16 k
C. 32 k
D. 64 k

**126.** Which of the following 4-bit numbers equals its 2's complement?
A. 1010
B. 0101
C. 1000
D. No such number exists

**127.** A computer uses 8-digit mantissa and 2-digit exponent. If $a = 0.052$ and $b = 28E + 11$, then $b + a - b$ will
A. result in an overflow error
B. result in an underflow error
C. be 0
D. be 5.28 E + 11

**128.** In previous Qn. 'a' will actually be stored as (the '/' is separating the mantissa and the exponent)
A. 00000000/00
B. 05200000/00
C. 52000000/-09
D. 52000000/-01

**129.** Suppose the largest n-bit binary number requires 'd' digits in decimal representation. Which of the following relations between 'n' and 'd' is approximately correct?
A. $d = 2^n$
B. $n = 2^d$
C. $d < n \log_{10} 2$
D. $d > n \log_{10} 2$

**130.** Which of the following is not typically found in the status register of a microprocessor?
A. Overflow
B. Zero result
C. Negative result
D. None of the above

**131.** The output F, of the circuit given in Fig. is given by

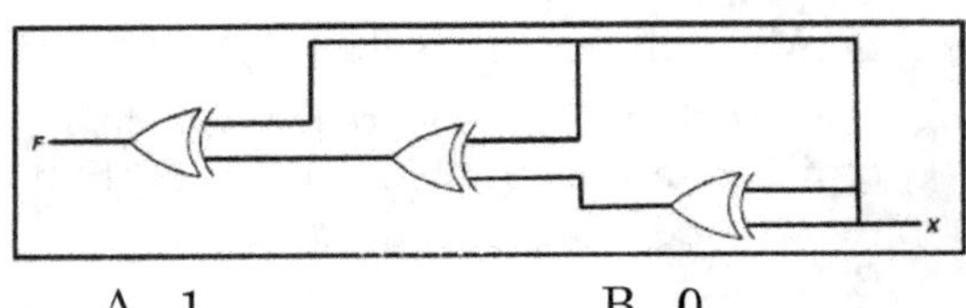

A. 1
B. 0
C. X
D. X'

**132.** The three main components of a digital computer system are
A. memory, I/O, DMA
B. ALU, CPU, memory
C. memory, CPU, I/O
D. control circuits, ALU, registers

**133.** Most of the digital computers do not have floating-point hardware because
A. it is costly
B. is it slower than software
C. floating-point addition cannot be performed by hardware
D. none of the above

**134.** 'n' flip-flops will divide the clock frequency by a factor of
A. $n^2$
B. $n$
C. $2^n$
D. $\log (n)$

**135.** A toggle operation cannot be performed using a single
A. NOR gate
B. AND gate
C. NAND gate
D. XOR gate

**136.** Micro program is
A. the name of a source program in micro computers
B. the set of instructions indicating the primitive operations in a system
C. a primitive form of macros used in assembly language programming
D. a program of very small size

**137.**
```
MVI B, 00
MVI A, 1ch
DCR B
DAA
STA TEMP
HLT
```

The content of the TEMP location after the execution of the above program is
A. 1Ch
B. 22h
C. 82h
D. 12h

**138.** A single instruction to clear the lower four bits of the accumulator in 8085 assembly language is
A. XRI 0FH
B. ANI F0H
C. XRI F0H
D. ANI 0FH

**139.** Which of the following instructions requires the most number of T-states?
A. MOV A, B
B. MOV A, M
C. LDAX B
D. DAD D

**140.** The number of RAM chips of size (256 K × 1) required to build a 1 Mbyte memory is
A. 8
B. 32
C. 10
D. 24

**141.** Consider the following program. Assume that the program is stored in R/W memory.

```
Initial condition :     (A000H) = 00H
8000 : 31 07 80         LXI SP, 8007H
8003 : 3E 76            MVI A, 76H
8005 : F5               PUSH PSW
8006 : 3A 00 A0         LDA A000H
8009 : F1               POP PSW
800A : 3A 00 A0         STA A000H
800D 76                 HLT
```

The content of the location A000H after the execution of the above program is
A. 76h
B. 00h
C. FFh
D. 55h

**142.** The μP may be made to exit from HALT state by asserting
A. RESET
B. any of the five interrupt lines
C. READY line
D. option (A) or option (B) or HOLD line

**143.** The 8085 μP enters into wait state after the recognition of
A. HOLD
B. *READY
C. *RESET-IN
D. INTR

**144.** Maximum number of I/O devices that can be addressed by Intel 8085 is
A. 65,536
B. 255
C. 512
D. 256

**145.** Pick out the matching pair.
A. READY : RIM
B. HOLD : DMA
C. SID : SIM
D. S0, S1 : Wait states

**146.** The minimum number of bits required to represent a character from ASCII code set is
A. 2
B. 5
C. 7
D. 8

**147.** Consider the following program:
```
            ORC    8000H
START :     LXI    H, 8000H
            MOVE A, L
            ADD H
            JM     XYZ
            RST    0
XYZ :       PCHL
            HLT
```

Pick out the correct statement from the following:
A. the program will branch to 0000H after JM XYZ
B. the program will branch to 0008H after JM XYZ
C. the program will halt the processor
D. the program will be repeated infinitely

**148.** The contents of the A15-A8 (higher order address lines) while executing "IN addr" instruction are
A. same as the contents of A7-A0
B. irrelevant
C. all bits reset (i.e. 00h)
D. all bits set (i.e. FFh)

**149.** The stack is nothing but a set of
A. reserved ROM address space
B. reserved RAM address space
C. reserved I/O address space
D. none of the above

**150.** S0 and S1 pins are used for
A. serial communication
B. indicating the processor's status
C. acknowledging the interrupt
D. none of the above

**151.** RST 3 instruction will cause the processor to branch to the location
A. 0000h     B. 0018h
C. 0024h     D. 8018h

**152.**
```
8000 :   START : LXI   H,    0001H
                 LXI   D,    8010H
                 XCHG
                 DCX   D
                 JZ    800C
                 PCHL
800 C :  JMP   8000
         NOP
         HLT
```
Referring to the above program, which of the following statements is true?
A. The program will loop infinitely
B. The program will reach halt state after the first pass
C. The program will reach halt state after 8010h times
D. None of the above

**153.** The only interrupt that is edge-triggered is
A. INTR     B. TRAP
C. RST 7.5     D. RST 5.5

**154.** Consider the following program fragment
```
DELAY :     LXI   H,   0 0 1 0 H
LOOP :      DCX   H
            MOV   A, L
            ORA   H
            XRA   A
            JNZ   LOOP
            RET
```
The number of times LOOP will be executed is
A. 16     B. 10
C. 1     D. infinite

**155.** Which one of the following interrupts is non-maskable?
A. TRAP     B. RST 7.5
C. INTR     D. RST 6.5

**156.** The execution of RST *n* instruction causes the stack pointer to
A. increment by two
B. decrement by two
C. remain unaffected
D. none of the above

**157.** The instruction used to shift right the accumulator contents by one bit through the carry flag bit is
A. RLC     B. RAL
C. RRC     D. RAR

**158.** Which one of the following instructions will never affect the zero flag?
A. DCR reg     B. ORA reg
C. DCX rp     D. XRA reg

**159.** Which of the following peripheral ICs is used to interface keyboard and display?
A. 8251     B. 8279
C. 8259     D. 8253

**160.** Which one of the following instructions may be used to clear the accumulator content (i.e. A = 00h) irrespective of its initial value?
A. CLR A     B. ORA A
C. SUB A     D. MOV A, 00h

**161.** A sequence of two instructions that multiplies the contents of the DE register pair by 2 and stores the result in the HL register pair (in 8085 assembly language) is
A. XCHG and DAD B
B. XTHL and DAD H
C. PCHL and DAD D
D. XCHG and DAD H

**162.** Assume that the 8255 gets selected whenever A15-A11 are high during I/O read or write cycles. The A2 and A1 are connected to A1 and A0 of 8255 chip. Then, the address for port C of 8255 is
A. 03h     B. FEh
C. FFh     D. FF03h

**163.** Which of the following instructions may be used to save the accumulator value onto the stack?
A. PUSH PSW     B. PUSH A
C. PUSH SP     D. POP PSW

**164.** In a vectored interrupt the
  A. branch address is assigned to a fixed location in memory
  B. interrupting source supplies the branch information to the processor through an interrupt vector
  C. branch address is obtained from a register in the processor
  D. none of the above

**165.** Which of the following statements is true?
  A. ROM is a read/write memory.
  B. PC points to the last instruction that was executed.
  C. Stack works on the principle of LIFO.
  D. All instructions affect the flag.

**166.** Assume that a slow memory device is interfaced with an 8085 microprocessor and an 1-wait state generating circuit is connected to READY input. Then, the execution time needed for the following program would be,

```
LDA    TEMP
ADD    B
LHLD   TEMP
```

  A. 43 T-states
  B. 30 T-states
  C. 40 T-states
  D. 33 T-states

# ANSWERS

| 1 | 2 | 3 | 4 | 5 | 6 | 7 | 8 | 9 | 10 |
|---|---|---|---|---|---|---|---|---|---|
| C | A | B | C | D | A | B,C | A,B | D | B |
| **11** | **12** | **13** | **14** | **15** | **16** | **17** | **18** | **19** | **20** |
| B,C | B | C | C | B | A | D | B | D | B |
| **21** | **22** | **23** | **24** | **25** | **26** | **27** | **28** | **29** | **30** |
| A | D | B | D | B,C | C | A | D | B,C | A |
| **31** | **32** | **33** | **34** | **35** | **36** | **37** | **38** | **39** | **40** |
| B | B | B | C | D | B,C | A | D | C | D |
| **41** | **42** | **43** | **44** | **45** | **46** | **47** | **48** | **49** | **50** |
| D | D | D | A,C | B,C | D | C | B,D | D | C |
| **51** | **52** | **53** | **54** | **55** | **56** | **57** | **58** | **59** | **60** |
| B,C | D | C | D | A,B | D | B | A | D | |
| **61** | **62** | **63** | **64** | **65** | **66** | **67** | **68** | **69** | **70** |
| D | C | D | D | A | A,B | A | C | A | D |
| **71** | **72** | **73** | **74** | **75** | **76** | **77** | **78** | **79** | **80** |
| A | C | A | B | D | B | B | B | A,B | D |
| **81** | **82** | **83** | **84** | **85** | **86** | **87** | **88** | **89** | **90** |
| C,D | C | D | B,D | D | D | D | C | D | A |
| **91** | **92** | **93** | **94** | **95** | **96** | **97** | **98** | **99** | **100** |
| B | C | A | A | A | C | C | C | D | D |
| **101** | **102** | **103** | **104** | **105** | **106** | **107** | **108** | **109** | **110** |
| A | C,D | D | B | B | C | B | C | D | D |
| **111** | **112** | **113** | **114** | **115** | **116** | **117** | **118** | **119** | **120** |
| B,D | C | B | D | D | C | B | B | A | C |
| **121** | **122** | **123** | **124** | **125** | **126** | **127** | **128** | **129** | **130** |
| B | D | C | D | D | C | C | D | D | D |
| **131** | **132** | **133** | **134** | **135** | **136** | **137** | **138** | **139** | **140** |
| B | C | A | C | B | B | B | B | D | B |
| **141** | **142** | **143** | **144** | **145** | **146** | **147** | **148** | **149** | **150** |
| B | D | B | D | B | C | D | A | B | B |
| **151** | **152** | **153** | **154** | **155** | **156** | **157** | **158** | **159** | **160** |
| B | B | C | C | A | B | D | C | B | C |
| **161** | **162** | **163** | **164** | **165** | **166** | | | | |
| D | B,C | A | A | C | A | | | | |

# 16.

1. Which of the following initiates the sequence of events that ultimately allows a user to `login`?
   A. `clri`      B. `sync`
   C. `login`     D. `init`

2. `getc(stdin)`
   A. results in run time error
   B. results in syntax error
   C. is equivalent to `getchar();`
   D. none of the above

3. Which of the following is not the work of a C-preprocessor?
   A. Macro expansion
   B. File inclusion
   C. Conditional compilation
   D. None of the above

4. Which of the following is used to write disk block images from memory to disk?
   A. `clri`      B. `sync`
   C. `mkfs`      D. `stty`

5. Choose the correct statement:
   A. To read successive characters from an open file, `getchar` and `scanf` can be used interchangeably
   B. To read successive characters from an open file, `getchar` and `read` can be used interchangeably
   C. The `read` system call reads from the buffer
   D. None of the above

6. The following program

```
main()

{
```

```
close(1);

print("How R U?");

}
```

   A. is syntactically incorrect
   B. results in a run-time error
   C. will wait indefinitely, if executed
   D. none of the above

7. The PID of the kernel process is:
   A. undefined      B. 0
   C. 1              D. 3

8. Choose the correct remarks.
   A. `exit` and `return` can be used interchangeably
   B. Use of `return` terminates the program
   C. Use of `exit` terminates the program
   D. `exit` returns a value to the system

9. Which of the following is an index to the array of open files maintained by the kernel for a user?
   A. i-node
   B. i-node number
   C. File descriptor
   D. File pointer

10. In which of the following directories does `init` reside?
    A. root       B. bin
    C. etc        D. usr

11. The command `cat > x`
    A. is invalid
    B. creates a file x and displays an error message

C. creates a file x and waits for the user to give input from the keyboard
D. none of the above

**12.** Which of the following are defined in `stdio.h` ?
A. EOF
B. NULL
C. BUFSIZE
D. None of the above

**13.** The `login prompt` can be changed by changing the contents of the file:
A. `inittab`  B. `init`
C. `passwd`  D. `gettydefs`

**14.** When the read system call encounters EOF, it returns:
A. some positive integer
B. some negative integer
C. 0
D. –1

**15.** Which of the following library functions do not return a pointer to the structure FILE?
A. `fopen`  B. `fclose`
C. `freopen`  D. `fwrite`

**16.** Which of the following processes are involved in the process of allowing a person to `login`?
A. `init`  B. `getty`
C. `login`  D. `kernel`

**17.** Which of the following system calls reads 8 bits from the standard input? (assume buff is a pointer to the buffer area)
A. `read (0, buff, 8)`
B. `read (1, buff, 8)`
C. `read (0, buff, 1)`
D. `read (1, buff, 1)`

**18.** Which of the following are implemented as macros (rather than functions)?
A. `getchar`  B. `getc`
C. `fgetc`  D. `fputc`

**19.** Choose the correct statements:
A. `errno` is an external variable available to any 'C' program

B. `errno` is set to a value when an error occurs
C. `errno` is cleared when a non-erroneous call is made
D. `errno` cannot be used to find the cause of an error

**20.** When the user responds to `login` prompt
A. `getty` forks `login` process
B. `login` process replaces `getty` process
C. a shell will be created
D. none of the above

**21.** To simulate the command "system", which of the system calls—`fork, wait` and `excel` is/are to be used?
A. `fork` and `wait`
B. `wait` and `excel`
C. `fork` and `excel`
D. all three

**22.** Consider the program

```
main ()
{
    print ("He arose a victor from/n"):
    system ("date");
    printf ("the dark domain");
}
```

If `a.out` is the executable code corresponding to the above source code, then the command `a.out > out f`
A. redirects the output of date to `file out f`
B. displays the output of date on the screen
C. prints everything on the screen
D. prints the two messages on the screen

**23.** The default permission bits of a file when it is created for the first time, is controlled by:
A. chmod value
B. fmask value
C. umask value
D. none of the above

**24.** Let x.c be a C source code. The command `cc x. c > y`

A. is equivalent to the command
```
cc x.c; mv a.out y
```
B. is equivalent to the command
```
cc -0 y x.c
```
C. serves no purpose
D. none of the above

**25.** Which of the following sections in the manual covers system calls?
A. 1       B. 2
C. 3       D. 4

**26.** Which of the following are not system calls?
A. chmod       B. open
C. iseek       D. getc

**27.** Choose the correct statements.
A. C programs can directly make system calls
B. System calls are functions used by the shell
C. Library functions use system calls
D. Library functions don't use system calls

**28.** Which of the following remarks about system calls, library functions and UNIX commands are true?
A. System call is a part of kernel, while the other two are not a part of kernel
B. Unlike library functions, system calls and Unix commands are stand-alone programs
C. Library functions and UNIX commands use system calls
D. Unlike system calls, library functions and UNIX commands are stand-alone programs

**29.** The 2 in the manual entry access (2)
A. implies access is a system call
B. implies access is a library function
C. refers to the section number
D. none of the above

**30.** If path is set to: .:/usr/x:/usr/bin, then:
A. the command one types will be first checked in the current directory, then /usr/x and /usr/bin.

B. if a command is found in both /usr/x and /user/bin, then the one in /usr/x will be executed
C. in the previous choice, what happens is unpredictable
D. if a command is found in both /usr/x and /usr/bin, then the one in /usr/bin will be executed

**31.** The command cd ./../.
A. serves no purpose
B. is invalid
C. is equivalent to cd..
D. none of the above

**32.** The UNIX tool awk
A. can do both numerical and string comparison
B. decides from the context whether the comparison is numerical or alphabetical
C. signals an error if an alphabet is compared with a number
D. all of the above

**33.** Which of the following strings will be matched by awk, if /(x+)*y!s/ is the specified pattern to be searched for?
A. x -x +x +y!$
B. x x x x y!$
C. x x xy!
D. none of the above

**34.** When awk encounters strings in arithmetic expressions,
A. it treats them as having the value 0
B. it treats them as having the value 1
C. it displays an error message
D. it is assigned an arbitrary value

**35.** Which of the following comments about awk are true?
A. It is a text processing language
B. Arrays can be indexed by string
C. It has features for redirecting its output
D. None of the above

**36.** Which of the following UNIX tools, receives input only from the standard input?

A. `awk`                    B. `grep`
C. `sed`                    D. `tr`

**37.** If `x.c` is a file, then `ed  x.c` creates a copy of `x.c` in:
A. `/etc`                   B. `/usr`
C. `/tmp`                   D. `/usr/bin`

**38.** The number of 3's in the output of the following C program

```
main()

(

   printf("1"); fork();

   printf("2"); fork();

   fork(); printf("3");

   )
```

is:
A. 1                        B. 8
C. 4                        D. 2

**39.** Which of the following processes has the PID 1?
A. kernel                   B. unix
C. init                     D. shell

**40.** Which of the following remarks about `fgrep` are true?
A. It is faster than `grep`
B. It is compact to use
C. It does not recognize any meta-character
D. It can simultaneously search for different patterns

**41.** When a process makes a system call, its mode changes from:
A. user to kernel
B. kernel to user
C. restricted to unrestricted
D. unrestricted to restricted

**42.** Choose the correct statements.
A. When a process makes a system call, a `context` switch is initiated
B. Kernel is not involved in servicing a system call
C. When a process making a system call has to wait for an event to occur, then

a process switch to the kernel process is initiated
D. System calls cannot be serviced in kernel mode

**43.** The command `ls > xy`
A. displays an error message, if `xy` exists and is write protected
B. if followed by `cat  xy`, lists `xy` also
C. redirects errors, if any, to `xy`
D. none of the above

**44.** Shell functions:
A. are another name for shell procedures
B. execute faster than shell procedures
C. are executed by a new shell
D. are not executed by a new shell

**45.** The `cc` command makes a total of:
A. 1 pass                   B. 2 passes
C. 4 passes                 D. 5 passes

**46.** Which of the following is not invoked when the `cc` command executes?
A. `/lib/cpp`               B. `/lib/cl`
C. `/bin/as`                D. `/bin/ld`

**47.** `creat` will fail, if:
A. there are too many open files
B. the `filename` is a directory
C. the named file already exists with its `write` permission off
D. the parent directory of the named file is `write` protected

**48.** Which of the following arguments to the open system call, will be discarded, if the named file already exists?
A. `O_TRUNC`                B. `O_APPEND`
C. `O_EXCL`                 D. `O_CREAT`

**49.** Under which of the following circumstances `rm /y/x`, cannot remove x?
A. If x is `write` protected, but y is not write protected
B. If x is not write protected, but y is `write` protected
C. If y has its execution permission bit off
D. All of the above

**50.** File pointer:
A. is a `long` integer
B. is of pointer data type
C. represents the position of the `read-write` head from the beginning of the file
D. none of the above

**51.** UNIX was developed by:
A. Bell Labs
B. Berkley Software Group
C. California University
D. American Defence Academy

**52.** Chocolate Chip is:
A. a latest Intel product
B. another name for BSD 4.2 Version
C. another name for System V
D. another name for System III

**53.** Which of the following features of UNIX may be used for inter process communication?
A. Signals
B. Pipes
C. Semaphore
D. Message Queues

**54.** Pick the incorrect statements.
A. Shell is a command interpreter
B. Shell is the interface between user and kernel
C. System can't work without a shell
D. Shell is a program

**55.** UNIX is:
A. a multi-user system
B. a real-time system
C. a multi-task system
D. name of a file in the root directory

**56.** Which of the following statements best explains a process?
A. It is a program
B. It is a program in execution
C. It is an instance of a program in execution
D. It is a program that uses system calls

**57.** In a system, if 5 people are currently using the vi editor, then the number of corresponding processes will be:
A. 1      B. 5
C. 2      D. 0

**58.** Kernel is not involved:
A. when a read operation is done
B. when a pressed key is echoed on to the screen
C. in resource allocation
D. none of the above

**59.** The command:
`echo welcome > /dev/tty`
A. echoes welcome in all the terminals that are switched on
B. echoes welcome in all the terminals that are logged on
C. echoes welcome only in the terminal in which it is run
D. signals the error message—Terminal number not specified

**60.** `/dev/null`
A. is a file
B. has write permission for all
C. is the UNIX built-in dustbin
D. none of the above

**61.** `m4`:
A. is a macro processor
B. can be used to preprocess C code
C. can be used to preprocess assembly language program
D. none of the above

**62.** The first thing that is searched when a command references a file is its:
A. i-node
B. i-node number
C. permission setting
D. none of the above

**63.** `cc` command sequentially invokes:
A. preprocessor, compiler and link editor
B. compiler and link editor
C. preprocessor, compiler, assembler and link editor
D. compiler, assembler and link editor

**64.** Among the directory entries, i-node and the file contents, which will be changed when a file is updated?
A. Only directory entry and file contents
B. Only i-node and file contents
C. All the three
D. None of the above

**65.** The `cc` command:
A. can take more than one argument
B. can act on files with `.c` or `.o` extension
C. creates `.o` files by default when more than one argument with `.c` extension is present
D. if provided with more than one argument, immediately terminates if the first argument fails to compile successfully

**66.** The `mv` command changes:
A. only the directory entry
B. only the directory entry and i-node
C. only the i-node number
D. none of the above

**67.** If 7 terminals are currently logged on, then the command

`date;who|wc-1`, displays:
A. `date` followed by 7
B. `date` followed by 8
C. `date` followed by 1
D. an error message

**68.** Choose the correct answers if the command `1s  -1/dev/mt0` displays `brw_rw_ _ _ _  1 root 3, 0 jan 18 11:05 mt0`
A. The 'b' indicates that it is a special file
B. `mt0` indicates that it is a tape drive
C. `mt0` indicates that it is a mounted tape
D. The 'b' indicates that data transfer is done in blocks

**69.** Choose the correct statements:
A. `1d x.o` is a valid command (assume `x.o` exists)
B. `1d x.o` is same as `cc x.o`

C. `cc x.s` is a valid command (assume `x.s` exists)
D. All of the above

**70.** `cat/dev/tty`
A. throws garbage onto the terminal `tty`
B. just echoes what you type, line by line
C. terminates if one types control `d`. at the beginning of a line
D. terminates if one types control `d`, anywhere in a line

**71.** Which of the following remarks about the `return` value of "wait" are true?
A. In case of normal termination (through `exit`), the lower byte of the `wait` status is set to zeroes
B. In case of abnormal termination, the lower byte of the `wait` status is set to zeroes
C. A core dump sets the seventh bit on
D. A process in `zombie` status sets the seventh bit on

**72.** The following C program

```
main()
{
    printf("WHATIZIT");
    system("date");
}
```

A. first prints `WHATIZIT` and then displays the output of `date` command in the next line
B. first prints `WHATIZIT` and then displays the output of `date` command in the same line
C. first displays the output of `date` command and then `WHATIZIT` in the next line
D. none of the above

**73.** The program

```
main()
{
    printf("x");
    fflush(stdout);
```

```
system ("date");
}
```

A. gives the same output as the program

```
main()
{
    printf("x\n");
    system(date);
}
```

B. prints x, before displaying date
C. prints x after displaying date
D. all of the above

**74.** An attempt to read from a locked file, results in:
A. prematured termination
B. a deadlock
C. an indefinite wait
D. none of the above

**75.** Which of the following is not a valid argument to the function `main` in a C program?
A. `errno`      B. `argc`
C. `envp`       D. `argv`

**76.** Mounting a file system results in the loading of:
A. boot block      B. super block
C. i-node table    D. all of these

**77.** Choose the correct statements.
A. If two users execute a file, two copies will be there in memory
B. Shareable programs are loaded into swap area
C. `chmod u+t filename`, is a valid command
D. None of the above

**78.** Go through the following C program

```
main()
{
    int i, n;
    for(i = 1; i <- n; ++i)
    fork();
    Printf("yes");
```

```
}
```

For what value of n, will `yes` be printed 24 times?
A. 3
B. 4
C. 5
D. Impossible to find such an n

**79.** Consider the following program

```
main()
{
    printf("God looks at the heart, not the hand/n");
    system ("date");
    printf ("The giver, not the gift");
}
```

If `a.out` is the executable file corresponding to the above program, then the command `a.out > x; cat x`
A. displays both the messages, with the output of `date` coming in between
B. displays the output of `date` before both the messages
C. does not display the first message
D. none of the above

**80.** The following program

```
main()
{
    if(fork()>0)
    sleep(100);
}
```

results in the creation of
A. an orphan process
B. a zombie process
C. a process that executes for ever
D. none of the above

**81.** A file x is created with the following contents

```
echo today is:
date
```

If you type x, then

A. it echoes the message, followed by date
B. it gives the desired output only if the `execute` permission of tile x is set
C. the desired output can be got by the command `sh x`, which works even if x has its `execute` permission not set
D. none of the above

**82.** Shell script is preferable to other forms of programming because it:
A. executes faster
B. enhances portability
C. occupies less space
D. makes programming task easier

**83.** Choose the incorrect statements.
A. Shell scripts can accept arguments
B. Shell scripts are interpreted
C. Shell is a programming language
D. Shell scripts are compiled

**84.** Files that store data in the same format as used in program are called:
A. binary files     B. source file
C. text file     D. core

**85.** To allow only one user to work with a particular file at a particular time, one has to use:
A. semaphore     B. critical region
C. locking     D. dedicated mode

**86.** Which of the following remarks about `realloc` are true?
A. It allocates memory of required size that need not be contiguous
B. It never shifts the existing block
C. It can work only with an existing block of memory
D. It may shift the existing block

**87.** The differences between `malloc()` and `calloc()` are:
A. `malloc` is used for dynamic allocation of memory, while `calloc` can't be used for that purpose
B. `malloc` needs only one argument, while `calloc` needs two
C. unlike `malloc`, `calloc` allocates memory and initializes it to 0.

D. `malloc` needs two arguments and `calloc` only one

**88.** The file that stores an integer as a sequence of characters is a:
A. text file     B. data file
C. binary file     D. core

**89.** If `cat x`, prints garbage, then x is probably a:
A. data file     B. binary file
C. text file     D. source file

**90.** Which of the following file names can be found in more than one directory?
A. `passwd`
B. `bin`
C. `date`
D. none of the above

**91.** The advantage of binary files over text files is that:
A. it is compact
B. it can be accessed faster
C. many commands (like cat) assume the named file to be a binary file
D. they are more reliable

**92.** The permission bits of a file `noname`, can be set to `_rws_ _x_ _x` by the command.
A. `chmod 711 noname`
B. `chmod go-rw noname`
C. `chmod 2711 noname`
D. none of the above

**93.** `/bin/passwd` has the user execution permission set to 's' because:
A. it is not executable
B. it should allow users who don't have write permission to `/etc/passwd` to write to it
C. `/etc/passwd` is `write` protected
D. this facility assigns to the user, permissions of the program owner, temporarily

**94.** If one doesn't want anyone else to read or write to a file named `datfile`, except through a program in file `filex`, then he may use:
A `chmod u+s filex; chmod go-rw datfile`

B. `chmod u+s datfile; chmod go-rw filex`

C. `chmod 4711 datfile; chmod go-rw filex`

D. `chmod 4711 filex; chmod go-rw datfile`

**95.** Writing a C program that accepts input from keyboard, rather than from a file is advantageous because:
A. keyboard is a file that is already open
B. it facilitates batch processing
C. it can be used in a pipe, if it writes to `stdout`
D. none of the above

**96.** Consider the following command that invokes the executable file `a.out`, with the following command line arguments

`a. out God loves you`

`argv[1][2]` corresponds to the character:
A. e          B. o
C. +          D. d

**97.** In the previous question after the operation argv++, the value of argv [1][2] will be:
A. e          B. d
C. v          D. undefined

**98.** Which of the following string functions can be used to find the last occurrence of a given character in a given string?
A. `strncmp`
B. `strncpy`
C. `strchr`
D. None of the above

**99.** Choose the correct statements:
A. The function `stat` refers a file by its name
B. The function `stat` refers a file by its file descriptor
C. The function `fstat` refers a file by its file descriptor
D. The function `fstat` refers a file by its name

**100.** Which of the following fields in the structure `stat`, has information about the permission setting of a file?

A. `st_gid`          B. `st_mode`
C. `st_ino`          D. `st_uid`

**101.** Which of the following shell script's looping features does not recognize the `break` command?
A. `while`
B. `until`
C. `for`
D. None of the above

**102.** Shell script:
A. needs no compilation
B. is ideal for manipulating a file, character by character
C. is not good in arithmetic operations
D. enhances portability

**103.** The desirable features of a new shell script you write is that:
A. it should take its input from `stdin`
B. on successful termination, it should exit with a non-zero value
C. it should not accept command line arguments
D. it does some cleaning up operation, on termination

**104.** Which of the following shell commands displays the contents of each of the command line arguments, one by one?
A. `cat $*`          B. `cat '$*'`
C. `cat "$"`          D. `cat "$*"`

**105.** The disadvantage of a pipe is that:
A. it is a one way communication channel
B. it dies along with the process that created it
C. it can't be shared by unrelated processes
D. none of the above

**106.** The state of signals are:
A. preserved across a `fork` call
B. not preserved across a `fork` call
C. not preserved across an `exec` call
D. preserved across an `exec` call

**107.** A `fork` system call with fail, if:
A. the previously executed statement is also a `fork` call

B. the limit on the maximum number of processes in the system would be exceeded

C. the limit on the maximum number of processes that can be under execution by a single user would be exceeded

D. all of the above

**108.** Which of the following options for the shell command `test` should be followed by the file descriptor?

A. `r`

B. `d`

C. `t`

D. `s`

**109.** Which of the following displays the `exit` status of the last executed command?

A. `echo $#`

B. `echo $$`

C. `echo $?`

D. `echo $!`

**110.** Which of the following file names cannot be displayed if `ls *` is run?

A. `-xy`

B. `?x`

C. `.x`

D. `hidden`

**111.** Which of the following results in an error?

A. `expr 4+5`

B. `expr 9-3`

C. `expr 2*3`

D. `expr 7/5`

**112.** Which of the following is not a command delimiter?

A. `new line`

B. `;`

C. `&`

D. `,`

**113.** A file `abc` has the following shell script in it.

```
cat $1 > $1.$$
```

The command `sh abc file1`

A. results in an error

B. is equivalent to `cp $1 $1.$$`

C. copies the contents of `file1` to another file that has the PID of the executing shell as its extension

D. none of the above

**114.** `*?*` will be the output of

A. `echo *?*`

B. `echo `*?*`'`

C. `echo "*?*"`

D. `echo *\?*`

**115.** Which of the following shell variables can be used to customize the editors (like `ex`, `vi`)?

A. PATH

B. IFS

C. HOME

D. EXINIT

Go through the following sequence of commands and answer the next two questions based on it.

```
$echo $x
$sh
$x=hai
$export x
$sh
```

**116.** `echo $x` will output

A. hai

B. garbage

C. an empty line

D. none of the above

**117.** If the command exit is run twice followed by running the command `echo $x`, the output will be:

A. hai

B. garbage

C. an empty line

D. none of the above

**118.** An orphan process:

A. is a child process that was terminated before the parent process

B. is adopted by the login shell

C. is adopted by the process dispatcher

D. will be denoted by the process status O

**119.** Which of the following calls never returns an error?

A. `getpid`

B. `fork`

C. `ioctl`

D. `open`

**120.** The following C program

```
main()
{
    fork();fork();printf("yes");
}
```

prints yes

A. only once      B. twice
C. 4 times      D. 8 times

**121.** The header files used in C programs are usually found in:
A. `/bin/include`
B. `/usr/bin/include`
C. `/dev/include`
D. `/usr/include`

**122.** The command `pwd` displays `/x/y`. After executing the command `chmod u-x`, which of the following commands will not work?
A. `cd..`      B. `ls`
C. `chmod u+x`      D. `pwd`

**123.** A C program should be compiled with `-g` option (like `cc -g x, c`) to use:
A. `prof`      B. `make`
C. `lprof`      D. `sdb`

**124.** The difference between a pipe and a regular file is that:
A. unlike a regular file, pipe is not a file
B. the data in a pipe is transient, unlike the contents of a regular file
C. pipes forbid random accessing, while regular files do allow this
D. all of the above

**125.** Choose the correct statements:
A. The default linking arrangement for `cc` is dynamic
B. Dynamically linked programs save disk storage
C. Dynamically linked programs enhances shareability of library routines
D. Dynamically linked programs can be fixed or enhanced without relinking the applications that depend on it

**126.** Context switch changes the process mode from:
A. user to kernel mode
B. kernel to user mode
C. kernel mode to the kernel process
D. kernel process to the kernel mode of some process

**127.** File `x.c` has 5 lines of code. The command
`date|tee abc|sort-x.c|wc -1,`
displays:
A. 5
B. 6
C. 0
D. an error message

**128.** Which of the following comments about the signals system call are true?
A. It takes up two arguments
B. The second argument, is a function call
C. The second argument is a pointer to a function
D. The first argument is an integer

**129.** `lint` can analyse the named source code for:
A. inconsistent usage
B. nonportability
C. suspicious constructs
D. none of the above

**130.** Which of the following characteristics of the original process are preserved when, the `exec` system call is executed?
A. The current working directory
B. The open files
C. PID
D. PPID

**131.** The shell command `cat x y > x`
A. doesn't work
B. replaces the contents of file x, by the contents of file y
C. does nothing, other than displaying an error message
D. none of the above

**132.** Which of the following return file descriptor?
A. `close`      B. `fopen`
C. `open`      D. `creat`

**133.** The simulate the who command, one has to access the file:
A. `/etc/passwd`
B. `/bin/.login`
C. `/etc/utmp`
D. `/usr/user_dat`

**134.** A file system in UNIX has the four sections—boot block, super block, I-list and data block that are arranged in the order:
  A. boot block, super block, I-list and data block
  B. boot block, data block, super block and I-list
  C. boot block, data block, I-list and super block
  D. super block, boot block, data block and I-list

**135.** `stderr, stdout, stdin` have the file descriptors:
  A. 0, 1, 2 respectively
  B. 0, 2, 1 respectively
  C. 1, 0, 2 respectively
  D. 2, 1, 0 respectively

**136.** Which of the following functions can be used to randomly access a file?
  A. `fgetc`          B. `getc`
  C. `fseek`          D. `ftell`

**137.** A manual entry of the form `xyz(3s)`
  A. implies `xyz` is a system call
  B. implies `xyz` is a library function
  C. means `xyz` is a library function that is part of the standard `i/o` package
  D. means `xyz` is a library function that is a part of the standard math library

**138.** The reference time adopted by UNIX is:
  A. Jan 1, 1970      B. Jan 1, 1980
  C. Jan 1, 1982      D. Jan 1, 1972

**139.** `perror()` can be simulated by using:
  A. `errno` and `sys_nerr`
  B. `sys_errlist` and `sys_nerr`
  C. `sys_errlist` and `errno`
  D. none of the above

**140.** A process that uses CPU, cannot continue to use it if:
  A. the CPU time slice expires
  B. a higher priority process arrives
  C. it has to wait for an event to happen
  D. it executes an `exit` statement

**141.** `/bin`
  A. is a bucket for storing information
  B. has files in binary code
  C. is a directory
  D. none of the above

**142.** The main reasons for the success of pipes are:
  A. the availability of many filter programs
  B. UNIX treats devices as files
  C. it provides a 2-way communication channel
  D. all of the above

**143.** Which of the following are not filter programs?
  A. `date`          B. `sort`
  C. `cat`           D. `grep`

**144.** Redirection in pipes can be achieved by using:
  A. `>`             B. `>>`
  C. `tee`           D. `lpr`

**145.** Choose the correct statements
  A. The symbols `>` and `|` are both processed by shell
  B. `>` can be used to direct output to a named file
  C. `|` can be used to direct output to programs
  D. Filter programs can be piped

**146.** The command `who|sort-file1 > file2`
  A. results in an error
  B. sorts the contents of `file1` and puts it in `file2`
  C. puts in `file2`, the sorted output of who, followed by sorted contents of `file1`
  D. none of the above

**147.** If the command `cat x`, is executed after successfully executing the command `time sort filename > x`, then:
  A. only the time details will be displayed
  B. only the sorted contents of the file `filename` will be displayed
  C. an error message will be displayed
  D. the sorted contents of the file

`filename`, along with the time information will be displayed

**148.** Which of the following information is not present in an i-node?
A. Contents of the file
B. Size of the file
C. Name of the file
D. Permission setting of the file

**149.** The system identifies a file by its:
A. name
B. absolute path
C. file owner
D. inode number

**150.** The system identifies the end of the file by the:
A. EOF character
B. file size
C. i-node number
D. none of the above

**151.** The command line argument `a.out x 'a b' 'c d'`
A. is acceptable
B. is acceptable if the double quotes are replaced by single quotes
C. is acceptable if the single quotes are replaced by double quotes
D. none of the above

**152.** Which of the following metacharacters will be recognized by the shell, even if it comes within double quotes?
A. $
B. *
C. ?
D. None of these

**153.** `lint` should be used:
A. before compilation
B. after compilation
C. to analyze a C code
D. none of the above

**154.** Environment variables can be accessed by:
A. system programs
B. C programs
C. shell scripts
D. none of the above

**155.** Which of the following are character special files?
A. Terminal
B. Printer
C. Modem
D. Tape Drive

**156.** If one exports a variable:
A. variables placed in the environment by a child process are not inherited by the parent process
B. it is passed to all its descendant processes
C. it dies when the shell that created it dies
D. only the first two choices are correct

**157.** Profilers are:
A. tools that analyze the run time behaviour of a program
B. tools that check a C code for cross file consistency
C. tools that keep track of evolving versions of a file
D. none of the above

**158.** The shell command:
A. does nothing
B. can be used to cause infinite looping
C. can take arguments but it cannot act on them
D. can be used to indicate a comment

**159.** Which of the following tools can be used to keep track of evolving versions of a file?
A. `make`
B. `yacc`
C. `sccs`
D. `dv`

**160.** The . (dot) shell command:
A. can take command line argument
B. will fork a child shell to execute the named shell script
C. can be used to change the environment of the current shell
D. all of the above

**161.** The C compiler can be modified to compile programs coded in other high level languages just by changing:
A. `/lib/ccom`
B. `/lib/c2`
C. `/lib/c1`
D. `/bin/as`

**162.** When a file is aliased:
A. a new directory entry is created
B. a new i-node is created
C. the i-node number is shared
D. none of the above

**163.** Setting the execute bit on has no meaning, if the file is a:
A. directory      B. shell script
C. C source code      D. symbol table

**164.** Which of the following sections of an executable binary file has all uninitialised data items?
A. `bss`      B. Data
C. Header      D. Symbol table

**165.** In which section of a process, the information about the arguments to the program are available?
A. Data      B. Text
C. Stack      D. User-block

**166.** Which of the following system calls transforms an executable binary file into a process?
A. `fork`      B. `exec`
C. `ioctl`      D. `longjmp`

**167.** UNIX was first installed in:
A. IBM-360      B. PDP/11
C. PDP/7      D. CRAY

**168.** PID is used by the system to identify:
A. a process
B. the file name
C. the i-node
D. all of the above

**169.** Choose the best answer:

Suspended processes are written onto a
A. swap area      B. dedicated area
C. ROM      D. critical area

**170.** Which of the following system calls, does not return control to the calling point, on termination?
A. `fork`      B. `exec`
C. `ioctl`      D. `longjmp`

**171.** Which of the following comments about semaphore are true?
A. It is an integer that can act as a counter
B. Its value depends on the number of resources to be shared
C. Its value is stored in the kernel

D. It can be used for resource synchronization

**172.** The following sequence of commands

```
grep x *.c > mn&
wc -1 mn&
rm mn&
```

produces the same result as the single command:
A. `grep x *.c | wc -1`
B. `wc -1 < grep x *.c`
C. `grep x *.c > wc -1`
D. none of the above

**173.** Choose the correct statements.
A. Kernel is non-preemptive
B. Interrupts are blocked when critical section of a code is being executed
C. No process can put another process to sleep
D. None of the above

**174.** Choose the correct statements:
A. A disk cannot have more than one file system stored in it
B. On the logical level, the kernel deals with disks rather than file system
C. The logical to physical device address mapping is done by the device driver
D. None of the above

**175.** Which of the following data structures is not maintained by the kernel?
A. User file descriptor table
B. File table
C. I-node table
D. None of the above

**176.** Choose the correct statements:
A. A file has only one associated i-node
B. I-node stands for index node
C. A particular i-node may correspond to more than one file
D. A file can have more than one associated i-node

**177.** The call `pipe(p);` is valid if p had been declared as:
A. `int p`      B. `int p[2]`
C. `char *p`      D. `FILE *p`

**178.** Choose the correct statements:
   A. When a program terminates, pipes are automatically closed
   B. If the `write` end of a pipe is closed then an attempted `read` from the other end results in a deadlock
   C. If the `write` end of a pipe is closed, then an attempted `read` from the other end, terminates the program
   D. None of the above

**179.** Consider the following program

```
#include<signal.h>

main()
{
    signal (SIGHT, mn);
    fork() ;
    fork() ;
    fork(; ;) ;
}
mn()
{
    printf("x/n");
}
```

Choose the correct statements.

Pressing the `<del>` key
   A. sends the signal, only to the parent process
   B. sends the signal, to all the four processes
   C. for the first time, prints x only once
   D. for the first time, prints x four times

**180.** Consider the following program

```
main()
{
    int p[2]
    pipe (p);
    fork();
}
```

Choose the correct statements.

   A. The pipe will be recognized only by the parent process
   B. `p[0]` is the file descriptor of the `write` end of the pipe
   C. There will be four file descriptors in memory
   D. The pipe will be shared by both the parent and the child processes

**181.** Which of the following remarks about `lex` are true?
   A. It generates a C program
   B. It produces a C code that consumes more memory than a C program that can be written separately to accomplish the same task
   C. It produces a C code that executes slower than a C program that can be written separately to accomplish the same task
   D. None of the above

**182.** Which of the following programs are not interactive?
   A. `passwd`        B. `date`
   C. `grep`          D. `sh`

**183.** `lex` can be used for:
   A. text processing
   B. code enciphering
   C. compiler construction
   D. collecting statistical data of different patterns

**184.** The number of errors in the following shell script

```
echo How are you?
read $answer
```

is:
   A. 0        B. 1
   C. 2        D. 3

**185.** The `read` in the previous question is a:
   A. library function
   B. system call
   C. shell command
   D. none of the above

**186.** If `lex.l` is a lex code then:
   A. the command `lex lex.l` invokes `lex` to act on `lex.l`

B. the command `lex lex.l` writes its output to the file `lex.yy.c`
C. `lex.yy.c` has the definition of the function `yylex`
D. `lex` library can be invoked by the compiler option `ll`

**187.** Choose the correct statements
A. Any process has an associated owner ID and group ID
B. Effective ID defines who you are for the duration of a process
C. Real ID defines who you are for the duration of a process
D. Effective ID is available in `/etc/passwd` file.

**188.** A file `hai` has the following shell script in it

```
echo oh! What a wonderful day
echo Day I will never forget 1>&2
echo Day I will never ever get
```

The command `sh hai > mn`:
A. puts all the three messages in mn
B. puts the second message both in mn and the screen
C. puts only the first and the third message in mn
D. results in an error

**189.** No shell script can take input from
A. `stdin`
B. the output of the previously executed command redirected to it
C. the file that holds the script
D. none of the above

**190.** The command `cc x.c && a.out`
A. is equivalent to `cc x.c;a.out`
B. means execute `a.out` only when `x.c` compiles successfully
C. means execute `a.out` only if `cc x.c` returns a value 0 to the system
D. all of the above

**191.** In UNIX, the status of a process may be:
A. `running`       B. `orphan`
C. `sleeping`      D. `zombie`

**192.** Consider the following program

```
main()
{
    int i = 7;
    if {0 == fork()}
    i += 10;
    else
    {
            wait(0);
            printf("%d", i);
    }
}
```

Choose the correct answers:
A. the statement `i += 10` is executed by the child only
B. The statement `i += 10` is executed by the parent only
C. The child can start executing, only after the termination of the parent process
D. None of the above

**193.** The value of i, printed by the above program will be:
A. 10
B. 7
C. 17
D. none of the above

**194.** The exception to the fact that any process in UNIX, has a parent is:
A. `dev`          B. `sh`
C. kernel         D. `login`

**195.** Which of the following are shared between a parent process and a child process?
A. External variables
B. Pointer variables
C. File pointers
D. Pipes

**196.** Consider the following C program

```
main()
{
```

```c
int j = 7, *i = &j;
if {0 == fork()}
*i = (*i + 10);
else
{
        wait(0);
        printf("%d", *i);
        }
}
```

The value of i that will be printed is:

A. 10
B. 7
C. 17
D. none of the above

197. In the previous question, if the declarations are made global (i.e. declared before `main()`), then the value of i that is printed will be:

A. 10
B. 7
C. 17
D. none of the above

198. Choose the correct statements:

A. Interrupts are caused by events that are external to a process
B. An exception condition is caused by an event external to a process
C. An exception condition happens in the middle of the execution of an instruction
D. An interrupts happens in the middle of the execution of an instruction

199. Consider the following program

```c
#include<signal.h>
mn();
main()
{
   signal (SIGINT, mn);
   for(; ;) ;
}
mn()
{
   printf("x/n");
}
```

On receipt of the signal SIGINT

A. the default action corresponding to SIGINT will be performed
B. the user defined function mn, will be executed
C. what happens depends on whether the signal is received for the first time or not
D. none of the above

200. In the previous question, if the statement `signal (SIGINT, mn);` is repeated thrice, then:

A. what happens depends on whether the signal is received for the first time or not
B. what happens depends on whether the signal is received for the fourth time or not
C. it cannot print the message more than three times
D. none of the above

## ANSWERS

| 1 | 2 | 3 | 4 | 5 | 6 | 7 | 8 | 9 | 10 |
|---|---|---|---|---|---|---|---|---|----|
| D | C | D | B | A | D | B | CD | C | C |

| 11 | 12 | 13 | 14 | 15 | 16 | 17 | 18 | 19 | 20 |
|----|-----|----|----|----|------|----|----|----|----|
| C | ABC | D | C | BD | ABCD | C | AB | AB | B |

| 21 | 22 | 23 | 24 | 25 | 26 | 27 | 28 | 29 | 30 |
|----|----|----|----|----|----|----|----|----|----|
| D | A | C | C | B | D | AC | AC | AC | AB |

| 31 | 32 | 33 | 34 | 35 | 36 | 37 | 38 | 39 | 40 |
|----|----|----|----|----|----|----|----|----|----|
| C | AB | D | A | ABC | D | C | B | C | BCD |
| **41** | **42** | **43** | **44** | **45** | **46** | **47** | **48** | **49** | **50** |
| AC | ABC | AB | BD | D | B | ABCD | D | BC | AC |
| **51** | **52** | **53** | **54** | **55** | **56** | **57** | **58** | **59** | **60** |
| A | B | ABCD | C | ACD | C | B | D | C | ABC |
| **61** | **62** | **63** | **64** | **65** | **66** | **67** | **68** | **69** | **70** |
| ABC | B | C | B | ABC | A | A | ABD | AC | BC |
| **71** | **72** | **73** | **74** | **75** | **76** | **77** | **78** | **79** | **80** |
| ACD | C | B | D | A | BC | ABC | D | B | B |
| **81** | **82** | **83** | **84** | **85** | **86** | **87** | **88** | **89** | **90** |
| BC | BCD | D | A | C | CD | BC | A | B | AB |
| **91** | **92** | **93** | **94** | **95** | **96** | **97** | **98** | **99** | **100** |
| ABD | D | BCD | AD | AC | D | C | D | AC | B |
| **101** | **102** | **103** | **104** | **105** | **106** | **107** | **108** | **109** | **110** |
| D | ACD | AD | AC | ABC | AC | BC | C | C | BC |
| **111** | **112** | **113** | **114** | **115** | **116** | **117** | **118** | **119** | **120** |
| C | D | BC | BCD | D | A | C | ACD | A | C |
| **121** | **122** | **123** | **124** | **125** | **126** | **127** | **128** | **129** | **130** |
| D | ABCD | D | BC | ABCD | AB | B | ACD | ABC | ABCD |
| **131** | **132** | **133** | **134** | **135** | **136** | **137** | **138** | **139** | **140** |
| B | CD | C | A | D | CD | BC | A | C | ABCD |
| **141** | **142** | **143** | **144** | **145** | **146** | **147** | **148** | **149** | **150** |
| BC | AB | A | C | ABCD | D | B | AC | D | B |
| **151** | **152** | **153** | **154** | **155** | **156** | **157** | **158** | **159** | **160** |
| A | A | AC | ABC | ABC | ABC | A | ABCD | C | C |
| **161** | **162** | **163** | **164** | **165** | **166** | **167** | **168** | **169** | **170** |
| A | AC | C | A | C | B | C | A | A | B |
| **171** | **172** | **173** | **174** | **175** | **176** | **177** | **178** | **179** | **180** |
| ABCD | D | ABC | C | D | ABC | B | AC | BD | CD |
| **181** | **182** | **183** | **184** | **185** | **186** | **187** | **188** | **189** | **190** |
| ABC | BC | ABCD | C | C | ABCD | AB | C | D | BC |
| **191** | **192** | **193** | **194** | **195** | **196** | **197** | **198** | **199** | **200** |
| ABCD | A | B | C | CD | B | B | AC | C | A |

1. When did the first ANSI programming language standard come out?
   A. 1949
   B. 1975
   C. 1958
   D. 1966

2. An electrical pathway within a computer is called _______.
   A. circuit
   B. line
   C. bus
   D. track

3. The fastest and most expensive type of storage device is a _______.
   A. electronic disk
   B. register
   C. cache
   D. magnetic tape

4. The PA-RISC 2.0 processors implement which cache architecture ?
   A. Harvard
   B. Von Neumann
   C. Crafton
   D. None of the above

5. How many multi-chip modules (MCM) are therein every node in the Cray XI ?
   A. 1
   B. 2
   C. 3
   D. 4

6. The four access modes that memory management of the VAX architecture uses are _______.
   A. general, executive, supervisor, and user
   B. kernel, executive, supervisor, and user
   C. kernel, executive, manager, and user
   D. kernel, executive, supervisor, and worker

7. Which of the following are features of the object-oriented approach to databases?
   A. The ability to develop database models based on location rather than state and behaviour.
   B. The ability to develop more realistic models of the real world.
   C. The ability to develop databases using natural language approaches.
   D. The need to split objects into their component parts.

8. One of the things that separates a "Terminal" from a "PC" is that the terminal does not have a what ?
   A. Keyboard
   B. Monitor
   C. Power cord
   D. CPU

9. The device that can convert images on a page to electronic signals that can be stored in a computer, is known as _______.
   A. scanner
   B. monitor
   C. plotter
   D. mouse

10. A package, which can be used for a short period before purchasing it is termed _______.
    A. try and buy
    B. freeware
    C. shareware
    D. borrow-ware

11. A spreadsheet is the BEST application for _______.
    A. handling simple accounts
    B. writing a report which include tables
    C. producing a grid-referenced map
    D. keeping an inventory of equipment used

12. Which piece of hardware do you need to connect to the Internet ?

A. An ISP account
B. A modem
C. A browser
D. Internet Explorer

**13.** Anti-virus software should be configured to ______.
A. start along with your system
B. stop when you connect to the Internet
C. start when selected from the Programs menu
D. stop when you are sending an e-mail

**14.** The term HTTP stands for ______.
A. hyper terminal tracing program
B. hypertext tracing program
C. hypertext transfer protocol
D. hypertext tracing protocol

**15.** Protocol is ______.
A. software that facilitates connection to the internet
B. a list of rules for transferring data over a network
C. software that allows file copying
D. a gateway calling program for internet bridging

**16.** People who break in computer systems for malicious purposes are known as ______.
A. hackers
B. thieves
C. crackers
D. security experts

**17.** During normal IP packet forwarding by a router, which of the following fields of the IP header is/are updated ?
A. Source address
B. Destination address
C. TTL
D. Checksum

**18.** In data communications, flow control:
A. can be implemented using the CSMA/CD protocol.
B. makes a channel an error free one.
C. enables two computers running at different speeds to ta to each other.
D. cannot be implemented on a simplex link.

**19.** A prdgram requests memory that the memory manager can't provide in Windows 9. This is referred to as a ______.
A. Page out
B. Page fault
C. Disk block
D. Rap block

**20.** Which of the following elements of an REA data model does not necessarily generate a relational table ?
A. Agents
B. Resources
C. Events
D. One to many relationships

**21.** Which type of software would you use to store medical records ?
A. Spreadsheet software
B. Database software
C. Desktop publishing software
D. Word processing software

**22.** The purpose of performance testing is to ______.
A. prove response times are acceptable
B. prove printed output is acceptable
C. find errors in software
D. test with invalid input data.

**23.** The data type and format of every data item in a system is held in a ______.
A. data dictionary
B. entity-matrix
C. domain list
D. data analysis grid

**24.** What is the process that uses hardware and software to "imitate" a computer system in order to run programs that would otherwise be incompatible?
A. Mapping
B. Cloning
C. Migration
D. Emulation

**25.** The approach to systems development that involves having someone else do part or all of the data processing activities for you is called ______.
A. prototyping
B. subcontracting
C. outsourcing
D. designing

26. System documents are important because ______.
    A. they serve as communication tools within the development team
    B. they are the only way of monitoring project progress
    C. they are intended to be used as a help file for the user
    D. they avoid repetition of work when a team member leaves the project

27. A syntax error is signalled by the :
    A. compiler
    B. linker
    C. editor
    D. run time system

28. A run-time error is ALWAYS caused by ______.
    A. division by zero
    B. incorrect logic
    C. error in syntax
    D. incorrect linkage

29. A translator that translates the entire source program into machine language before executing any of the instructions, is known as ______.
    A. compiler
    B. interpreter
    C. query language
    D. high-level language

30. The first generation computers were general purpose computing machine in which ______ technology was used.
    A. Vacuum Tube
    B. Transistors
    C. Integrated circuits
    D. Registers

31. The Central Processing Unit (CPU) constitutes ______.
    A. Arithmetic Logic Unit (ALU) only
    B. Control Unit (CU) only
    C. Both ALU & CU
    D. Operational registers, ALU and CU

32. The descending order of a data hierarchy is ______.
    A. Bit-Byte-Record-File-Field-Database
    B. Database-File-Record-Field-Byte-Bit
    C. Byte-Bit-Field-Record-Database-File
    D. None of the above

33. Computers have been classified under following classes, mark the wrong choice if any ______.
    A. Micro Computers
    B. Mini Computers
    C. Mainframes
    D. All of the above

34. A program whose function is to start the computer software operating when power is turned on is known as ______.
    A. Loader
    B. Compiler
    C. Linker
    D. Boot strap loader

35. Which of the following is correct?
    A. Serial transmission is faster than parallel transmission
    B. Serial transmission is slower than parallel transmission
    C. Communication between computers are always parallel
    D. All of the above

36. Macromedia is a name of a company related with ______
    A. Hardware        B. Software
    C. Periperals      D. Services

37. What is the name of the series of Laptop computers manufactured by IBM called?
    A. LapPad          B. ThinkPad
    C. Aptiva          D. Notepaq

38. Which company did SCO sue for using code UNIX in its Operating System?
    A. RedHat          B. SuSE
    C. IBM             D. Microsoft

39. Who is the founder of BSD Unix?
    A. Bill Gates
    B. Dennis Ritche
    C. Bill Joy
    D. Linux Torvalds

**40.** Which computer periperal manufacturer quotes - Empowering your PC_______
A. Canon
B. Epson
C. Mercury
D. Samsung

**41.** Nortel is a company into manufactures -
A. Software
B. Processors
C. Cables
D. Network equipment

**42.** Who among the following is a Personal Computer manufacturer from Taiwan—
A. Sony
B. IBM
C. Samsung
D. Acer

**43.** Direct X is a _______
A. Computer Part
B. Software that drives Graphic hardware
C. A User Interface
D. None of these

**44.** A Pixel is_______
A. A computer program that draws picture
B. A picture stored in secondary memory
C. The smallest resolvable part of a picture
D. None of these

**45.** In a high resolution mode, the number of dots in a line will usually be—
A. 320
B. 640
C. 760
D. 900

**46.** Which of the memories below is often used in a typical computer operation?
A. RAM
B. ROM
C. FDD
D. HDD

**47.** Time taken to move from one cylinder of a hdd to another is called
A. Transfer rate
B. Average seek time
C. Latency
D. Roundtrip time

**48.** Who is the founder of Oracle Corporation?
A. Bill Gates
B. Lars Ellison
C. Andrew S Grove
D. Marc Anderson

**49.** The dominant graphical scheme for OOAD is _______.
A. UML
B. IML
C. GUI
D. MFC

**50.** _____________ diagrams in UML show relationships between classes.
A. collaboration
B. structure
C. class
D. inheritance

**51.** What is the intersection of set A {1, 2, 3} and set B {2, 3, 4}?
A. {1, 2, 3, 4}
B. {2, 3}
C. {1, 4}
D. {1, 2, 2, 3, 3, 4}

**52.** How many shades of red are there in the RGB color scheme?
A. 16
B. 64
C. 256
D. 512

**53.** For each item in a list, which tag is used?
A. <ITEM>
B. <LI>
C. <DL>
D. <OL>

**54.** Which tag in a definition list precedes each term?
A. <DL>
B. <DD>
C. <DT>
D. <TERM>

**55.** What color is represented by "#FF0000"?
A. Bright green
B. Black
C. Bright Red
D. Bright Blue

**56.** Which of the following examples of escaping from HTML to PHP is incorrect?
A. <?php echo("Hello World"); ?>
B. <$ echo("Hello World"); $>
C. <? echo("Hello World"); ?>
D. <% echo("Hello World"); %>

**57.** Which of the following is not a basic data type in PHP?
A. boolean
B. string
C. integer
D. date time

**58.** Which of the following is an invalid variable name in PHP?
A. $CT216
B. $ct216
C. $216ct
D. $ ct216

**59.** How is a variable's data type specified in PHP?
- A. A data type is declared for each variable in the source code.
- B. A data type is automatically determined when the variable is first assigned to.
- C. There are no data types in PHP.
- D. Data types are determined through a super-global array.

**60.** Which two methods can be used to submit data to a web server?
- A. GET and POST
- B. GET and API
- C. POST and API
- D. None of the above.

**61.**
```php
<?php
$a = "3";
$b = '4';
$c = '5$a';
$d = "$c$b";
?>
```

After the above PHP code is executed, what is the value of $d?
- A. $c$b
- B. 5$a4
- C. 534
- D. None of the above

**62.** Which one of the following is not typically provided by Source Code Management software?
- A. Synchronisation
- B. Versioning and revision history
- C. Syntax highlighting
- D. Project forking

**63.** In HTTP communications, what role does the web browser play?
- A. As a client
- B. As a server
- C. Both A and B
- D. None of the above

**64.** Which of the following is not found in a URL?
- A. path
- B. post
- C. protocol
- D. port

**65.** Which of the following character combinations are used to separate name/value pairs in a HTTP query string?
- A. $ and &
- B. = and &
- C. / and =
- D. $ and /

**66.** Which statement is false?
- A. Not all internet servers are part of the World Wide Web.
- B. The default port number for HTTP is 80.
- C. HTTP responses always return HTML.
- D. None of the above.

**67.** Who was the father of Punched Card Processing?
- A. J. Presper Eckert
- B. Charles Babbage
- C. Dr. Herman Hollerith
- D. Blaise Pascal

**68.** A factor which would strongly influence a business person to adopt a computer is its:
- A. Accuracy
- B. Reliability
- C. Speed
- D. All of these

**69.** In which year were chips used inside the computer for the first time?
- A. 1964
- B. 1975
- C. 1977
- D. 1981

**70.** The first microprocessor built by the Intel Corporation was called:
- A. 8008
- B. 8080
- C. 4004
- D. 8800

**71.** What was the name of the first commercially available microprocessor chip?
- A. Intel 8008
- B. Intel 8080
- C. Intel 4004
- D. Motorola 6809

**72.** When was the first minicomputer built?
- A. 1965
- B. 1962
- C. 1971
- D. 1966

**73.** The first digital computer built with IC chips was known as:
- A. IBM 7090
- B. Apple-1
- C. IBM System/360
- D. VAX-780

**74.** Which one of the following is the first second-generation computer?
A. IBM 7090
B. IBM 801
C. IBM 7070
D. IBM 650

**75.** Which computer was the first to use the magnetic drum for memory?
A. IBM-650
B. IBM-7090
C. IBM-701
D. PDP-1

**76.** What is the name of the British gentleman who was the first to put forward in 1952 the idea for the integrated circuit?
A. Jack S. Kilby
B. G.W. Dummer
C. William Shockley
D. John Bardeen

**77.** The magnetic tape consists of a plastic tape with a surface coating of magnetic material. When was it invented?
A. 1968
B. 1964
C. 1956
D. 1946

**78.** In the third generation of computers:
A. Distributed data processing first became popular
B. An operating system was first developed
C. High-level procedural languages were first used
D. On-line, realtime systems first became popular

**79.** To produce high-quality graphics (hardcopy) in colour, you would want to use a/an:
A. RGB monitor
B. Plotter
C. Ink-Jet printer
D. Laser printer

**80.** The personal-computer industry was started by:
A. IBM
B. Apple
C. Compaq
D. HCL

**81.** The word size of a microprocessor refers to:
A. The amount of information that can be stored in a byte
B. The amount of information that can be stored in a cycle
C. The number of machine operations performed in a second
D. The maximum length of an English word that can be input to a computer

**82.** When was the IBM XT microcomputer released in the market?
A. 1970
B. 1971
C. 1987
D. 1986

**83.** Bar codes store information using:
A. Punch holes
B. Thick and thin lines
C. Magnetized spots
D. Bits

**84.** A group of integrated parts is called:
A. system
B. swapping
C. circuits
D. system analysis

**85.** Which is an electronic device that can store temporarily a single bit of data.
A. Accumulator
B. Buffer
C. Memory
D. Latch

**86.** The first generation computers were characterised by:
A. Micro processor chips
B. Thermionic valves
C. Transistors
D. Integrated circuits

**87.** The speed of third generation computer is:
A. 10 sec
B. 5 nano sec
C. 25 sec
D. 64 sec

**88.** Which type of computers accuracy is superhigh.
A. Optical
B. Hidden
C. Hybrid
D. Digital

**89.** A modern digital computer has:
A. Extremely high speed
B. Large memory
C. Almost unlimited array
D. All of these

**90.** Which company is the biggest player in the microprocessor industry?
A. Motorola
B. IBM
C. Intel
D. AMD

**91.** What is the full form of COBOL?
A. Common Business Objective Language
B. Command Byte Oriented Language
C. Common Business Oriented Language
D. Character Business Oriented Language

**92.** Find the invalid combination:
A. Dot Matrix Printer - Impact Printer
B. Laser Printer - Non Impact Printer
C. Daisy wheel printer - Non Impact Printer
D. Inkjet printer - Non Impact Printer

**93.** In which generation of computers, Transistors were used?
A. First generation computers
B. Second generation computers
C. Third generation computers
D. Fourth generation computers

**94.** Which computer system is mainly used in Weather forecasting and Disaster control?
A. Super computer
B. Mainframe computer
C. Micro computer
D. Personal computer

**95.** Which of the following devices can be used to directly input 'Text books'?
A. OCR
B. OMR
C. MICR
D. None of these

**96.** Ascending order of a data hierarchy is:
A. Bit-byte-record-field-file-database
B. Bit-byte-field-record-file-database
C. Byte-bit-record-file-database
D. None of the above

**97.** Personal computers are also called:
A. Desktop computers
B. Portable computers
C. Advanced computers
D. Palmtop computers

**98.** ENIAC stands for
A. Electronic Number Instruction and Code
B. Electronic Number Integrated and Calculator
C. Electronic Number Instruction Access Calculator
D. None of these

**99.** An IP address contains four sets of numbers ranging from:
A. 1 to 100
B. 1 to 1000
C. 0 to 255
D. 1 to 500

**100.** *X-MP* is Models of:
A. Micro Computer
B. Mini Computer
C. Main Frame Computer
D. Super Computer

**101.** Which of the following is an example of nonvolatile memory?
A. ROM
B. VLSI
C. LSI
D. RAM

**102.** Which is used for manufacturing chips?
A. Bus
B. Control unit
C. Semiconductors
D. A and B only

**103.** The computer code for the interchange of information between terminals is:
A. ASCII
B. BCD
C. EBCDIC
D. All of these

**104.** A byte is comprised of:
A. one bit
B. four bits
C. eight bits
D. sixteen bits

**105.** The CPU chips used in a computer is partially made up of:
A. copper
B. iron
C. gold and silver
D. silica

**106.** The silicon chips used for data processing are called:
A. RAM chips
B. ROM chips
C. micro processor
D. PROM chips

**107.** The hardware in which data may be stored for a computer system is called:
A. Registers
B. Bus
C. Control unit
D. Memory

**108.** A half byte is known as:
A. Data
B. Bit
C. Half byte
D. Nibble

**109.** The most common binary code in use today is the 8 bit ASCII code. What do the letters ACII stand for?
A. American Standard Code for International Interchange

B. American Standard Code for Information Interchange

C. American Standard Code for Intelligence Interchange

D. American Scientific Code for Information Interchange

**110.** One thousand bytes represent a:
 A. mega byte
 B. giga byte
 C. kilo byte
 D. None of these

**111.** CD-ROM is a:
 A. Semiconductor memory
 B. Memory register
 C. Magnetic memory
 D. None of these

**112.** Which of the following is the user programmed semiconductor memory?
 A. SRAM
 B. DRAM
 C. EPROM
 D. All of the above

**113.** Which of the following is not a primary storage device?
 A. Magnetic tape
 B. Magnetic disk
 C. Optical disk
 D. None of the above

**114.** A name or number used to identify a storage location is called:
 A. A byte
 B. A record
 C. An address
 D. All of these

**115.** A memory bus is mainly used for communication between:
 A. processor and memory
 B. processor and I/O devices
 C. I/O devices and memory
 D. input device and output device

**116.** Which chips are erasable by ultra-violet rays after removing them from the main circuit?
 A. EPROM chips
 B. EEPROM chips
 C. PROM chips
 D. All of these

**117.** EPROM consists of:
 A. bipolar transistors
 B. easily erasable
 C. MOSFETs
 D. Diodes

**118.** Which of the following is used only for data entry and storage, and never for processing?
 A. Mouse
 B. Dumb terminal
 C. Microcomputer
 D. None of these

**119.** Different components on the motherboard of a PC processor unit are linked together by sets of parallel electrical conducting lines. What are these lines called?
 A. Conductors
 B. Buses
 C. Connectors
 D. None of these

**120.** Where have the program and data to be located before the ALU and control unit of a computer can operate on it?
 A. Internal memory
 B. Secondary memory
 C. Microprocessor
 D. Magnetic tapes

**121.** What is the name of the logic circuit which can add two binary digits?
 A. Full adder
 B. Half adder
 C. Buffer
 D. Register

**122.** A microcomputer has primary memory of 640K. What is the exact number of bytes contained in this memory?
 A. $64 \times 1000$
 B. $640 \times 100$
 C. $640 \times 1024$
 D. either B or C

**123.** Two new types of semiconductor memories are:
 A. Magnetic disks
 B. Charge-coupled devices
 C. Magnetic bubble memory
 D. Both B and C

**124.** Magnetic tape is used for:
 A. Historical storage
 B. Computer input
 C. Both A and B
 D. Neither A nor B

**125.** A characteristic of the ASCII code is:
A. its use of the zone code 1010, 1011 and 1100
B. its limitation to a maximum of 96 character configurations
C. its independence from the Hollerith code
D. All of the above

**126.** A temporary storage area, attached to the CPU, for I/O operations is a:
A. Chip
B. Buffer
C. Register
D. Core

**127.** In magnetic disks, data is organized on the platter in a concentric sets of rings called:
A. Sector
B. Track
C. Head
D. Block

**128.** A dumb terminal can do nothing more than communicate data to and from a CPU of a computer. How does a 'smart' terminal differ from a dumb terminal?
A. It has a primary memory
B. It has a cache memory
C. It has a microprocessor
D. It has an input device

**129.** A code used for standardizing the storage and transfer of information amongst various computing devices is called:
A. CRT
B. CPU
C. ASCII
D. dvorak

**130.** What is the name of the storage device which is used to compensate for the difference in rates of flow of data from once device to another?
A. Cache
B. Concentrator
C. Buffer
D. I/O device

**131.** Which is the most popular medium for direct-access secondary storage of a computer?
A. Magnetic tape
B. Magnetic disk
C. RAM
D. ROM

**132.** The standard size reel of magnetic tape is:
A. 120 feet in length
B. 240 feet in length
C. 1200 feet in length
D. 2400 feet in length

**133.** Conversion of decimal number $89_{10}$ it's binary number equivalent is:
A. $1011011_2$
B. $1100111_2$
C. $1011001_2$
D. $10011_2$

**134.** A type of semiconductor memory that usually has small capacity but very fast access is:
A. PROM
B. RAM
C. scratchpad
D. ROM

**135.** A single primary storage location in the processor unit:
A. can hold several different data items at the same time
B. can hold data items but not program instructions
C. is identified by a built-in and unique number called an address
D. is identified by a number that varies with the contents in the location

**136.** A storage device where the access time is dependent upon the location of the data is:
A. Random access
B. Serial access
C. Sequential access
D. Transaction access

**137.** A memory that holds microprograms is:
A. core memory
B. ROM
C. RAM
D. control memory

**138.** Octal numbers are used:
A. In computer hardware
B. When binary numbers are too long
C. Internal to the computer
D. In perference to 'hex' number

**139.** Binary numbers need more places for counting because:

A. They are always big numbers
B. Any no. of 0's can be added in front of them
C. Binary base is small
D. 0's and 1's have to be properly spaced apart

**140.** Any type of storage that is used for holding information between steps in its processing is:
A. CPU
B. Primary storage
C. Intermediate storage
D. Internal storage

**141.** *PROM* is a type of computer memory. What does *PROM* stands for?
A. Powered Read Only Memory
B. Programmable Read Only Memory
C. Permanent Read Only Memory
D. Powered Read Only Memory

**142.** Which one of the following is not a correct definition?
A. SRAM→Static Random Access Memory
B. PROM→Programmable Read Only Memory
C. DRAM→Dynamic Random Access Memory
D. SAM→Static Access Memory

**143.** Which of the following are the type of the secondary storage?
A. Floppy Disk & Hard Disk
B. Floppy Disk & ROM
C. Hard Disk & RAM
D. None of the above

**144.** Who defined the binary number system?
A. Pascal
B. A.D. Leibniz
C. Newton
D. Aristotle

**145.** Find the valid statements:
A. A floppy has more capacity than a hard disk
B. Hard disk is a primary memory device
C. RAM stands for read access memory
D. ROM is a permanent memory

**146.** Which statement is not correct about Third Generation computer?
A. The computers were relatively inexpensive than second generation computers.
B. Replaced transistors with ICs (integrated Circuits)
C. The size of the computer was same as fourth generation computer
D. None of these

**147.** Pentium, Power PC was/were the example(s) of:
A. First Generation Computers
B. Second Generation Computers
C. Third Generation Computers
D. Fourth Generation Computers

**148.** Which of the following is/are not correct statement(s) about the third generation computer?
A. The third generation computers replaced small scale integrated circuits and medium scale integrated circuits with the microprocessors chip.
B. The hard-disks are available of the sizes up to 200 GB. The RAID technology (Redundant Array of Inexpensive Disks) gives storage up to thousands of GB.
C. Computer cost came up rapidly in this generation.
D. Application of computers is increased in various areas like visualization, parallel computing, multimedia etc.

**149.** Name the first calculating device developed by Chinese:
A. Abacus
B. Napier Bones
C. Analytical Engine
D. Pebbles

**150.** What is the full form of ATM?
A. Auto Tailoring Machine
B. Any Time Money
C. Automatic Teller Machine
D. All Time Money

**151.** Who is known as father of electronics communication age?
A. Charles Babbage
B. George Boole
C. Claude Shannon
D. John Napier

**152.** In which computers, computation are carried out with physical quantities?
A. Digital
B. Analog
C. Hybrid
D. All of the above

**153.** A hybrid computer——
A. Resembles digital computer
B. Resembles analog computer
C. Both of these
D. None of these

**154.** Which generation of computers is covered by the period 1964-77?
A. First
B. Second
C. Third
D. Fourth

**155.** An Integrated Circuit (IC) is:
A. Fabricated on a tiny silicon chip
B. A complicated circuit
C. Much costlier than a single transistor
D. An integrating device

**156.** Where was the India's first computer installed and when?
A. Institute of Social Science, Agra, 1955
B. Indian Institute of Statistics, Delhi, 1957
C. Indian Statistical Institute, Calcutta, 1955
D. Indian Institute of Science, Bangalore, 1971

**157.** The first electronic digital computer contained?
A. Electronic valves
B. Vacuum tubes
C. Transistors
D. Semiconductor memory

**158.** The first computer made available for commercial use was:
A. Mark-I
B. ENIAC
C. EDSAC
D. UNIVAC

**159.** The fifth generation digital computer will be:
A. extremely low cost
B. very expensive
C. versatility
D. artificial intelligence

**160.** The third generation of computer covers the period:
A. 1971-1982
B. 1982-1994
C. 1959-1964
D. 1964-1977

**161.** First generation computers are characterized by:
A. vacuum tube and magnetic drum
B. magnetic tape and transistors
C. micro computers
D. All of the above

**162.** What was the computer conceived by Babbage?
A. Analytical Engine
B. Arithmetic Machine
C. Donald Knuth
D. All of the above

**163.** The first IBM PC did not have any:
A. disk drive
B. RAM
C. ROM
D. Port

**164.** The process of starting or restarting a computer system by loading instruction from a secondary storage device into the computer memory is called:
A. Duping
B. Booting
C. Padding
D. All of the above

**165.** Who invented the microprocessor?
A. Marcian E Huff
B. Herman H Goldstein
C. Joseph Jacquard
D. All of the above

**166.** When was the first IBM microcomputer called IBM PC with 16-bit microprocessor introduced?
A. 1979
B. 1981
C. 1982
D. 1984

**167.** In which year were chips used inside the computer for the first time?
A. 1964      B. 1975
C. 1977      D. 1981

**168.** What was the name of the first commercially available microprocessor chip?
A. Intel 8008      B. Intel 8080
C. Intel 4004      D. Motorola 6809

**169.** When was the first minicomputer built?
A. 1965      B. 1962
C. 1971      D. 1966

**170.** Third generation computers are those which are built with integrated circuits. What was the name of the first third-generation computer and when was it introduced?
A. IBM-1620, 1964      B. 1960, USA
C. CDC-6600, 1962      D. PDP-1401

**171.** IBM 7000 digital computer:
A. belongs to second generation
B. uses VLSI
C. employes semi conductor memory
D. has modular construction

**172.** The proper definition of a modern digital computer is:
A. an electronic automated machine that can solve problems involving words and numbers
B. a more sophisticated and modified electronic pocket calculator
C. any machine that can perform mathematical operations
D. a machine that works on binary code

**173.** Which out of the following is the least expensive computer?
A. Home computer
B. Laptop microcomputer
C. Personal computer
D. Desktop computer

**174.** In analog computer:
A. input is first converted to digital form
B. input is never converted to digital form

C. output is displayed in digital form
D. All of the above

**175.** All of the following became popular during the fourth generation of computers except:
A. Minicomputers
B. Semiconductors
C. CRT terminals
D. Personal computers

**176.** The first generation of computers available was based on the bit micro processors.
A. 4      B. 8
C. 16      D. 64

**177.** Data processing computer built to conventional architecture is known as:
A. Super computer      B. Mainframe
C. Micro computer      D. Mini computer

**178.** The speed of third generation computer is:
A. 10 sec      B. 5 nano sec
C. 25 sec      D. 64 sec

**179.** The memory capacity of an old mini computer was:
A. 640 KB      B. 256 KB
C. 250 KB      D. 1024 KB

**180.** Third generation computers:
A. were the first to use integrated circuitry
B. were the first to use built-in error detecting devices
C. used transistors instead of vacuum tubes
D. All of the above

**181.** In which generation did magnetic disk started being used for storage?
A. First generation computer
B. Second generation computer
C. Third generation computer
D. Fourth generation computer

**182.** Operating System concept started in———.
A. First generation computer
B. Second generation computer
C. Third generation computer
D. Fourth generation computer

**183.** The time period of third generation computer is:
A. 1965-75
B. 1942-1955
C. 1956-1964
D. 1976 onwards

**184.** A German mathematician who invented a calculator, for addition, subtraction, multiplication and division, his name was ————.
A. Napier
B. Pascal
C. Leibniz
D. Hollerith

**185.** Who invented analytical machine?
A. Charles Babbage
B. Hollerith
C. Pascal
D. Napier

**186.** Modern computers are very reliable but they are not:
A. Fast
B. Powerful
C. Infallible
D. Cheap

**187.** A complete microcomputer system consists of:
A. Microprocessor
B. Memory
C. Peripheral equipment
D. All of the above

**188.** Modem is a/an ————.
A. input device
B. output device
C. both A and B
D. storage device

**189.** Computer peripherals do not include:
A. UPS
B. Speaker
C. Microphone
D. Microwave

**190.** This device helps us to change our voice into electronic signals, is called:
A. Speakers
B. Mouse
C. Microphone
D. Motherboard

**191.** Which one of the following is Essential Peripheral?
A. Printer
B. Keyboard
C. Mouse
D. All of the above

**192.** Which is not a 'Computer Peripherals'?
A. Scanner
B. Speaker
C. CPU
D. Printer

**193.** ———— is an input device used for playing computer games.
A. Scanner
B. Joystick
C. Light pen
D. Microphone

**194.** ———— is a small pen—like device that has a large storing capacity.
A. Light pen
B. Joystick
C. Pen drive
D. Bar code reader

**195.** The output that is printed on paper is called:
A. Hard copy
B. Soft copy
C. Both A and B
D. None of the above

**196.** In which kind of printers, a light beam is used to print?
A. Dot-matrix printers
B. Line printers
C. Inkjet printers
D. Laser printers

**197.** ———— printers are used for very good quality printout.
A. Dot-matrix
B. Line
C. Inkjet
D. Laser

**198.** Mouse, Keyboard, Monitor and Printer etc are examples of:
A. Software
B. Memory
C. Peripherals
D. CPU

**199.** Which kind of hardware is used the most in the input phase of a computer?
A. Keyboard
B. Storage devices
C. Monitor
D. Hard disk

**200.** Which is not an input device?
A. CRT (Cathode Ray Tube)
B. Optical scanners
C. Voice recognition devices
D. COM (Computer Micro film)

**201.** Which is considered a direct entry input device?
A. Optical scanner
B. Mouse
C. Light pen
D. All of the above

**202.** What of the following terms is related to a monitor?
A. Screen
B. Monochrome monitor
C. RGB monitor
D. Video display

**203.** The computer device primarily used to provide hardcopy is the:
A. CRT
B. line printer
C. computer console
D. card reader

**204.** Which of the following is a non-impact printer?
A. Daisy wheel printer
B. Drum printer
C. Laser printer
D. All of the above

**205.** The input unit of a computer ————.
A. feeds data to the CPU or Memory
B. retrieves data from CPU
C. directs all other units
D. All of the above

**206.** Direct entry data devices include:
A. telephone, communications and bar codes
B. keyboards, cartridges and bar code reader
C. machine communication, keyboards and data collection devices
D. analog computers, digital computers and time clocks

**207.** A disadvantage of the laser printer is:
A. It is quieter than an impact printer
B. It is very slow
C. The output is of a lower quality
D. None of these

**208.** Which of the following is used only for data entry and storage, and never for processing?
A. Mouse
B. Dumb terminal
C. Microcomputer
D. Dedicated data entry system

**209.** From among the following, pick out the item that does not belong to computer:
A. Mouse
B. OCR
C. MICR
D. Plotter

**210.** General purpose computers are those that can be adopted to countless uses simply by changing its:
A. Keyboard
B. Printer
C. Program
D. Display screen

**211.** A kind of serial dot-matrix printer that forms characters with magnetically-charged ink sprayed dots is called:
A. Laser printer
B. Inkjet printer
C. Drum printer
D. Chain printer

**212.** Which of the following is classified as an impact printer?
A. Jet printer
B. Daisywheel printer
C. Thermal printer
D. Laser printer

**213.** What is the name of the hardware/software boundary that permits communication between people and computer?
A. Interface
B. Keyboard
C. VDT
D. Monitor

**214.** In a computer system, which device is functionally opposite of a keyboard?
A. Mouse
B. Trackball
C. Printer
D. Joystick

**215.** What is the name of the screen symbol that shows the placement of the next character?
A. Mouse
B. Cursor
C. Track ball
D. Graphic tablet

**216.** The bar code which is used on all types of items, is read by a scanning device directly into the computer. What is the name of this scanning device?
A. Laser scanner
B. Wand
C. OCR
D. MICR

**217.** Program execution time would be minimum if the programs are written in:
A. Machine language
B. Assembly language
C. High level language
D. All of the above

**218.** Which of the following is non-impact printer?
A. Drum printer    B. Line printer
C. Chain printer    D. Laser printer

**219.** Which of the following printer can be classified as a page-a-time printer?
A. Laser printer
B. Dot-matrix printer
C. Thermal printer
D. Inkjet printer

**220.** Which of the following is a device that changes data from coded form to clear form:
A. Keyboard    B. Decoder
C. Mnemonics    D. Bar code

**221.** An input device that reads printed text employing optical character pattern matching is known as:
A. Scanner    B. Magnetic disk
C. Mouse    D. Magnetic tape

**222.** A hand-help device which reads marks or characters on paper by detecting photo-sensitivity is known as:
A. light pen    B. optical wand
C. plotter    D. All of the above

**223.** A stand-alone system which produces one page of printed output at a time is:
A. Page printer
B. Line printer
C. Laser printer
D. Dot matrix printer

**224.** A mouse is used as:
A. a way to entertain children
B. a pointing device
C. an easy way to input information in your computer
D. both B and C

**225.** Which device can produce the final product of machine processing in to a form usable by human?
A. Storage    B. Input device
C. Output device    D. Control

**226.** A peripheral device in which the storage medium used in magnetic tape is:
A. Keyboard    B. VDU
C. Punched card    D. Tape deck

**227.** The devices attached to the computer and controlled by computers control unit are known as:
A. Peripheral devices
B. Program
C. Software
D. Utility

**228.** A peripheral device:
A. tears easily on the dotted line
B. is another name for an add-on component of a computer system
C. sits on the sidelines and never gets involved
D. None of these

**229.** Where does a computer add and compare data?
A. Hard disk    B. Floppy disk
C. CPU chip    D. Memory chip

**230.** The word computer usually refers to the Central Processor Unit plus:
A. External memory
B. Internal memory
C. Input devices
D. Output devices

**231.** Which is not true for primary storage?
A. Information must be transferred to primary storage
B. It is relatively more expensive
C. It allows very fast access to data
D. It is not a part of the CPU

**232.** Everything that computer does is controlled by its:
A. RAM    B. ROM
C. CPU    D. Storage devices

**233.** Conversion of decimal number $61_{10}$ to its binary number equivalent is:
A. $111101_2$
B. $1111100_2$
C. $110011_2$
D. None of the above

**234.** The most popular secondary storage today is:
A. Magnetic tape
B. Floppy disk
C. Mass storage
D. Semiconductor

**235.** Which of the following is not used in the storage phase of a computer-based information system?
A. Magnetic tape
B. Keyboard
C. Diskette
D. Hard disk

**236.** CD-ROM is:
A. Semiconductor memory
B. Memory register
C. Magnetic memory
D. None of the above

**237.** Dot-matrix is a type of:
A. Tape
B. Printer
C. Disk
D. Bus

**238.** What is the name of the screen symbol that shows the placement of the next character?
A. Mouse
B. Cursor
C. Track ball
D. Graphic tablet

**239.** A computer program consists of:
A. System flowchart
B. Program
C. Algorithms written in computer's language
D. Discrete logical steps

**240.** An assembler is a:
A. Program
B. Person who assembles the parts
C. Symbol
D. Language

**241.** The most popular language for interactive use is:
A. COBOL
B. PASCAL
C. FORTH
D. FORTRAN

**242.** Programming errors generally fail into which category(ies):
A. Syntax errors
B. Execution Errors
C. Logical Errors
D. All of the above

**243.** Which of the following is a type of systems software used on microcomputers?
A. Apple DOS
B. MS-DOS
C. UNIX
D. All of the above

**244.** Which of the following is not applications software?
A. Word processing
B. Spreadsheet
C. UNIX
D. Desktop publishing

**245.** Which of the following is not a relational data base?
A. dBase II
B. $4^{th}$ Dimension
C. Oracle
D. Reflex

**246.** Data items grouped together for storage purposes are called a:
A. record
B. title
C. list
D. string

**247.** A computer consists of:
A. A central processing unit
B. A memory
C. Input & output units
D. All of the above

**248.** A computer is a box full of electronic:
A. Switching devices
B. Chips
C. Circuits
D. Registers

**249.** Which computer memory is essentially empty?
A. RAM
B. ROM
C. EPROM
D. PROM

**250.** Which of the following is not a Sequence Storage device?
A. Magnetic disk
B. Magnetic tape
C. Paper tape
D. All of the above

**251.** In a Computer System, which device is functionally opposite of a Keyboard?
A. Mouse
B. Trackball
C. Printer
D. Joystick

**252.** A source program is written in which language?
A. English
B. Symbolic
C. High-level
D. Machine

**253.** A folder inside a folder is called ————.
A. Mini Directory
B. Sub Directory
C. Root Folder
D. Child Folder

**254.** A mouse is this kind of device:
A. Input
B. Output
C. Network
D. Storage

**255.** All deleted files go to ———— .
A. My Computer
B. Desktop
C. Recycle Bin
D. My Documents

**256.** With a CD you can ————.
A. Read
B. Write
C. Both A and B
D. Save a file

**257.** A reusable CD is labelled as:
A. R
B. W
C. HD
D. RW

**258.** ———— is the process of carrying out commands.
A. Fetching
B. Storing
C. Executing
D. Decoding

**259.** An error in a program is also known as ————.
A. Bug
B. Debug
C. Cursor
D. Icon

**260.** What is the default file extension for all Word documents?
A. txt
B. wrd
C. doc
D. ppt

**261.** If text was highlighted and 'Edit' 'Copy' was clicked, what would happen?
A. Text would be copied from the document and placed in the clipboard
B. Text would be removed from the document and placed in the clipboard
C. Text from the clipboard would be placed in the document at the place where the cursor is blinking
D. Only B and C

**262.** The background of any Word document:
A. is always white colour
B. is the colour you preset under the Options menu
C. is always the same for the entire document
D. can have any colour you choose

**263.** What do you use to create a chart?
A. Pie Wizard
B. Excel Wizard
C. Data Wizard
D. Chart Wizard

**264.** To move at the beginning of a line inside a document, press:
A. End key
B. Home key
C. Ctrl + End
D. None of these

**265.** You click at B to make the text:
A. Italics
B. Underlined
C. Both A and B
D. Bold

**266.** You can keep your personal files/folders in:
A. My Folder
B. My Documents
C. My Files
D. My Text

**267.** The base of binary number is:
A. 2
B. 8
C. 10
D. 16

**268.** A ———— contains specific rules and words that express the logical steps of an algorithm.
A. programming language
B. syntax
C. programming structure
D. logic chart

**269.** The term bit is short for:
A. megabyte
B. binary language
C. binary digit
D. binary number

**270.** Hardware of computer system is consists of:
   A. CPU and storage devices
   B. System unit and application programs
   C. Operating system and all application programs
   D. System unit and all attached peripheral devices to the unit

**271.** Function of ALU is:
   A. To control the execution of instruction
   B. To perform arithmetic and logical operation on data
   C. To store the result in main memory
   D. All of the above

**272.** The ———— gives specific information about the type of file.
   A. File name
   B. File path
   C. File extension
   D. File content

**273.** 'Print' command is found inside the ——— menu.
   A. View          B. Edit
   C. Tools         D. File

**274.** A saved document is known as—
   A. File          B. Program
   C. Folder        D. Icon

**275.** A file can be created using ——— command.
   A. Save          B. Open
   C. New           D. Edit

**276.** In Word you can force a page break—
   A. by positioning your cursor at the appropriate place and pressing the F1 key
   B. by positioning your cursor at the appropriate place and pressing Ctrl + Enter
   C. by using the Insert/Section Break
   D. by chaning the font size your document

**277.** Which of the following refers to a small, single-site network?
   A. LAN          B. DSL
   C. RAM          D. USB

**278.** By default, your documents print in-mode.—
   A. Landscape
   B. Portrait
   C. Page Setup
   D. Print View

**279.** How do you prevent e-mailed word documents from always opening in the Reading Layout?
   A. From the Tools Menu > Options > General Tab > uncheck the 'Allow starting in Reading Layout'
   B. From the View Menu > Reading Layout > General Tab > uncheck the 'Allow starting in Reading Layout'
   C. From the Format Menu > Autoformat > Edit Tab > uncheck the 'Use with e-mailed attachments'.
   D. All the above

**280.** Which of these is a quick way to copy formatting from a selected cell to two other cells on the same worksheet?
   A. Use CTRL to select all three cells, then click the Paste Button image button on the Standard toolbar.
   B. Copy the selected cell, then select the other two cells, click Style on the Format menu, then click Modify
   C. Click Format Painter Button image on the Formatting toolbar twice, then click in each cell you want to copy the formatting to
   D. Use Alt to select all three cells, then click the Paste Button image button on the Standard toolbar

**281.** Select the odd one out—
   A. Interpreter
   B. Operating System
   C. Compiler
   D. Assembler

**282.** Which of the following places the common data elements in order from smallest to largest?
   A. Character, file, record, field, database
   B. Character, record, field, file, database

C. Character, field, record, file, database

D. Bit, byte, character, record, field, file, database

**283.** The Assistant is—
A. an application that allows you to take notes and save them in a file
B. an animated character that provides help and suggestions
C. a button on the standard Toolbar that executes the Print command
D. a collection of frequently mis-spelled words in a dictionary file

**284.** Suppose you have coloumns of data span more than one printed page. How can you automatically print the column headings on each page?
A. Click Page Setup on the File menu, click the Sheet tab, and enter the row that contains these column headings under Print titles
B. Click Page Setup on the File menu, click the Page tab, click the Options button, then enter your choices
C. Click Page Preview on the File menu, click the Sheet tab, and enter the row that contains these column headings under Print titles
D. Click Page Setup on the File menu, click the Sheet tab, and make a selection under the Print heading

**285.** Which of the following describes a relational database?
A. It provides a relationship between integers
B. It consists of separate tables or related data
C. It retrieves data related to its queries
D. It provides a relationship between floats

**286.** What do you press to enter the current date in a cell?
A. CTRL + ; (semicolon)
B. CTRL + SHIFT + : (colon)
C. CTRL + F10
D. CTRL + F11

**287.** What happens when you press Ctrl + V key?
A. A Capital V letter is typed into your document at the cursor point
B. The selected item is pasted from the Clipboard
C. The selected item is pasted from the Clipboard
D. The selected drawing objects are distributed vertically on the page

**288.** CRM means—
A. Customer Relationship Management
B. Customer Retention Manager
C. Customers' Relatives Meet
D. Channel Route Market

**289.** The term PC means—
A. Private Computer
B. Personal Computer
C. Professional Computer
D. Personal Calculator

**290.** Silicon Valley of India is located in—
A. Dehradun          B. Bangalore
C. Hyderabad         D. Srinagar

**291.** Collection of two or more computers that are located within a limited distance of each other and that are connected to each other directly or indirectly?
A. Innernet
B. Intranet
C. Local Area Network
D. Wide Area Network

**292.** Part of a database that holds only one type of information?
A. Report          B. Record
C. File            D. Field

**293.** Which of the following is true?
A. Plotters are not available for microcomputer systems
B. Micro-computer are not programmed like conventional computers
C. Mini-computers are task-oriented
D. The contents of ROM are easily changed

**294.** ROM is composed of—
A. Magnetic cores
B. Micro-processors
C. Photoelectric cells
D. Floppy disks

**295.** The computer code for interchange of information between terminals is—
A. ASCII
B. BCD
C. BCDIC
D. Hollerith

**296.** A temporary storage area, attached to the CPU, for I/O operations, is a—
A. Channel
B. Buffer
C. Register
D. Core

**297.** Which one of the following is a file?
A. Floppy disk
B. Magnetic drum
C. Magnetic tape
D. None of these

**298.** An I/O device which provides photographic outputs for printing galleys, is the—
A. Camera printer
B. Automatic typesetter
C. Radix printer
D. All of these

**299.** A term used interchangeably with diskette is—
A. Disk cartridge
B. Disk pack
C. Floppy disk
D. Packette disk

**300.** A peripheral device used in a word processing system is—
A. Floppy disk
B. Magnetic card reader
C. CRT
D. All of these

## ANSWERS

| 1 | 2 | 3 | 4 | 5 | 6 | 7 | 8 | 9 | 10 |
|---|---|---|---|---|---|---|---|---|---|
| C | C | B | A | D | B | B | D | C | C |
| **11** | **12** | **13** | **14** | **15** | **16** | **17** | **18** | **19** | **20** |
| A | B | A | C | B | A | C | C | B | D |
| **21** | **22** | **23** | **24** | **25** | **26** | **27** | **28** | **29** | **30** |
| B | A | A | D | C | A | A | A | A | A |
| **31** | **32** | **33** | **34** | **35** | **36** | **37** | **38** | **39** | **40** |
| D | B | D | D | B | B | B | D | B | C |
| **41** | **42** | **43** | **44** | **45** | **46** | **47** | **48** | **49** | **50** |
| D | D | B | C | B | A | B | B | A | D |
| **51** | **52** | **53** | **54** | **55** | **56** | **57** | **58** | **59** | **60** |
| A | C | D | C | C | B | D | C | B | A |
| **61** | **62** | **63** | **64** | **65** | **66** | **67** | **68** | **69** | **70** |
| B | C | A | B | B | C | C | D | B | C |
| **71** | **72** | **73** | **74** | **75** | **76** | **77** | **78** | **79** | **80** |
| C | A | C | A | A | B | D | D | B | B |
| **81** | **82** | **83** | **84** | **85** | **86** | **87** | **88** | **89** | **90** |
| B | C | B | C | D | B | B | D | D | C |
| **91** | **92** | **93** | **94** | **95** | **96** | **97** | **98** | **99** | **100** |
| C | C | B | A | A | B | A | B | C | D |
| **101** | **102** | **103** | **104** | **105** | **106** | **107** | **108** | **109** | **110** |
| A | C | A | C | D | C | D | D | B | C |

| 111 | 112 | 113 | 114 | 115 | 116 | 117 | 118 | 119 | 120 |
|-----|-----|-----|-----|-----|-----|-----|-----|-----|-----|
| D | C | D | C | A | A | C | A | B | A |
| 121 | 122 | 123 | 124 | 125 | 126 | 127 | 128 | 129 | 130 |
| B | C | D | C | C | B | B | C | C | C |
| 131 | 132 | 133 | 134 | 135 | 136 | 137 | 138 | 139 | 140 |
| B | D | C | C | C | B | C | C | C | C |
| 141 | 142 | 143 | 144 | 145 | 146 | 147 | 148 | 149 | 150 |
| B | D | A | B | D | C | D | D | A | C |
| 151 | 152 | 153 | 154 | 155 | 156 | 157 | 158 | 159 | 160 |
| A | B | C | C | A | C | A | A | D | D |
| 161 | 162 | 163 | 164 | 165 | 166 | 167 | 168 | 169 | 170 |
| A | A | A | C | A | B | B | C | A | B |
| 171 | 172 | 173 | 174 | 175 | 176 | 177 | 178 | 179 | 180 |
| D | A | A | B | A | B | B | B | B | A |
| 181 | 182 | 183 | 184 | 185 | 186 | 187 | 188 | 189 | 190 |
| B | C | A | C | A | C | D | C | D | C |
| 191 | 192 | 193 | 194 | 195 | 196 | 197 | 198 | 199 | 200 |
| B | C | B | C | A | D | D | C | A | D |
| 201 | 202 | 203 | 204 | 205 | 206 | 207 | 208 | 209 | 210 |
| D | D | B | C | A | B | D | B | D | C |
| 211 | 212 | 213 | 214 | 215 | 216 | 217 | 218 | 219 | 220 |
| B | B | B | C | B | A | A | D | A | B |
| 221 | 222 | 223 | 224 | 225 | 226 | 227 | 228 | 229 | 230 |
| A | B | A | D | C | D | A | B | C | A |
| 231 | 232 | 233 | 234 | 235 | 236 | 237 | 238 | 239 | 240 |
| B | C | A | B | B | D | B | B | D | A |
| 241 | 242 | 243 | 244 | 245 | 246 | 247 | 248 | 249 | 250 |
| B | D | D | C | A | A | D | C | A | A |
| 251 | 252 | 253 | 254 | 255 | 256 | 257 | 258 | 259 | 260 |
| C | C | B | A | C | A | D | C | A | C |
| 261 | 262 | 263 | 264 | 265 | 266 | 267 | 268 | 269 | 270 |
| A | B | D | B | D | B | A | A | C | D |
| 271 | 272 | 273 | 274 | 275 | 276 | 277 | 278 | 279 | 280 |
| B | C | D | A | C | B | A | B | A | C |
| 281 | 282 | 283 | 284 | 285 | 286 | 287 | 288 | 289 | 290 |
| B | C | B | A | B | A | B | A | B | B |
| 291 | 292 | 293 | 294 | 295 | 296 | 297 | 298 | 299 | 300 |
| C | C | C | B | A | B | D | D | C | D |